Creating CRITICAL Classrooms

K–8 Reading and Writing with an Edge

Permissions

Creating CRITICAL Classrooms

K–8 Reading and Writing with an Edge

Mitzi Lewison
Christine Leland
Jerome C. Harste
Foreword by Linda Christensen

LEA Lawrence Erlbaum Associates
Taylor & Francis Group

New York   London

Lawrence Erlbaum Associates
Taylor & Francis Group
270 Madison Avenue
New York, NY 10016

Lawrence Erlbaum Associates
Taylor & Francis Group
2 Park Square
Milton Park, Abingdon
Oxon OX14 4RN

© 2008 by Taylor & Francis Group, LLC
Lawrence Erlbaum Associates is an imprint of Taylor & Francis Group, an Informa business

Printed in the United States of America on acid-free paper
10 9 8 7 6 5 4 3 2 1

International Standard Book Number-13: 978-0-8058-6231-7 (Softcover)

Library of Congress Cataloging-in-Publication Data

Lewison, Mitzi.
    Creating critical classrooms : K-8 reading and writing with an edge / Mitzi Lewison, Christine Leland, and Jerome Harste.
        p. cm.
    Includes bibliographical references and index.
    ISBN-13: 978-0-8058-6231-7 (alk. paper)
    1. Language arts (Elementary)--Case studies. 2. English language--Study and teaching (Elementary)--Case studies. 3. Critical pedagogy--Case studies. I. Leland, Christine. II. Harste, Jerome C. (Jerome Charles) III. Title.

LB1576.L52 2008
818'.309--dc22   2007016048

Visit the Taylor & Francis Web site at
http://www.taylorandfrancis.com

and the LEA Web site at
http://www.erlbaum.com

For teachers everywhere who dare to make a difference

*For the incredible teachers in Bloomington, Indiana,
who became colleagues in a joint quest to understand
critical literacy, and in memory of Rob Kling*

M. L.

*For our amazing colleagues and friends at both the "old"
and "new" Center for Inquiry in Indianapolis. You rock!*

C. L. and J. C. H.

Contents

Creating Critical Classrooms—Reading and Writing with an Edge

LINDA CHRISTENSEN

As a teacher I make dozens of decisions daily—from the books I choose to the way I respond to my students' papers. Sometimes these decisions come from an examination of my classroom practice—a close watching of what works and what does not—but sometimes my practice relies on a tradition that has not been examined. I taught *Huckleberry Finn* and *The Scarlet Letter* year after year without questioning whether these were the books my students needed to read. I also did not ask myself questions about why they were not reading them; I blamed the students for being lazy.

The first rethinking of my classroom practice happened more than 20 years ago at Jefferson High School, located in Portland, Oregon's pre-dominantly working-class African American neighborhood. Jefferson's administration granted Bill Bigelow and me permission to team teach a two-period, interdisciplinary class in the coming year: "Literature and U.S. History." Before our first summer planning meeting, I gave Bill a list of my class books to read in preparation for our initial discussion: *The Crucible, The Scarlet Letter, The Red Badge of Courage, My Antonia, The Great Gatsby,* and *Grapes of Wrath.* To be fair, I did insert a Native American unit and a unit on the Harlem Renaissance, but my attempt at including multicultural literature amounted to tokenism, not a thought-ful weaving of diverse writers.

Bigelow's question during that first meeting was, "What do you want students to learn from *Red Badge of Courage?*" It provided an illuminating moment in my teaching career. I fumbled about for an answer: "the brutality of war …." But to be honest, I taught *The Red Badge of Courage* and the rest of the books because they were part of the literary canon, acknowledged classics taught or supplied by folks who I figured knew a lot more than I did. After all, I was just a teacher. They were the books I had read in high school, and they were the books I studied again as a literature major in college.

At that time, I taught out of tradition and assumptions rather than out of conviction for what I believed students at Jefferson needed to learn—or out of what I thought might contribute to needed social change. I did not have a curricular center, a staging platform of core beliefs to anchor my teaching. I followed unexamined assumptions about curriculum because I did not feel important enough, smart enough, or empowered enough to make those decisions on my own.

During this time, Bigelow and I also started a critical pedagogy group with like-minded teachers. We got together every other Sunday night to study books by Paulo Freire and Ira Shor. We used our group as a sounding board as we developed curriculum to engage our students in literacy and history by critically examining their lives and the world.

The group became my curricular conscience. Instead of leaping from book to book, my years of working in a critical collaborative community taught me to construct curriculum around big ideas that matter—that connected students to their community and world. I learned to pull books, stories, poems, and essays that helped students critically examine the world rather than to consume it one classic at a time.

Creating Critical Classrooms: Reading and Writing with an Edge provides a curricular conscience to teachers. The collection of vignettes, theories, thought pieces, and invitations pulls out a chair at the table as teachers and professors discuss classroom practice in light of critical literacy. The imaginative format of the book allows the reader to join a conversation as classroom teachers discuss specific examples of their practice through vignettes, which illuminate their theoretical frameworks and provide a kind of topographical map for readers to follow. The work—from morning meetings to debates on social artifacts to risky books and museum exhibits—demonstrates exemplary literacy practices, but it also demonstrates education that liberates instead of domesticates or alienates. The work is culturally sensitive, critically astute—and absolutely essential for teachers and teacher educators today.

This work flies in the face of contemporary, paced, scripted, top-down curriculum that deskills teachers. These chapters show teachers who think, teachers who write, teachers not only who understand what they are teaching but also who can articulate why. As the editors note, "A conscious awareness of the theories that influence our teaching enables us to be more reflective about our practice." And it is that reflection that moves us to change our strategies, content—even our theories—as the teachers and teacher educators in this text do. This state of reflection, instead of mindless following of past practice, is the place I want to live in as a teacher because it is where new questions are born. It is where teachers learn to trust their own paths of inquiry instead of looking to outside authorities for approval. I was struck by Jerry Harste's statement, "The state of uncertainty is not one of indifference …. Good teachers must have doubts. Good teachers must know that it is the lack of certainty that opens up the space wherein he or she just might discover effectiveness. Only an uncertain person can learn."

Books about critical literacy and social justice teaching swagger on my bookshelf, boasting of more than they provide. Most offer less than they promise. They rush students to action on a cause without getting them to critique social hierarchies that privilege some and oppress others. *Creating Critical Classrooms* does not boast, it does not swagger; it delivers both theory and practice on how to construct lessons that "disrupt the commonplace, consider multiple viewpoints, focus on the socialpolitical, and take action to promote social justice." This book dares to ask educators to construct counternarratives to challenge the mainstream propaganda dished up by television news, curriculum departments, and presidents.

I attempt to keep my vision—and hope—alive by participating in critical teaching groups. These groups help me think more carefully about issues inside as well as outside the classroom, from literacy practices to top-down curricular policies. Our sometimes-heated discussions about articles, books, and curriculum hone my ability to evaluate my work. I carry these voices—and the solidarity of these teachers—like a Greek chorus in my mind. They remind me to question and sometimes to defy those in authority when I am told to participate in practices that harm children. They nettle me when I fall into easy patterns and point out when I deliver glib answers to difficult problems. *Creating Critical Classrooms: Reading and Writing with an Edge* will join that Greek chorus, becoming, in Toni Morrison's words, "a friend of my mind" who I return to when I am troubled, when I need someone who has thought deeply and wisely about education.

Mitzi Lewison is associate professor of language education at Indiana University, Bloomington. She teaches literacy methods courses in the elementary teacher education program, master's level literacy and children's literature courses, and doctoral seminars centered on issues in language education. Her research interests include critical literacy, critical discourse analysis, and writing instruction in elementary classrooms. She is currently part of a National Science Foundation grant studying student discourse during small-group problem-solving conversations in mathematics and is the English director of the United States Agency for International Development (USAID) Afghanistan Higher Education Project, designed to begin rebuilding teacher education institutions in Afghanistan. Before coming to Indiana University, Lewison spent five years developing and implementing a language arts curriculum and accompanying professional development program for the GALAXY Classroom, a nonprofit foundation with students and teachers in 400 schools across the United States, Mexico, and Canada. Prior to this, she held positions in the Montebello Unified School District—a large, urban district in Southern California—as bilingual teacher, reading and language specialist, middle school assistant principal, and district language arts consultant.

Christine (Chris) Leland is professor of language education at the Indiana University School of Education at Indiana University–Purdue University, Indianapolis (IUPUI). She teaches graduate and under-graduate literacy courses and works with master's and doctoral students. Her research focuses on urban schools and the role that critical literacy and inquiry can play in supporting the development of all children as empowered learners. She has worked with many teachers in the Indianapolis area through the study group model of professional development. One group that she and Jerry Harste worked with over a number of years developed the Center for Inquiry (CFI), a successful public magnet school that continues to challenge stereotypes about urban children and their families. The CFI has been an anchor school in the Learning to Teach/Teaching to Learn Teacher Education Program at

IUPUI for many years. Leland currently serves as associate dean for Academic Affairs in her unit and works with a team of socially conscious colleagues who engage in the ongoing process of creating and recreating field-based programs that prepare teachers and other leaders for schools in the city and beyond. Before coming to IUPUI, she spent 12 years teaching grades 1, 4, 5, and 6 in several communities in Massachusetts.

Jerome (Jerry) C. Harste is emeritus professor of language education at Indiana University, Bloomington, where he was the first member of that faculty to hold the Martha Lea & Bill Armstrong Chair in Teacher Education. His book *Language Stories and Literacy Lessons* (Heinemann, 1984), coauthored with Carolyn Burke and Virginia Woodward, was awarded the David H. Russell Research Award for Outstanding Contributions in the Teaching of English. Jerry is a coauthor of *Creating Classrooms for Authors* (Heinemann, 1988) and *Creating Classrooms for Authors and Inquirers* (Heinemann, 1996) as well as host and developer of several videotape series including *The Authoring Cycle* and *Visions of Literacy* (available from Irwin in Canada and Heinemann in the United States 1986 and 1990–2, respectively). He sees this volume as extending both the work begun in these earlier volumes as well as his work with teachers in creating curricula that highlight multiple ways of knowing, inquiry-based learning, and critical literacy. Twelve years ago Chris Leland, a group of teachers from the Indianapolis Public Schools, and Jerome created a new public K–8 school called the Center for Inquiry (CFI), dedicated to creating curriculum based on the inquiry questions of learners. Because of its success, other CFIs have sprung up nationally, and the Indianapolis Public Schools opened a second CFI in fall 2006. "Jerome C.," as he is known in academic circles—because of the way he signs his name in professional publications—has served on the board of the International Reading Association and is past president of the National Reading Conference, the National Conference on Research in Language and Literacy, the Whole Language Umbrella, and the National Council of Teachers of English.

Lee Heffernan has taught in elementary schools for more than 20 years. She and her sixth-grade students are reading and writing texts that focus on the question, "Is the pen mightier than the sword?" Heffernan is the author of *Critical Literacy and Writer's Workshop: Bringing Purpose and Passion to Student Writing* (International Reading Association, 2004). She is currently a doctoral student at Indiana University and is writing her dissertation, titled *A Dangerous Job: Teacher as Editor*. Lee is also proud to say that she has taught nearly all 90 of her students to knit during recess this year.

Katie Van Sluys is assistant professor of literacy at DePaul University. She teaches courses for preservice and practicing teachers focusing on issues of language, literacy, culture, and classroom inquiry. Her research examines the issue of identity and who teachers and students become as they inquire into critical literacies, multilinguism, and what it means to teach and learn in urban contexts. As a researcher, teacher, and scholar Van Sluys works closely to build collaborative relationships with schools such that literate futures can be studied, revised, and reimagined together.

Kate Kuonen-Bakhtiary is a teacher in a fifth-and-sixth-grade combination classroom at the new Center for Inquiry, an Indianapolis Public Schools magnet option. She and her students are exploring political cartoons as well as designing action pieces in response to their findings. A graduate of the Learning to Teach/Teaching to Learn Teacher Education Program at Indiana University–Purdue University, Indianapolis, Kuonen-Bakhtiary is most interested in helping kids read, talk, listen to, and write about the world around them critically and purposely. She integrates critical literacy throughout the curriculum using drama, art, social action, debate, and writing. Creating an arena for kids to interrogate issues they find relevant is at the core of Kuonen-Bakhtiary's philosophy of education.

Kimberly Huber is a first-grade teacher at North Salem Elementary School in the North West Hendricks School Corporation in North Salem, Indiana. She is currently examining the relationship between the use of critical literacy in her rural classroom and the evolving social dynamics that occur simultaneously with the use of critical literacy texts on a regular basis. Huber was a member of the first Learning to Teach/ Teaching to Learn cohort during her undergraduate work at Indiana University–Purdue University, Indianapolis (IUPUI). Later she completed her master's degree at IUPUI and focused her thesis on using critical literacy in her first-grade classroom.

Amy Wackerly teaches in a second-and-third-grade multi-age classroom at the Center for Inquiry in the Indianapolis Public Schools. She is interested in using critical literacy in the classroom to encourage social action with her students. One of her current interests is learning about the Primary Years Program of the International Baccalaureate Organization. She is coauthor of an article titled "Community, Choice and Content in the Urban Classroom," which appeared in the National Council of Teachers of English publications *Primary Voices K-6* and *Literacy as Social Practice*. Wackerly is involved in the Indiana Partnership for Young Writers and is on the executive board of Indiana Council of Teachers of English. She worked with Chris Leland and Jerry Harste while in the Learning to Teach/Teaching to Learn Teacher Education Program at Indiana University–Purdue University, Indianapolis.

Emily McCord is a seventh- and eighth-grade social studies teacher at Batchelor Middle School in Bloomington, Indiana. McCord's eighth-grade curriculum consists of a thematic exploration of U.S. history from its origins to the era of Reconstruction. Her seventh-grade curriculum focuses on examining the physical geography of Asia, Africa, and Oceania, as well as the histories and cultures of the diverse peoples living in these areas. McCord received an arts baccalaureate from Bowdoin College and a master of arts for teachers of social studies from Indiana University. She has a passion for the study of globalization and current events, which deeply influences her teaching. She also has studied in the areas of gifted and talented education, service learning, and cultural competency.

Dana Hubbard works for the Indianapolis Public Schools with children designated as in the autistic spectrum. He is a single father who resides in downtown Indianapolis. Hubbard is also a graduate of the Learning to Teach/Teaching to Learn Teacher Education Program at Indiana University–Purdue University, Indianapolis (IUPUI) and worked with Chris and Jerry over a two-year period while he was in the program. He is currently enrolled in a master's program at IUPUI.

Gerald Campano is assistant professor at Indiana University, Bloomington. His research interests include practitioner inquiry, urban education, and immigrant identities in the contexts of schooling. Campano has taught elementary school for a number of years in Houston, Texas, and California's Central Valley. He is also a Carnegie scholar and author of *Immigrant Students and Literacy: Reading, Writing, and Remembering* (Teachers College Press, 2006).

Creating Critical Classrooms

MITZI LEWISON, CHRISTINE LELAND, AND JEROME C. HARSTE

As educators, we are living in hard times. Stories of outstanding teachers and principals leaving the profession are not uncommon. After a decade of teaching, Katherine Bomer (2005) began to feel that her classroom curriculum was not her own. Instead of focusing on student needs, interests, and meaning-based literacy strategies, she faced mandates that emphasized skill-based instruction, basal readers (not real literature), and various regimes of testing:

> When I decided to resign from my beloved profession of teaching, I told my principal that my bottom line had been crossed. I told her that a decade of fighting increased district, federal, and state intrusion into my classroom, and decreased trust in my ability and expertise as a teacher, had left me feeling like a used tube of toothpaste, squeezed and rolled up to that last sad, thin smear on the toothbrush. (Bomer, 2005, p. 168)

We have witnessed Katherine's spectacular teaching and know that her exit from the classroom is a great loss.

Sadly, it is not just teachers who are leaving the profession, but also principals:

New York's most experienced principals have been fleeing the system in alarming numbers. Over the last five years, more than half have left their jobs. Most retired, but union statistics—which don't include detailed reasons for leaving—show that more than 200 left for reasons "other than retirement." As a result, a city system that once viewed educators with even 10 years' experience as too green to lead a school has grown increasingly dependent on young people—some still in their 20s—who have spent relatively little time in the school system. … The principals' union, for its part, says that some people have left the job because they have not been given enough administrative help to meet their new responsibilities. (Editorial, "The Principals Vanish," *NY Times*, May 27, 2006)

This is not surprising. Good principals will leave the profession when they are burdened with more and more accountability measures that they see as artificially inflated in importance and not focused on the real meat of schooling. These include topics like phonics, phonemic awareness, and making significant gains on one standardized test. Some have reported that they have become educational police officers rather than educational leaders.

One-size-fits-all mandates restrict classroom curricula. There is less and less time in the school day devoted to the arts, to student-centered instruction, to critical thinking, and critical inquiry. As documented by Bomer and the *New York Times* editorial, stringent restrictions have been the impetus for some of our best and brightest leaving teaching.

But despite hard times and a plethora of reductionist mandates, there are some talented and courageous teachers and principals who have managed to find ways to work in the margins. They ask questions and find ways to disrupt or subvert top-down curricular decrees. These teachers often focus on equity issues, seeking to understand why certain groups of students are privileged and why others are marginalized—simply by arriving at school with a set of resources gained at home that aren't valued in classrooms. The narratives of teachers who are striving for more equitable, relevant, and critical classroom practices are the inspiration for this book.

Background

We have been working together for the past 10 years on an array of projects focused on defining, conceptualizing, and implementing critical literacy practices in elementary and college classrooms. As a collective, our work began as members of the Indiana Study Group. For one of our projects, we took on the responsibility of identifying and reviewing children's books and adolescent novels that raise important social issues. The idea behind this project was that by making these social issues books an integral part of the English language art curriculum, teachers could use literacy as a way to open up spaces in their classrooms for important conversations about critical issues. Every three years we were responsible for identifying 50 titles for a chapter on critical literacy in the volume *Adventuring with Books* (Harste et al., 2000; Leland & Harste, 2002) published by the National Council for Teachers of English (NCTE). To date, members of the Indiana Study Group have produced two chapters and several articles on the use of social-issue books in the classroom (many of which are available online at http://php.indiana.edu/~harste/recpub; see specifically "Supporting critical conversation in classrooms" and "Taking a critical stance: It's not just the books you choose").

Chris and Jerry worked with a group of teachers in the Indianapolis Public Schools to start a new school, the Center for Inquiry. Now in its second decade, the center has expanded to two buildings and includes a middle school. The center was designed to create a curriculum for the 21st century for both public elementary education and teacher education. The curriculum focuses on multiple ways of knowing, inquiry-based learning, and critical literacy. Teachers in both buildings continue to work with Chris and Jerry through study groups.

While Chris and Jerry were working with teachers in the Indianapolis area, Lewison and Amy Flint were working with teachers in Bloomington. Through several Indiana University and state-funded grants, Mitzi and Amy were able to sponsor eight years of teacher–researcher study groups, where teachers explored how they might put a critical edge on their teaching of reading and language arts.

We have found small but powerful groups of teachers in different parts of the state whose teaching "takes your breath away." They are engaged in blue teaching in a red state with critical practices permeating their teaching.

A Model of Critical Literacy Instruction

As we have worked with teachers over the years, the question, "What is critical literacy?" has arisen time after time. A number of frameworks are available that describe critical literacy: Luke and Freebody's (1997) four-resource model, Shannon's (1995) critical literacy framework, Janks's (2002) synthesis model, and the four dimensions of critical literacy (Lewison, Flint, & Van Sluys, 2002). Each of these frameworks proposes important ways of understanding critical practices, but we felt none was sufficient in representing the complexity of what it means to implement critical literacy in elementary and middle school classrooms. This volume is the result of our struggle to articulate a theory of critical literacy—in all its complexity. The model we developed is our best thinking at this time. Not only did we revise the model numerous times ourselves, but we also had the privilege of presenting it at several conference sessions

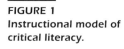

FIGURE 1
Instructional model of critical literacy.

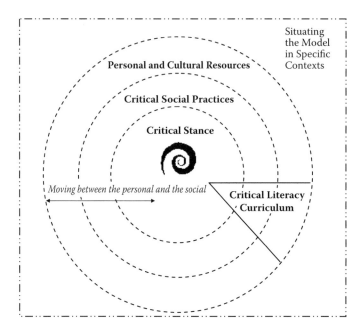

Situating the Model in Specific Contexts

Personal and Cultural Resources

Critical Social Practices

Critical Stance

Moving between the personal and the social

Critical Literacy Curriculum

at the annual NCTE meetings and the annual National Reading Conference. The feedback we received from the audiences at these two venues helped us further refine the model (Figure 1).

In Chapter 1 of this book, we describe the various components of the model by featuring the work of third-grade teacher-researcher Lee Heffernan. In a vignette that highlights the content of the first chapter, Lee lays out the problems and potentials of transforming morning meeting time from a consumerist show-and-tell forum to a classroom space where important critical work gets done. By using her narrative, we are able to illustrate the interaction among (1) personal and cultural resources; (2) critical social practices; (3) critical stance; (4) movement between the personal and the social; and (5) the context in which this model is situated.

Personal and Cultural Resources

Personal and cultural resources, the outside ring of our model, are what students and teachers draw on to create the content of curriculum. Three chapters in this book are devoted to exploring the various personal and cultural resources that teachers and students use in critical classrooms.

In Chapter 2, Katie Van Sluys describes how she and teacher Rïse Reinier worked in a multi-age (grades 4–6) classroom "to build a curriculum based on kids' lives, passions, and needs." We use Rïse and Katie's narrative to highlight their commitment to recognizing all students as capable—each bringing a wide range of experiential, cultural, and linguistic resources to the classroom. They are committed to regularly using these resources and giving them a place of prominence in what counts in the classroom. Katie and Rïse are very concerned with creating a curriculum that is relevant to students' interests and knowledge—building connections between the classroom and life outside of school. From a rich description of their classroom practices, we also begin to theorize the notion that people must see themselves in literacy to become literate.

In Chapter 3, fourth-grade teacher Kate Kuonen-Bakhtiary describes how she used popular culture as a resource to build curriculum. What is especially interesting about Kate's narrative is her realization that just because she finds something interesting in popular culture, it does not necessarily mean her students are interested in the same thing. Through listening to her students' conversations, Kate comes to understand that school can provide a site for interrogating cultural texts and repositioning oneself and that repositioning is not just a goal for students but for teachers as well. Through her inquiry with her students into Bratz dolls she comes to understand that literacy keeps changing and that to be able to question and examine new literacies and popular culture, children need to develop what Shannon (1995) calls the language of critique.

In Chapter 4, first-grade teacher Kim Huber describes her reluctance to use books about tough social issues and how she worked with other teachers as a form of support to help her begin using nontraditional content in her classroom. Kim's narrative also illustrates how tension drives the learning process. Even though she was very worried about using social issues books in her classroom, Kim was amazed by the transformation in her students' attitudes after she started introducing risky texts. She also began to understand that when she used nontraditional children's literature in her classroom she could not just read the book, have a short discussion, and go on to something else. Social issues books require us to help students linger in text, to visit and revisit these powerful cultural resources, and to encourage children to make connections between the books and their lives and communities.

Critical Social Practice

The second ring of our model, critical social practices, includes the specific social practices in which students and teachers engage as they create critical curricula. We use four dimensions of critical social practice (Lewison, Flint, and Van Sluys, 2002): (1) disrupting the commonplace; (2) interrogating multiple viewpoints; (3) focusing on sociopolitical issues; and (4) taking action to promote social justice. Chapters 5 through 8 each focus on one of the dimensions of critical social practice.

In Chapter 5, "Disrupting the Commonplace," Chris and Jerry describe their visit to the Smithsonian National Museum of American History in Washington, D.C., and the exhibit titled "The Price of Freedom: Americans at War." Their vignette shows how no texts are neutral—particularly at this museum. They highlight the ways they analyzed the language used in the exhibit—looking at how phrases like *wars erupted* were designed to position patrons to see war as natural, as something that just happens. Using the museum example as a springboard, Chris and Jerry emphasize a number of ways students can interrogate the language of everyday texts in classrooms. They firmly believe that critical language study needs to be an integral part of the elementary and middle school curriculum. But interrogation of language is not enough. If students see inequity or one-sidedness as they engage in critical language study, it is our job to encourage them to write counternarratives.

In Chapter 6, "Interrogating Multiple Viewpoints," Chris and Amy Wackerly describe the varied ways that Amy helps the students in her multi-age second-and-third-grade urban classroom try to understand and empathize with the perspectives of others. Through strategies such as role playing, inner dialogues, dramatizing bullying scenarios, and creating "I statements" for characters, Amy's students began to go beyond stereotypes and snap judgments of others and attempted to understand why people and book characters act in certain ways. From this narrative, they theorize how multiple perspectives complicate what we know and that this complexity, like life, is not always neat and tidy but is of key importance in creating critical curriculum. Chris and Amy's narrative also emphasizes the need to expand the curriculum by bringing in people and ideas not prominent in traditional school culture. This means finding ways to weave diversity and difference into the fabric of curriculum rather than treating them as isolated topics.

In Chapter 7, "Focusing on the Sociopolitical," middle school teacher Emily McCord discusses how attending a summer institute on global change helped her understand that multiple, interconnected factors work together to cause any given event. She also came to realize that if there are multiple interconnected causes, one could positively impact a problem by working at the site of any one of the causes. With her seventh-grade students, Emily created a curriculum on world hunger that emphasized inquiry into tough sociopolitical issues. From her narrative, we theorize that complexity is something to expect, insist on, and encourage when focusing on the sociopolitical. We also see from Emily's narrative that one of the most fruitful ways to encourage students to engage in sophisticated critical practices is to have their teacher actively involved in the same practices, providing demonstrations of the technical processes needed to engage the issues at hand.

In Chapter 8, "Taking Action to Promote Social Justice," Dana Hubbard describes how he used the invitation of a state senator to transform the typical fifth-grade social studies topic "How laws get made" into an inquiry about the violence kids encounter in their own community. After an invitation from the senator and lots of discussion with Dana, the students decided to write a bill that would give people money to turn in their guns. This narrative is a reminder of how education is never neutral: It either liberates, domesticates, or alienates. We theorize how creating critical curricula often means delving into risky topics that surround students' lives and argue that it is not enough to treat critical literacy as a topic of conversation; we have to go out and do something as well.

Critical Stance

Critical stance, at the core of our model, consists of the attitudes and dispositions we take on that enable us to become critically literate beings. We have identified four dimensions of adopting a critical stance: (1) consciously engaging; (2) entertaining alternate ways of being; (3) taking responsibility to inquire; and (4) being reflexive. In Chapter 9, former fifth-grade teacher-researcher Gerald Campano explores the stance he adopted when looking back on how he worked with a group of migrant children for literacy instruction. We focus on how each of the four dimensions of critical stance plays out in Gerald's narrative. Although it was a difficult lesson, Gerald came to realize how traditional school curricula "may function to exclude or devalue the cultural resources" children bring to school. We also explore how Gerald used inquiry and tension as a resource and took on a reflexive stance to move his practice forward.

Although Chapters 1 through 9 explain the model in detail, this model addresses two additional issues that are worth a brief note here: (1) moving between the personal and the social; and (2) situating the model in specific contexts.

Moving Between the Personal and the Social

In our model of critical literacy, arrows on the diagram show curriculum moving between the personal and the social. Kamler, as the title of her book suggests, (2001) describes this process as "relocating the personal." This concept entails remembering that students bring many valuable interests and cultural resources to school; it is irresponsible if we treat kids like empty vessels to be filled with our knowledge. We see curriculum as a negotiation between what kids want to learn and our own goals. By building on kids' personal knowledge and issues, we have the potential to create powerful, transformative curricula. But it is never enough to leave curricular content in the personal. There are always social, political, cultural, and economic dimensions to any event or issue we might first describe as personal. It is also important to note that there are times, especially when dealing with difficult issues such as racism, that it is easier to start with something out there (i.e., the social) and then eventually have students start making personal connections to the issue at hand. This movement between the personal and the social often complicates the ways we envision curriculum. At its best, curriculum is always infused with personal and social dimensions.

Introduction

Situating the Model in Specific Contexts

We have placed our model of critical literacy in a box called *context*. We are very aware from our work with teachers that the culture and norms of a particular school can support or hinder moves to develop critical practices. In schools where reductive mandates are held up as the curriculum, we have discovered there are teachers who find great support in study groups where they work with peers from less restrictive schools. Even with support, creating critical curricula is not easy. By placing our model in the political context of real-world schools and classrooms, we move away from romanticizing about the implementation of critical practices.

Map of the Chapters

Chapters 2 through 9 each elaborate on a different aspect of the critical literacy model. Although each chapter was reviewed by the entire team and went through multiple revisions, Lewison was lead author on the Introduction and Chapters 1, 2, 7, and 9. Leland was the lead author on Chapters 3, 4, 5, 6, and 8.

Vignettes

Each chapter begins with a vignette written by a teacher-researcher. The vignette highlights an example of how the model of critical literacy instruction works in real life. Nearly all of the authors of these narratives have been members of a critical literacy study group.

Theories That Inform Practice

After each vignette in Chapters 2 through 9, we present the theories we see as informing the classroom practice of the teacher-researcher featured in the vignette. These theories make explicit the assumptions that guided the choices the teacher made with students and also provide insight into the underlying beliefs that this teacher associated with enacting a critical literacy curriculum. We strongly believe that a conscious awareness of the theories that influence our teaching enables us to be more reflective about our practice.

Critical Literacy Chart

In each chapter, a chart is provided that reviews the classroom vignette and explicates which cultural resources were drawn on, what critical social practices were enacted, and how the teacher took up a critical stance (Table 1).

Map Showing Movement Between the Personal and the Social

Each chapter also includes a map that shows the ways the teacher helped students move between the personal and the social.

TABLE 1 Critical Literacy Chart		
Cultural Resources Drawn On	Critical Practices Enacted	How the Teachers Took Up a Critical Stance

Thought Pieces

Harste was the lead author on nine thought pieces, each related to the chapter theme. In these essays, he urges us to step back and interrogate everyday assumptions about teaching and learning. The essays are as follows:

- Chapter 1: Do Methods Make a Difference?
- Chapter 2: Uncertainty in the Teaching of Reading and Writing
- Chapter 3: Visual Literacy
- Chapter 4: Risky Texts
- Chapter 5: Teacher Talk: Critical Choices
- Chapter 6: Understanding Reading: Multiple Perspective, Multiple Insights
- Chapter 7: Having Our Hands in the Cookie Jar
- Chapter 8: School Posters
- Chapter 9: "May You Live in Interesting Times": The Politics of Eclecticism

Invitations for Disruption

These invitations are mini-inquiries designed for teachers. They are related to the theories that teacher-researchers employed in each vignette and also related to the thought pieces. It is our hope that readers will take the time to conduct these inquiries. Although they can be done alone or with a colleague, they are also interesting topics for study groups to pursue.

Invitations for Students

At the end the book, there is a series of invitations for students that can be used in conjunction with a particular aspect of our model of critical literacy instruction or with any other part of your curriculum. Each invitation is based on a particular social issue such as name calling or consumerism and consists of a rationale, needed materials, and how

TABLE 2
Invitations

Elements of Invitations	Description
Rationale	Sets the stage for getting started with students and gives background information about the content of the invitation
Materials	What you will need to implement the invitation in classrooms
Getting Started	The step-by-step description of how to implement this invitation as a whole-class engagement
Learning Center Extension	This is a different teaching strategy based on the same theme but designed to be used in a learning center. It is written in center-card format so that it can be reproduced and used directly by students.
Learning Center Materials	What you will need to implement the center in classrooms
Taking Action	Suggestions for how you and your students might take action following the invitation. These are meant to serve as a springboard for you and your students developing your own action plans.

to get started. Invitations are written with a whole-class focus and are followed by a learning center extension, designed for groups of students to do on their own. As you will see, it takes little work to convert a whole class engagement into a learning center and vice versa. We invite readers to think of these invitations as springboards to your own engagements or as organic entities that can grow and change based on the needs of your class. Each Invitation consists of the elements shown in Table 2. As an accompaniment to the invitations in this book, we recommend *What If and Why? Literacy Invitations for Multilingual Classrooms* (Van Sluys, 2005).

As we have already noted, creating critical curricula can be challenging, complex, and, at times, risky. What we have not addressed is the level of engagement and enthusiasm we have witnessed time and again on the part of students when they have the opportunity to delve into meaty, real-world topics and activities that they care about. We, and the teachers with whom we work, believe that the results are definitely worth the effort. It is our hope that this book will be a partner with you on your journey to creating and recreating critical classrooms.

Overview

Why Do We Need an Instructional Theory of Critical Literacy?

Vignette

Morning Meeting: Contradictions and Possibilities*

Lee Heffernan

Morning meeting is a time for building classroom community, an opportunity to address important personal as well as political issues. Though I shared this vision with my students, many still saw morning meeting as a type of show and tell. The meeting sometimes evolved into a consumerist forum as kids brought in prized possessions and the rest of the class looked on with envy. We sat watching as classmates displayed and described trendy artifacts, rare baseball cards, trip souvenirs.

This year, I made the decision to transform morning meeting. I explained to my students that morning meeting was not a time for show and tell but rather was a time to share information that was of value and concern to all present. One day, as a contributor and participant in these meetings, I announced that I had received a notice from the principal that students in all grades were required to sit in assigned seats while in the cafeteria because of rowdiness (food fights and too much yelling). In this lunchroom, students normally could sit wherever they wanted, usually with friends. The kids' first reaction to the announcement was to protest the unfairness of assigned seats since the students claimed they were not causing any problems. I had no idea

---

*Adapted from L. Heffernan (2003). Morning Meeting: Contradictions and possibilities. *School Talk* Copyright July 2003, 8, by the National Council of Teachers of English. Reprinted with permission.

if this was true. As we began to discuss possible configurations for assigned seating, one kid groaned, "Boy–girl, right?" The general negative reaction to the possibility of a mixed-gender seating arrangement led to a discussion about student perceptions of a mandated boy–girl configuration as punishment. The kids discussed the risks of sitting boy–girl—if a girl and boy sat together they could count on being teased. But sitting with friends was also problematic. Often kids saved seats so students could not always sit where they wanted to anyway. There were a lot of complex issues coming to the surface—the lunchroom was definitely a place of contestation and conflict.

I introduced the idea of *coresearching* the lunchroom-seating rule. As coresearchers, we would spend time during morning meeting investigating the interactions of a commonplace site, our lunchroom. We talked about the situation in the lunchroom and audiotaped our conversations. As we listened to our tapes, we made a chart of topics that evoked a strong emotional reaction to the issue. We crafted the topics into inquiry questions.

Research Questions

- What causes food throwing? Is this a problem? What causes "no trashbacks"?
- What happens when people save seats? How many people save seats?
- What makes the lunchroom loud? What is too loud?
- How does a chain reaction happen? What is a chain reaction?
- What do people like about the lunchroom?
- What do people like about that space?

We also went into the field to observe lunchroom behaviors and interactions. Students were divided into randomly assigned research teams and were asked to report back on specific research questions. We viewed the *Teaching Tolerance* website (http://www.tolerance.org) where we read information about a Mix It Up action project. Mix It Up is a national project that provides information to students and teachers about the importance of reaching across borders and reconfiguring social groupings in school cafeterias. My students were surprised to learn that high schoolers also had lunchroom problems. We wrote in our notebooks about the ideal lunchroom, spent a week planning a Mix It Up lunch of our own, and participated in this lunch in our classroom. One of the prominent features of our Mix It Up lunch was the procedure of students coming into the room and picking a stick with a random table number designating where they were to sit. The children also wrote plays about the lunchroom issue and presented them in readers' theater format to other classes. The plays focused on differ-ent lunchroom problems the students uncovered in their inquiries—gendered teasing about where kids sit, "boys' tables and girls' tables," popularity and the lunchroom, and wanting to escape the lunchroom to go outside. It was pretty amazing to see the kids problematizing the gendered practice of sitting with friends. This was what they had most passionately protested being taken away from them after I first read the principal's announcement. Now they were interrogating the practice and trying to change it.

Our morning meetings have evolved, but there is still work to do. Recently, during one of our meetings, I noticed that all the boys sat on one side of the circle, and all the girls sat on the other side. When I commented on the contradiction between our talk about mixing it up and how we sat at morning meeting, the kids started laughing and scurrying to new spots in the circle. Kamler (1999, p. 212) believes that these contradictions are important moments in classroom research: "Contradictions are a sign of struggle and struggles are ultimately hopeful; they indicate discourse in flux, shifting subjectivities and hence enable us to imagine the possibilities of change."

> Morning meetings provide opportunities for bringing real events into the classroom. They can also be sites where groups can act as coresearchers into the norms of the social institutions they inhabit. It is a place of possibilities, where the contradictions and tensions between the personal and the social can be addressed and reimagined.

Despite national efforts to homogenize the elementary literacy curriculum and to reduce it to a set of skills to be learned, Lee Heffernan and other teachers across the country and internationally are resisting pressures to conform to top-down instructional mandates and are courageously incorporating critical practices into their teaching. Lee's description of morning meeting in her third-grade classroom is a good example of what critical literacy in action looks like.

What Is Critical Literacy?

Over the past five years, Mitzi Lewison and Chris Leland facilitated two study groups of elementary teachers who met regularly to support each other in their efforts to infuse critical approaches into their curriculum. Lee has been a long-time group member. One question that came up repeatedly in early meetings was, "What is critical literacy?" From our perspective, critical literacy practices encourage students to use language to question the everyday world, to interrogate the relationship between language and power, to analyze popular culture and media, to understand how power relationships are socially constructed, and to consider actions that can be taken to promote social justice. Lee's morning meeting vignette highlights many of these practices. She, like other study group teachers, encourages students to analyze spoken, written, visual, and real-life texts (e.g., the lunchroom) to uncover whose interests are served and whose are being marginalized. These practices are substantively different from what are commonly referred to as *critical thinking* approaches. Although critical thinking approaches have focused more on logic and comprehension, critical literacies have focused on identifying social practices that keep dominant ways of understanding the world and unequal power relationships in place.

Critical literacies are rooted in principles of democracy and justice, of questioning and analysis, of resistance and action (Edelsky, 1999)—all uncommon in traditional pedagogies that define a teacher as a transmitter of knowledge. It is interesting that even though democratic principles are highly touted in textbooks and political rhetoric, they are often not taken up in classroom routines (Giroux, 1994). The work that Lee and her students engaged in with the lunchroom project is an inspiring example of how critical practices can be enacted in daily school life.

Chapter One
Overview

TABLE 1.1
Kinds of Citizens

Personally Responsible Citizen	Participatory Citizen	Justice-Oriented Citizen
	Description	
• Acts responsibly in his or her community • Works and pays taxes • Obeys laws • Recycles, gives blood • Volunteers to lend a hand in times of crisis	• Active member of community organizations or improvement efforts • Organizes community efforts to care for those in need, to promote economic development, or to clean up environment • Knows how government agencies work • Knows strategies for accomplishing collective tasks	• Critically assesses social, political, and economic structures to see beyond surface causes • Seeks out and addresses areas of injustice • Knows about democratic social movements and how to effect systemic change
	Sample Action	
Contributes food to a food drive	Helps to organize a food drive	Explores why people are hungry and acts to solve root causes
	Core Assumptions	
To solve social problems and improve society, citizens must have good character; they must be honest, responsible, and law abiding members of the community.	To solve social problems and improve society, citizens must actively participate and take leadership positions within established systems and community structures.	To solve social problems and improve society, citizens must question, debate, and change established systems and structures when they reproduce patterns of injustice over time.

Source: Westheimer and Kahne (2004, p. 240).

The Role of Theory in Critical Practice

Creating critical citizens is often listed as one of the goals of critical pedagogy. The work of Westheimer and Kahne (2004, p. 240) is useful in helping us to understand how our theories about the world, in this case citizenship, can make huge differences in the type of social practices we enact in our classrooms. Table 1.1 describes three models of democratic citizenship—personally responsible, participatory, justice oriented—and the assumptions that underlie each.

Examining the core assumptions of personally responsible, participatory, and justice-oriented citizens helps us to see how our theories about how to improve society make a difference in the ways we act in the world. The underlying assumptions that lead a teacher to encourage students to contribute to a food drive, help organize a food drive, or explore why people are hungry and act to solve root problems are very different. In critical literacy instruction, our theories and cultural models about what critical literacy is make a difference in the resources we use in the classroom, the social practices we enact, and the stance we take as teachers.

Creating Critical Classrooms

Lee's underlying assumptions about citizenship and social action were leaning toward Westheimer and Kahne's (2004) justice-oriented category. Students in her classroom questioned established systems and structures (i.e., lunchroom discipline and seating practices), analyzed the current structures to see beyond surface causes, developed research questions, and sent out inquiry teams to find answers. They also gained initial understandings of the historical causes of boy–girl seating in the lunchroom and learned about how others have worked to solve similar problems by researching the Mix It Up website. Finally, the students attempted to change established systems by developing and implementing their own Mix It Up activity and writing and presenting plays to educate other students and teachers in the school. In their plays they depicted the dilemma that every seating arrangement both marginalizes some students and privileges others. It is not an accident that this project moved students toward justice-oriented citizenship. "Any pedagogical choice implies some kind of theory …. Neither pedagogical practice nor personal experience can be assumed to be unmediated by theoretical standpoints" (Pennycook, 1999, p. 342).

A Model of Critical Literacy Instruction

After 10 revisions and dozens of conversations, we developed a model of critical literacy instruction. This model is not set in stone, but rather it is our best thinking at this time. We see critical literacy instruction as a transaction among the personal and cultural resources we use, the critical social practices we enact, and the critical stance that we and our students take on in classrooms and in the world. Because of the multifaceted nature of the model, we can use it as a planning tool and also as a lens from which to examine our teaching. For example, imagine that a teacher decided to read aloud a picture book like *White Wash* (Shange, 1997), which depicts racial bullying, verbal and physical violence, and neighborhood kids taking action to protect the victim. Simply reading this book does not guarantee that the teacher is enacting a critical curriculum. Granted, *White Wash* does have the potential to be part of critical literacy instruction, but unless the teacher and students are involved in critical social practices and are working from a critical stance, there is no assurance that there will be anything critical about the *White Wash* read-aloud. Figure 1.1 is a graphic representation of how we visualize a theory of critical literacy instruction and how the various components of the model interact with each other.

Personal and Cultural Resources

Personal and cultural resources, the outside ring of our model, are what students and teachers draw on to create the content of curriculum. The list of possible resources is endless. It can include personal experience;

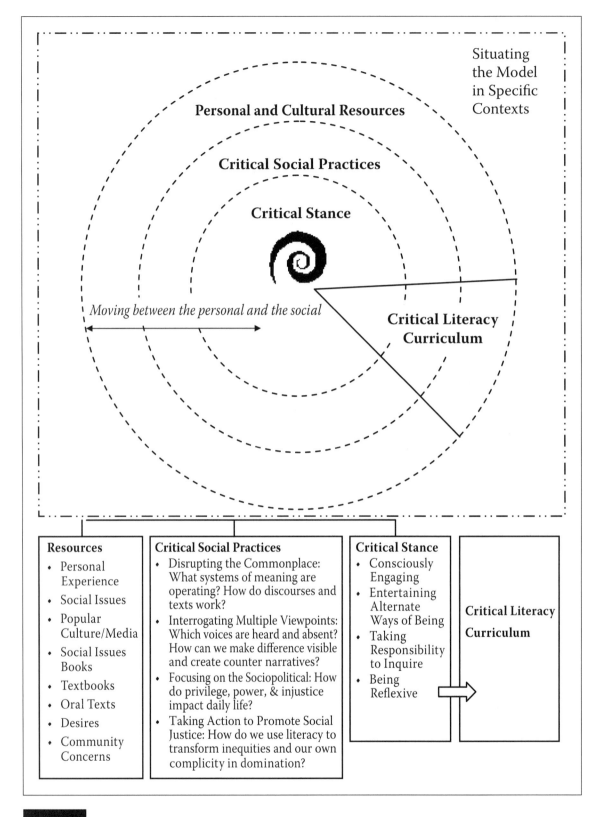

FIGURE 1.1
An Instructional Model of Critical Literacy

social issues books; popular culture and media; home literacies; textbooks; oral texts; competence in a language other than English; student desires and interests; and community, national, and international issues.

In the case of Lee's classroom, lunchroom discipline procedures (i.e., boy–girl seating as punishment) became the stuff from which curriculum was built. This is particularly important because this work deals with gender issues. In discussing teaching English to speakers of other languages (TESOL), Pennycook (1999, p. 340) reminds us that "issues such as gender, race, class, sexuality, and postcolonialism [are] so fundamental to identity and language that they need to form the basis of curricular organization and pedagogy." We believe this applies not only to the content of TESOL classes but also to the content of literacy curricula at all levels of schooling.

Critical Social Practice

The second ring of our model, critical social practices, includes the specific social practices that students and teachers engage in as they create critical curricula. As we saw in Lee's vignette, the social practices she encouraged in her classroom reflected her theories about what is appropriate curriculum for third-grade students, what characteristics of literate beings she values and encourages in students, and what commitments she makes to promote social justice.

By making a decision to use critical social practices, teachers create spaces that have the potential for students to disrupt what is considered to be normal by asking new questions, seeing everyday issues through new lenses, demystifying naturalized views of the world, and visualizing how things might be different (Giroux, 1994). Critical literacy practices support students in gaining a greater understanding of how social and cultural forces shape their choices and their lives.

Lewison, Flint, and Van Sluys (2002) reviewed a range of definitions of critical literacy that appeared in the research and professional literature over the last 30 years. They synthesized these into four dimensions of critical social practice: (1) disrupting the commonplace; (2) interrogating multiple viewpoints; (3) focusing on sociopolitical issues; and (4) taking action and promoting social justice. These four dimensions, like our model of critical literacy, are not meant to be the sole definition of critical social practices, but they are useful tools to use when planning curricular engagements. The four dimensions are interrelated; none are sufficient, nor do they stand alone.

Dimension 1: Disrupting the Commonplace

Routines, habits, beliefs, and theories about how the world works and what it takes to be successful guide all aspects of our lives. These factors impact the social groups we join, how we spend our time, and the careers we pursue. Without a critical perspective, these beliefs and assumptions

Invitation for Disruption 1:

What Is a Literate Being?

What we believe about literacy makes a difference. Even though our definitions of literacy are never fixed and always changing, it is important to go back regularly and revisit our current thinking.

- Jot down your current definition of a literate person.
- Which of your students does this definition value and privilege? Which students are marginalized by the definition?
- What characteristics might be added to this definition to create a greater number of literate, critical citizens in your classroom?

are seen as sensible and innocent, often just the way things are, and not in need of examination (Hinchey, 1998). A critical viewpoint requires a step outside of one's usual modes of perception and comprehension using new frames to understand experience. Shannon (1995) argues for the development of a language of critique. This language can then be used to disrupt what is considered to be normal by asking new questions, seeing everyday issues through new lenses, demystifying naturalized views of the world, and visualizing how things might be different (Giroux, 1994). One way a language of critique can be developed is through the study of language itself. This includes analyzing how language is socially situated, how it shapes identity, and how words, grammar, and cultural discourses work in terms of agency, passivity, and power (Gee, 1999).

Another aspect of critical social practices that focuses on interrogating the everyday world is for individuals and groups to examine how cultural and historical influences have shaped all aspects of life including the experience of schooling (Shor, 1987). Using education as an example, it is possible to open up pedagogy and curricular content for critique by asking why some groups benefit from current forms of education more than others. Critical educators encourage investigation of a wide range of commonly held assumptions like beliefs that boys are better at sports or math than girls, students who live in poverty do not have many cultural resources to bring to school, and competitive sports build character. In an environment where teachers focus on expanding critical literacies, students are also encouraged to interrogate classroom and environmental texts by asking questions about authors' intentions and what they want readers to believe (Luke & Freebody, 1997).

Disrupting the everyday also involves an examination of how social norms are communicated through the various arenas of popular culture and how identities are shaped by these experiences. People in today's world are bombarded with powerful images from television, radio, computer games, the Internet, and numerous forms of print media. Critical literacy practices lead to an examination of how individuals and groups are positioned and constructed by popular culture and media. Cultural icons like Pokémon and Barbie are studied to understand the messages they convey about what is or should be valued. This leads to an analysis of how the media and consumer culture are always shaping our collective perceptions, responses, and actions.

As a way of interrogating the commonplace, Freire (1970) called for a problem-posing rather than a problem-solving curriculum where classroom engagements are grounded in the lives and interests of students. He urged educators to present information to students that was directly related to questions raised in the classroom community and not in a prescribed curriculum. In this model, teachers and children negotiate curriculum, allowing space for real-life issues and popular culture to become topics of study. Students play a major role in planning, gathering resources, and assessing learning. The goal is for teachers to become partners with students in meaningful inquiry.

Disrupting the Commonplace During Morning Meeting   Although there are a number of examples of disrupting the commonplace in Lee's vignette, here we focus on one: her decision to interrupt the traditional show-and-tell consumerist forum of morning meeting by changing it into a space where members of the classroom community "share information that is of value and concern to all present." We believe this seemingly small step is actually very radical. Morning meeting or sharing time is an extremely ritualized classroom structure (Cazden, 1988; Horsch, Chen, & Nelson, 1999; Kamler, 1999). Each morning, through the primary years, many students expect to gather in a circle to hear daily announcements, to share a personal event or artifact, and to answer questions from peers and their teacher. The particular kinds of talk and behavior emphasized in most morning meetings focus on telling a certain kind of personal story, being courteous, quietly listening, not interrupting, and asking polite questions.

So what is wrong with this type of sharing time or morning meeting? Do we not expect these common practices to take place in primary classrooms? We believe that no curricular practices are neutral and unproblematic. This is especially true for those taken-for-granted powerful school structures like morning meeting that are historically embedded, appear to be innocent, and take place in classrooms day after day, week after week, year after year. This traditional version of morning meeting prepares children for a transmission model of education, not a critical one. And it is not only the children who are compliant in accepting the dominant discourses, subjectivities, and ideologies that are constructed in common curricular practices like morning meeting, but so are we, as teachers. In addition, show-and-tell practices privilege those students who have lots of cool stuff or experiences to bring to class and share. It marginalizes students who do not have these high-status items or experiences to present to their peers. We all have memories of students who felt they had to fabricate stories to gain prestige among their peers during show and tell, and sadly, these episodes usually ended disastrously for the student.

In her effort to transform morning meeting, Lee stepped outside of what is perceived as normal or natural and made quite a significant change in her classroom. It is important to note the incredible durability of commonplace, ritualized curricular structures, like sharing objects during morning meeting. Even for a knowledgeable teacher like Lee, interrogating and transforming morning meeting did not happen until she had been incorporating critical practices in her classroom for several years.

Invitation for Disruption 2:

Cultural Models of Teachers in Literature

With a colleague, read and discuss any of the following books that highlight teachers' work.

- *The Year of Miss Agnes* (Hill, 2000)
  Educating Esmé: Diary of a Teacher's First Year (Codell, 2001)
  The Freedom Writers Diary (The Freedom Writers & Gruwell, 1999)
- How would you characterize the frames and cultural models that guide these teachers' actions?
- Which of the methods they use make a positive difference in students' lives?

Dimension 2: Considering Multiple Viewpoints

We are continually involved in interactions where we make judgments about what has occurred, who is powerful, what is right, and what is just (Comber, 2001). These assessments are usually made from our own perspectives. By taking on critical literacy as a social practice, we strive to appreciate multiple realities as we attempt to stand in the shoes of others—to understand experience and text not only from personal experience but also from the viewpoints of others. We ask ourselves and our students to consider various views concurrently as we seek to gain richer and more complete understandings of the issue at hand. This often means juxtaposing multiple and contradictory textual accounts of an event (Luke & Freebody, 1997). For example, readers might interrogate a text by paying attention to whose voices are heard and whose are missing and to consider how a story would be different if it was told from a different perspective such as the from the voice of a farm worker rather than a farm owner.

In selecting materials for classroom use, educators who are attempting to develop a critical literacy curriculum seek out texts that give voice to those who have been silenced or marginalized: the migrant farm worker, the unemployed father, the ridiculed child, the genocide victim (Harste, et al., 2000). In this way, students can compare historical accounts from textbooks in relation with accounts written by those described in other texts. Teachers who implement critical practices have students examine competing narratives that describe social and political realities and construct counternarratives that challenge dominant discourses. By encouraging students to pay attention to multiple perspectives and realities, these teachers seek to make difference visible—creating a curriculum that honors and highlights difference rather than one that strives for consensus and conformity (Harste, et al., 2000).

Considering Multiple Viewpoints by Interrogating Disciplinary Practices in the Lunchroom   In the process of collecting data to answer their questions on the problems in the lunchroom, Lee's students observed and took field notes about what was happening in the lunchroom at their school. They found out the various reasons that kids threw food and saved seats. They also discovered what kids at the school liked and did not like about the lunchroom. They were confronted with a variety of explanations and viewpoints on lunchroom issues. This type of data complicates curriculum, but it also forces kids to try to make sense of various viewpoints. In attempting to understand more about lunchroom issues, Lee's students also found information from a variety of schools on the Mix It Up section of the Teaching Tolerance website. Before planning their ideal lunchroom and writing plays to present to other classes, students had to wrestle with the messiness of making sense of multiple and often contradictory perspectives about the problem.

Dimension 3: Focusing on the Sociopolitical

Advocates of critical literacy suggest that although teaching is a non-neutral form of social practice, it often takes place with no conscious awareness of the sociopolitical systems and power relationships that are part of every teaching episode (Edelsky, 1999; Lankshear & McLaren, 1993). Studying how language works can be a tool for deconstructing and reconstructing the relationships between language and power. In studying how language works, Janks (2000) identifies the interrelated concepts of domination, access, diversity, and design. Taking a critical literacy perspective requires an analysis of how language is used to maintain domination, how nondominant groups can gain access to dominant forms of language without devaluing their own language and culture, how diverse forms of language can be used as cultural resources, and how social action can change existing discourses.

As a result of researching and analyzing language and power, educators with critical perspectives challenge the legitimacy of unequal power relationships, question existing hierarchies, and examine social structures that keep power in the hands of a few. They interrogate privilege and status, not just in lives of others but in their own lives as well (Hinchey, 1998). They investigate oppression-—especially forms of oppression that appear to be natural or part of the status quo. This means that their students study a wide scope of power relationships ranging from issues of why some children are marginalized on the playground to why some groups of people are marginalized in the larger society. Through these investigations, participants gain an understanding of the complexities surrounding power relationships and begin to imagine how things might be different. Students and teachers explore the use of resistance, dialogue, and public debate as tools to engage in the politics of daily life (Fairclough, 1989; Lankshear & McLaren, 1993).

Focusing on the Sociopolitical in Morning Meeting   Soon after Lee announced the school-wide policy of boy–girl seating as a disciplinary measure for lunchroom rowdiness, issues of gender politics came to the forefront in student questions. Why was boy–girl seating a punishment? Why was there a lot of gender-based teasing about where kids sit at lunchtime? Why are there boys' tables and girls' tables at our school? The students discussed and debated these issues in morning meeting as well as authored plays about the issues. By creating a space (i.e., morning meeting) where critical social practices were encouraged, a simple edict from the principal had turned into an in-depth class inquiry into the underlying social and political issues regarding gender and the lunchroom. This type of interrogation of real-life issues is a powerful curricular tool.

In a previous year, Lee's students also interrogated the segregated nature of boy–girl seating in the lunchroom (Heffernan & Lewison, 2005). In interviews that took place a year after the students had attempted to desegregate the lunchroom, all reported vivid memories of the experience and spoke about the impact of the project, even if they were not avid proponents of the desegregation movement. This was a school experience that made a significant impression on how these kids engaged in the politics of daily life at school.

Dimension 4: Taking Action to Promote Social Justice

Another aspect of enacting critical social practices in the classroom means using language and other sign systems to get things done in the world. This is exemplified by Freire's (1970) call for becoming actors in the world rather than spectators. He also stresses the importance of praxis—reflection and action that transforms the world. This sense of agency is strengthened when students compose their own narratives, counternarratives, letters, essays, reports, poems, commercials, posters, plays, and webpages to promote social change. They participate in discussions that focus on issues of oppression, fairness, and transformation. They use a variety of literacies to conduct surveys and gather data to explain, expose, and find solutions for real-world problems (Hinchey, 1998). They use the arts to express critical understandings and to get messages of justice and democracy out into the world. Instead of being positioned as helpless victims, students use critical social practices to rewrite their identities as social activists who challenge the status quo and demand changes (Leland & Harste, 2000). They use cultural resources and critical literacies to develop powerful voices and to speak out collectively against injustice.

Focusing on Taking Action in the Lunchroom The students in Lee's classroom took action or were engaged in what Janks (2000) calls *design* in a number of ways. After discussing all of the different visions that students had of an ideal lunchroom, they decided to try it out on a small scale in their own classroom. They had lunch in their classroom, and as the kids came into the room they were given a number of a table to sit at. In this way, they were able to have conversations with kids with whom they might not normally interact. They could leave to go out to play when they were done with lunch, or they could stay and read or play games if they preferred. They could also take their time about eating, which was very important to some students. All and all it was a success, although admittedly a small one. This was when the class decided to write plays to present to other classrooms in the school to educate their peers on the problematic dynamics of the lunchroom and how things might be different. We believe that it is often more productive to delve into the local than to focus mainly on big, national or global transformations (Kamler, 2001). The lunchroom project is a good example of this. Table 1.2 summarizes the four dimensions of critical literacy and their associated social practices.

Critical Stance

Critical stance, at the core of our model, consists of the attitudes and dispositions we take on that enable us to become critically literate beings. "Taking a critical approach ... does not entail introducing a 'critical element' into a classroom but rather involves an attitude, a way of thinking and teaching" (Pennycook, 1999, p. 340). We have identified four dimensions of adopting a critical stance: consciously engaging, entertaining alternate ways of being, taking responsibility to inquire, and being reflexive. Figure 1.2 represents how these dimensions occur in a cyclical fashion, leading to renaming (Freire, 1970) and retheorizing, which reactivate the critical stance cycle.

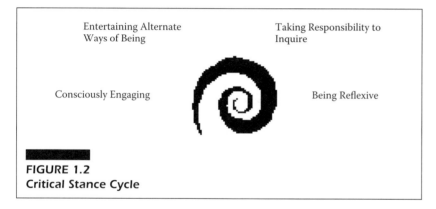

Entertaining Alternate
Ways of Being

Taking Responsibility to
Inquire

Consciously Engaging

Being Reflexive

**FIGURE 1.2
Critical Stance Cycle**

Consciously Engaging

When we take on a mindset of conscious engagement—the first aspect of adopting a critical stance—we do not just respond to events in our lives, but we thoughtfully decide how to respond. One way to start this process is by what Freire (1970, p. 76, emphasis in original) refers to as *naming*: "To exist, humanly, is to *name* the world to change it." We characterize naming as articulating thoughts that are outside of commonplace notions of what is natural—"to call an *ism* an *ism*" (Wink, 2000, p. 64) and to recognize commonsense power relationships that privilege certain people over others (Fairclough, 1989). Naming does not take place in isolation—we do not name alone. It is a social act and takes place as we dialogue and negotiate with others.

We also want to emphasize that naming is no easy task, especially if we take into account work from cognitive science demonstrating that humans think using unconscious frames (Lakoff, 2004, p. xv): These frames are "mental structures that shape the way we see the world . . .

TABLE 1.2
Four Dimensions of Critical Literacy

Dimension	Description
Disrupting the Commonplace	In this dimension, critical literacy is conceptualized as seeing the "everyday" through new lenses. We use language and other sign systems to recognize implicit modes of perception and to consider new frames from which to understand experience. From this dimension, critical literacy is seen as a way of (1) problematizing all subjects of study and understanding existing knowledge as a historical product (Shor, 1987); (2) interrogating texts by asking questions such as "How is this text trying to position me?" (Luke & Freebody, 1997); (3) including popular culture and media as a regular part of the curriculum for purposes of pleasure and for analyzing how people are positioned and constructed by television, video games, comics, toys, etc. (Marsh, 2000; Shannon, 1995; Vasquez, 2000); (4) developing the language of critique and hope (Shannon, 1995); and (5) studying language to analyze how it shapes identity, constructs cultural discourses, and supports or disrupts the status quo (Fairclough, 1989; Gee, 1999).
Considering Multiple Viewpoints	Authors who describe the multiple viewpoints dimension of critical literacy ask us to imagine standing in the shoes of others—to understand experience and texts from our own perspectives and the viewpoints of others and to consider these various perspectives concurrently. In this dimension we engage in a process of (1) reflecting on multiple and contradictory perspectives (Lewison, Leland, & Harste, 2000; Nieto, 1999); (2) using multiple voices to interrogate texts by asking questions such as "Whose voices are heard and whose are missing?" (Luke & Freebody, 1997); (3) paying attention to and seeking out the voices of those who have been silenced or marginalized (Harste, et al., 2000); (4) examining competing narratives and writing counter-narratives to dominant discourses (Farrell, 1998); and (5) making difference visible (Harste, et al., 2000).
Focusing on the Sociopolitical	Teaching is a nonneutral form of social practice, yet often it takes place with little attention focused on how sociopolitical systems, power relationships, and language are intertwined and inseparable from our teaching. From this dimension, critical literacy is seen as (1) going beyond the personal and attempting to understand the sociopolitical systems to which we belong (Boozer, Maras, & Brummett, 1999); (2) challenging the unquestioned legitimacy of unequal power relationships (Anderson & Irvine, 1993) by studying the relationship between language and power (Fairclough, 1989; Gee, 1999); (3) using literacy to engage in the politics of daily life (Lankshear & McLaren, 1993); and (4) redefining literacy as a form of cultural citizenship and politics that increases opportunities for subordinate groups to participate in society—literacy is an ongoing act of consciousness and resistance (Giroux, 1993).

the goals we seek, the plans we make, the way we act." To illustrate this, Lakoff (2004) describes the metaphor of the nation as a family—an overarching frame held by both conservatives and progressives in this country. He also points out how important distinctions in this metaphor become apparent when moving from generalities to particulars. Lakoff argues that conservatives believe in the model of a strict father family and progressives in a nurturant parent family (p. 6). There is a whole string of competing ideas, values, beliefs, and cultural models associated with each of these metaphors. Lakoff artfully points out how framing accounts for the ways that different groups of people understand a particular event in vastly different ways.

Without conscious engagement, we simply respond to events using our unconscious, commonsense frames, which make it challenging to assume a critical stance. Reframing is difficult. In fact, Lakoff (2004) believes that reframing is social change. It requires bringing our unconscious frames into awareness and then using new language and new points of view to modify our cultural models. One way to get at reframing is to pay attention to the language we use, focusing our awareness on how it shapes identity, constructs cultural discourses, and supports or disrupts the status quo (Fairclough, 1989; Gee, 1999). When we are cognizant of the options we have in interpretation, response, and action we move toward conscious engagement.

In Lee's case, she was consciously aware of how the show-and-tell nature of morning meeting was not supporting critical practices in her classroom. By the third grade, students were strongly enmeshed in traditional understandings of how to do morning meeting, making its reframing a difficult task. Lee took on a critical stance as she steered morning meeting away from a consumerist forum into a space for building classroom community as well as for addressing important personal, cultural, and political issues.

Chapter One
Overview

Entertaining Alternate Ways of Being

A second aspect of taking on a critical stance involves creating and trying on new discourses. This is something Lee did when she helped students engage in new types of talk during morning meeting. The traditional discourse of show and tell was no longer appropriate in this transformed setting. To participate, students had to try on new topics and ways of being during morning meeting. This meant experimenting with new identities and taking up new positions.

Along with entertaining new discourses, risk taking also supports adopting a critical stance. This means coming to an understanding that parts of what we believe about teaching, learning, and curriculum may not be working. We do not go about our work in classrooms with a "true believer" attitude, ignoring the anomalies that do not fit into our model of the world. Rather, we are aware of the partiality of our understandings, staying open to the possibility that our best thinking at a particular moment in time may be wrong—that we may need to imagine a new approach. Lee had been satisfied with the show-and-tell ritual for many years, but when she began using critical literacy as a lens to take a fresh look at this tried-and-true practice, she became uncomfortable. Despite the fact that morning meeting looked like it was working well to outsiders, it became increasingly difficult for Lee to maintain it in its traditional form. She took on a new challenge by revising her theory of morning meeting, a practice that no one else at her school had questioned.

Using tension as a resource also supports adopting a critical stance. Lee took a mandate from the principal regarding cafeteria discipline and turned it into curriculum—a bold move on her part. Questioning boy–girl seating arrangements as punishment brings to the surface the tensions between child and adult understandings of appropriate behavior, between group and individual rights, and of students interrogating a principal's mandate. In this case, tension served as an important resource in adopting a critical stance.

Another way of entertaining alternate ways of being is to understand the multimodal and multimediated nature of literacies and their relationship to power. When students in Lee's classroom inquired into lunchroom discipline, they decided they wanted to educate other students in the school about their findings. They were keenly aware of the power of language and its potential for getting things done in the world. These young people made a conscious decision to use drama as the genre that would be most likely to get their ideas across to other students at the school. They believed a dramatic storyline would be more likely to hook their audience than simply giving a talk or making a PowerPoint presentation. These students had a sophisticated understanding of how each medium or form of literacy offers both opportunities and constraints.

Taking Responsibility to Inquire

Inquiry, interrogation, and investigation are always at the forefront in adopting the third dimension of a critical stance. In short, we ask lots of questions. Why did a certain event happen in a particular way? Who benefits from things being like this, and who is marginalized? Part of our responsibility to inquiry means understanding that all knowledge is constructed from particular perspectives and that getting at multiple and contradictory viewpoints enriches our perceptions of the world. In curricular terms, we focus on asking questions that make a difference, interrogating the everyday, and not viewing knowledge as something static to be learned. Peirce (1931–58) wisely noted that knowledge is beliefs at rest. In adopting an inquiry stance, we push our beliefs out of their resting positions and engage in a cycle where new knowledge provokes new questions and where new questions generate new knowledge.

In a conversation with António Faundez in *Learning to Question* (Freire & Faundez, 1989, p. 227), Paulo Freire and Faundez discuss how questioning is "profoundly democratic" and how "surprise" plays a key role in lifelong learning: "…Precisely when someone loses the capacity to be surprised, they sink into bureaucratization." We see this happen when our teaching becomes routinized, when we implement someone else's answers, and when creativity is no longer part of the adventure of teaching.

Lee assisted students in taking on an inquiry stance by introducing the idea of coresearching the lunchroom and creating research teams to help them understand the issues at hand. Students began collecting data from a wide range of informants to get a more complete picture of what was going on in the lunchroom. By listening to their audiotaped conversations about the lunchroom at morning meeting, these young inquirers had a second level of data—their own talk about the issues—to use in creating a list of important topics to find out more about when they go back into the field to research. These kids were being real researchers, studying an important issue in their school lives.

Too often we develop curriculum from memory—from what we taught the previous year or from what we think is fundamental at a particular grade level. We also develop curriculum from mandated curricular frameworks, standards, and textbooks. The problem with these stances—aside from the way they, at times, lead us to teach nonsense—is that our students are positioned as consumers rather than participants in their education. They understand disciplinary knowledge as a set of facts to be learned rather than as alternate perspectives on understanding the world (Short, Harste, & Burke, 1996). In a consumerist model of education, students never get a chance to think, reason, and act like a mathematician, a historian, a psychologist, a geographer. They simply memorize what others have already found out.

In contrast, students in Lee's classroom took on the work of intellectuals and social scientists. They used the questions, tools, and methods of educational researchers in their lunchroom inquiry. Instead of learning about conflict resolution through a prepackaged curriculum, these students engaged in inquiry to confront the real-world issues that impacted their lives. They were participants in constructing knowledge, not consuming it.

Being Reflective

Reflexivity, the fourth aspect of adopting a critical stance, means being aware of our own complicity in maintaining the status quo or systems of injustice. Even though we may be committed to social change, we often are implicated in perpetuating oppression. Being aware of how we have our hand in the cookie jar is an important aspect of adopting a critical stance. During morning meeting, Lee pointed out that despite all of their work on gender desegregation, the boys and girls were sitting on different sides of the circle. With this comment, she gave the students a vivid demonstration of what it means to be reflexive. The kids' laughter and their scurrying to get into a more emancipatory seating arrangement mirrors our own surprise and often embarrassed feelings when we realize we are talking the talk but not walking the walk. As Kamler (1999) points out, catching ourselves in incongruent and contradictory behavior is hopeful. It is a sign that we are engaged in the struggle of trying on new identities and discourses.

Pennycook (1999, p. 331) asks us to consider, "To what extent does the work [in this case critical literacy] constantly question common assumptions, including its own?" He argues for seeing critical approaches "not as a static body of knowledge but rather as always being in flux, always questioning, restively problematizing the given, being aware of the limits of their own knowing, and bringing into being new schemas of politicization" (p. 329). It is not enough to be aware of our own complicity; we also need to engage in an active and systematic process of questioning and evaluating our critical practices.

Another way to understand reflexivity is through renaming or retheorizing. Freire (1970, p. 76) points out that "once named, the world in its turn reappears to the namers as a problem and requires of them a new naming." Notice that Freire uses the word *namers*. Naming and renaming are social activities that happen in dialogue and debate with others. In this dialogue, we use ourselves and others to outgrow ourselves. This renaming cycle is retheorizing—scrutinizing our assumptions about how the world works and, if necessary, changing our beliefs and understanding. But changing beliefs without action is not enough. Hooks (1994, p. 60) argues for "theory as intervention, as a way to challenge the status quo." Freire's call for praxis—reflection and action on the world—is the cornerstone of reflexivity.

Table 1.3 summarizes the four dimensions of taking a critical stance.

TABLE 1.3
Four Dimensions of Taking a Critical Stance

Dimension	Examples
Consciously Engaging	• Not just responding, but deciding how to respond • Paying attention to the language we use • Being cognizant of options in interpretation, response, and action
Entertaining Alternate Ways of Being	• Creating and trying on new or secondary discourses and identities • Risk taking • Using tension as a resource • Understanding the multimodal and multimediated nature of literacies and their relationship to power
Taking Responsibility to Inquire	• Understanding that all knowledge is constructed from particular perspectives • Creating a problem-posing rather than a problem-solving curriculum where students are participants and not just consumers • Being aware that knowledge is beliefs at rest • Moving beyond initial understandings
Being Reflexive	• Being aware of our own complicity in maintaining the status quo or systems of injustice • Questioning the practices of critical literacy • Using ourselves and others to outgrow ourselves • Renaming and retheorizing

Moving Between the Personal and the Social

In our model of critical literacy (Figure 1.1), we have an arrow showing how curriculum moves between the personal and the social—a key concept in our theory of critical literacy instruction. We believe it is important that we create curriculum by starting with students' personal knowledge, interests, and issues—that these become useful resources and social capital (Bourdieu, 1986) that are valued and used to accomplish school tasks in the classroom. But even though we start with the personal, it is always embedded in the social, and never enough. In a critical curriculum we emphasize how understandings are never individual or autonomous—that they always have social, cultural, and political dimensions. So although we often value and start with the personal, we think it is essential to move beyond it, to understand the forces that have shaped our experiences rather than just relying on experience itself (Kamler, 2001, p. 166).

There are also times when curriculum moves from the social to the personal and then back to the social. Some issues are so close to home that it is easier to begin conversations about someone else's concerns. For example, some teachers find it difficult to address incidents of racism that occur at their schools head on, but they are willing to

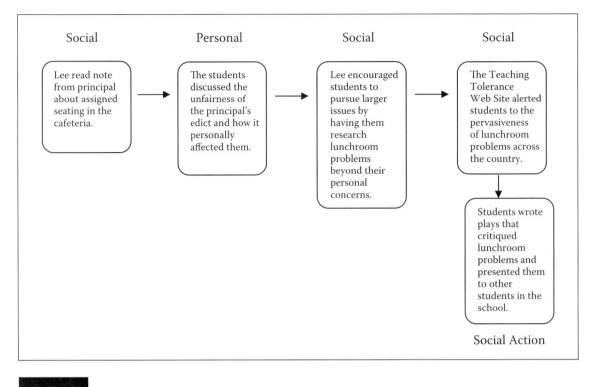

Social	Personal	Social	Social

Lee read note from principal about assigned seating in the cafeteria. → The students discussed the unfairness of the principal's edict and how it personally affected them. → Lee encouraged students to pursue larger issues by having them research lunchroom problems beyond their personal concerns. → The Teaching Tolerance Web Site alerted students to the pervasiveness of lunchroom problems across the country.

Students wrote plays that critiqued lunchroom problems and presented them to other students in the school.

Social Action

FIGURE 1.3
Moving between the personal and the social

start by reading aloud stories about racism, such as the book *White Wash* (Shange, 1997) mentioned earlier in the chapter. After students have discussed issues in the book, teachers ask questions like the following:

▮ Does anything like this happen at our school? How does it relate to what happened in *White Wash*?
▮ Have you ever been afraid of other kids at our school or in your neighborhood? Why were you frightened? Were you able to find an ally to help?
▮ What are the main problems we have at our school? How might we label them? What could we do to change them?

Figure 1.3 shows how Lee started a discussion about the note from her principal and then encouraged students to move from this social incident to the personal, then back to the social, and finally to social action.

Situating the Model in Specific Contexts
Our model of critical literacy instruction is situated in a context box. By physically placing the model in this box, we emphasize that implementing critical literacy in classrooms does not take place in a vacuum—that the context in which teachers find themselves makes a difference. Systemic forces always impact what we do and do not do in our classrooms. There is

Creating Critical Classrooms

no denying that if we want to implement critical practices in classrooms, working at a school where administrators demand the use of specific mandated, one-size-fits-all materials is much more difficult than working in schools where the staff has resisted standardized curricula. The contexts in which we work can support or hinder critical teaching.

For those who work in less supportive schools, we have found teacher study groups to be one of the most effective ways to begin impacting the contexts that influence our classrooms (Birchak, et al., 1998; Lewison, 1995; Lewison & Holliday, 1999). Dialogue with those who have similar interest in creating critical classrooms can build support and strength by learning and working together. Fairclough (1989), who studies language and power, sees communication (i.e., public discourse) as one of the few ways to struggle against domination where unequal power relationships exist. In many of our schools, we need to find ways to begin to take back our roles as intellectuals and professionals—to begin changing the way we have been positioned as transmitters of set curricula. Teacher study groups are a promising way to build solidarity and strategies for making our schools the kind of places in which we want to live and work. These groups also allow us to reflect on practice and the particular methods we use. The thought piece "Do Methods Make a Difference" directly addresses the connections among reflection, practice, and theory.

Lingering Questions

▌ Which aspects of the model of critical literacy are you already comfortable with? Which areas do you rarely address?
How might you start planning curriculum with more features of the model evident in classroom engagements?

▌ What moves can we make to support colleagues in schools where one-size-fits-all curricula are mandated?

Thought Piece

Do Methods Make a Difference?

Jerome C. Harste

The great debate in literacy has been over which instructional approach is best able to "solve" student reading and writing problems. Critical theorists say methods do not make the difference. Great-debate arguments, they say, miss the point.:

> Many of us working from sociological and cultural perspectives on literacy education have tried to change the subject of the great debate, to shift it sideways. We have argued that there is no "right" way of teaching reading and writing, but that different curricular approaches—and their attendant textbooks, classroom events, assessment instruments and adjunct materials—shape literacy as social practices differently. The ways that literacies are shaped have uneven benefits for particular communities .... (Luke, 1998, p. 305)

Critical theorists base their argument on research that shows that schools for working-class children are very different from schools for children coming from affluent neighborhoods (Anyon, 1997; Finn, 1999). Although the topics covered may be the same, the level of engagement by teachers and pupils differs drastically. The social practices of working-class schools prepare students for labor that is mechanical and routine. The social practices of schools located in affluent neighborhoods prepare students for work as artists, intellectuals, legal and scientific experts, and other professional roles that involve creativity, are intrinsically satisfying, and are rewarded with social power and high salaries. The children's capacity for creativity and planning in working-class schools is often denied or ignored, while at the same time the children's capacity for creativity and planning in schools in affluent neighborhoods is encouraged.

To understand critical theorists' argument it is important to unpack the phrase *social practices*. Following Gee's (1996) distinction between big "D" *Discourse* and little "d" *discourse*, it is useful to think of big "S" *Social Practices* and little "s" *social practices*. Social Practices are systems of meaning at work in society of which we may or may not be conscious. Men, despite "the women's movement" and all of the progress women have made, are still more valued in our society, for example. Women's pay remains lower even when educational attainments are the same. Men are, more often than not, thought of as the head of the household. Men still hold most of the very top jobs in government and business. This, then, is a Social Practice. A social practice would be the disuse of "he" in writing as a generic referencing form or the change in language use from *chairman* to *chairperson* in memos.

With this distinction in mind, the methods point being made by critical theorists is that Social Practices overpower social practices, where social practices are methods, and Social Practices are these larger forces of meaning that are operating in society. They say that bigger systems of meaning, like social class differences, are shaping schools and schooling more than methods. But by not making a distinction between Social Practices and social practices, I argue that social theorists confuse themselves and fail to understand that methods do indeed make a difference.

I have some proof. The Center for Inquiry, an inner-city public school, with which I have been associated for the past 10 years, regularly outperforms suburban schools on the Indiana State Test of Education Progress (Harste, Leland, Schmidt, Vasquez, & Ociepka, 2004). The same Social Practices of race, class, and poverty are in place here as in other parts of the country. I attribute the Center for Inquiry's success to a drastic change in social practices, or methods.

The Anyon (1997) study, cited by critical theorists, found that creativity and personal development were important goals in schools in affluent neighborhoods but not nearly so important in schools in working-class neighborhoods. My argument is that this goal was enacted through method. For example, in Finn's (1999) discussion of Anyon's research, he notes that social studies was taught to emphasize higher concepts, that students were invited to pursue their own inquiry questions, that a lot of time was devoted to understanding current events, that knowledge was seen as open to discovery, and that children were encouraged to use the arts and the new media to make and share meaning. I want to argue that these are not Social Practices issues but social practices, issues, or methods.

In fact, my experience with urban schools bears out both their Social Practices observations as well as their social practices observations. Teachers, I have found, often talk very differently to children from working-class homes than to children attending schools in affluent suburbs—a Social Practice issue—but this very fact is why the issues being talked about need to be disentangled and why methods do make a difference. From my perspective, methods are *social practices*. They may not be social practices in the sense of the larger systems of meaning that are operating in society—though they often reflect these—but rather the social practices that take place in the classroom. They are the social practices that matter to children and teachers because they are up close and personal.

Whereas other people may see methods as formulaic step-by-step procedures for how things are to be taught, this is not the way I think about methods. Such thinking, however, has given *methods* a bad name. That is more than unfortunate. Methods are too important to be walked away from, abandoned, or dismissed. Methods are, from my perspective, instructional practices derived from theory.

How learners and the learning process are viewed affects—and rightfully ought to affect—how to go about supporting learners and the learning process. The social practices someone puts in place, based on his or her beliefs, are what I see as methods. And in my view, methods make a big difference.

If learning is seen as an active process, then the social practices put in place need to allow children choice as well as agency. If learning is a social process, then collaboration and the opportunity to learn from and with others is important. If language is a meaning-making process (very few people I know learn to read for the sheer pleasure of sounding out words or learn to write to see how many words they can spell correctly), then language is presented for purposes of instruction makes a difference. If we want children to question the authority of text and how it positions them, then what we do to support this taking on of a critical perspective makes a difference. It does not make a difference every once in a while. It makes a difference all of the time. This, for me, is method as it suggests a set of social practices that characterize how we teach and how we engage students.

Teachers often complain that issues like this are too theoretical. What they want are practical ideas that work. I would argue that nothing is more practical than theory.

In fact, theory and practice go hand in hand. What every educator should aim for, in my estimation, is theoretical practice, or said differently, a sound set of beliefs on which to base the instructional decisions that are made in the classroom.

Do not get me wrong—it is not always theory to practice. Sometimes it is grounded theory, or theory evolving from practice, but for that to happen the social practices we engage in have to be reflected upon and some larger theoretical premise has to be generated. That is why I associate methods and theory with some of the best teachers I know. Following Schön (1983), I call them *reflective practitioners*.

Just because something works does not make it worthwhile. Worksheets work. They keep students busy, but do they teach what we want students to be learning? Smith (1982) says that the problem is not learning. Students are learning all of the time. The problem is that what they may be learning is not what we thought we were teaching. Children learn to hate reading, for example, by the very way we teach reading. If we want to create literate individuals who read, we need to teach reading—engage in sets of social practices in the classroom—in such a manner so that children come to value this form of literate activity and see its benefit. This is method as well as practical theory and theoretical practice.

A theory is a system of beliefs that we have developed over time and through experience. With more and more experience, our theories of the world as well as our theories of teaching become more and more fleshed out. There is a difference between acting on experience, however, and acting reflectively based on experience. The first is dangerous—we repeat something because it worked. The second is generative. We now have a bigger principle we understand that can help us modify as well as generate bigger and better social practices. We do not have to be conscious of a theory to have one, but we have to be conscious of a theory to use it to outgrow ourselves.

Both teachers and children hold theories of reading, whether or not they are aware that they hold these theories. Just watch them. Their behaviors always point to the types of theories they hold. Children who see reading as a sounding-out process display reading behaviors that differ from the behaviors displayed by children who see reading as a meaning-making process. Similarly, teachers who see reading, for "these children," as a matter of "breaking the letter–sound code" teach differently than teachers who see reading, for "these children," as a meaning-making process. Our beliefs about reading, our beliefs about children, and our beliefs about social class all interact. That is why teaching and learning look so different in schools in working-class neighborhoods as opposed to schools located in affluent neighborhoods. And trust me, even the critical theorists who say methods are not important think they are, or they would have no argument for advocating one type of school experience over another, one kind of literate being over another. Barnes (1975, p. 7) said it succinctly: "Not only what we teach, but how we teach affects what is learned." That is method.

Chapter 2

Personal and Cultural Resources

Using Life Experiences as an Entrée into Critical Literacy

Vignette

Writing Respect

Katie Van Sluys

Risë Reinier and I are both teachers and researchers. We have worked together for four years in a multi-age (grades 4–6), multilingual classroom in a public school. Through observations, field notes, and conversations, we regularly discussed what it meant to build a curriculum based on kids' lives, passions, and needs.

As with any class, on the first day of school in Room 4, the students brought with them a wide range of experiences. There were the recent immigrants from Mexico, Israel, Korea, and Northern Africa. There were the kids who could speak languages other than English—12 in all. There were the students who lived in traditional or single-parent families as well as those who lived with grandparents, stepparents, or adoptive parents. Our goal for the year was to make the classroom community feel comfortable to all students—especially newcomers. As a way to honor students' experiences and first languages, we decided to revise the writing curriculum to put students at the center of the curriculum. Risë and I envisioned writer's workshop as a curricular tool that would help us learn about the lives and interests of our students. We knew if we based curriculum on what was important to students and not on our preplanned lessons, we would need to be prepared to face uncertainties in what happened in the classroom. We understood that we would not be able to anticipate specific outcomes when students started writing. The stories of two sixth-grade girls show a glimpse of what life was like for students in Room 4.

Sara's Story

Sara arrived in this country from Algeria speaking Berber, Arabic, and French. She did not speak English. At first she did a lot of watching and observing what the other kids were doing. Things were very different in the United States for Sara—there were no familiar rows of desks or class-mates walking home for lunch. Instead there were tables, riding buses to school, and eating together in the lunchroom. The teacher did not stand on a podium in front of the class, and, maybe most surprising to Sara, her classmates were always talking.

On the day Risë launched writer's workshop with a minilesson on writer's notebooks, she also wrote the following in Sara's notebook to her father: "A notebook is a tool for thinking…a place to keep ideas. Today we talked about 'firsts' but again the topic is not mandated. Please encourage Sara to write at home each night and in class when we have notebooks out."

Risë hoped that Sara's father, who could read English, would take time to talk with Sara about what was happening in her classroom and how she might make links between home and school.

The Lonely Fish
by Sara

The fish in the big tank
Was not moving much.
I wonder what's
   wrong with him
Because the other fish
Seem to be having
   a good time
Moving a lot.
I thought a lot about
   the big fish
Not sharing the
   excitement.

Sara started filling the pages of her notebook with Arabic text. She also used Arabic to make connections with other students. Steve, a classmate of Sara's, suggested that they could focus on the map of the world and write about what they saw. In her notebook, Sara drew a compass rose with the four points and lengthy explanations written in Arabic. Later in the year, using her Arabic notebook entries, Sara carried on a discussion in English with her tablemates about the differences between schooling and life in the United States and Algeria. She also used Arabic to create a poem, "The Lonely Fish," which grew out of her own early experiences in the classroom. Her father worked at home with Sara on the English version of the poem.

Eventually, Sara was writing in both Arabic and English. Her writer's notebook became a key connection between home and school.

Rachel's Story

Another sixth grader in Room 4 was Rachel, an African American girl, the oldest of her mother's six (soon-to-be seven) children. Though accustomed to this school, Rachel was new to Room 4. From past school experience, she questioned her academic abilities and seemed wary of what was to come during her sixth-grade year. She often mentioned how in prior years she was teased by peers and lamented her past academic struggles of "catching up on stuff." Rachel started using her notebook to write about her strong and proud ties to family. Early entries in Rachel's notebook contained childhood stories of at-home haircuts between siblings, times when her dog bit her and would not let go, family outings to her cousin's football game, and the anticipation of a new baby. She also wrote about the days and nights she spent at camp with her class—where she wrote that "[everything was] okay, except for one thing I'm missing here, my family." Rachel treasured her family, and her writer's notebook was a place to bring this affection into the classroom and the curriculum. This family focus continued as she copied the words her mother had written on her birthday card into her writer's notebook. She also set aside pages to write about each of her siblings.

As her confidence grew through writer's workshop, Rachel began to talk about herself as someone like Grace in Alice Hoffman's (1991) *Amazing Grace*. She worked for weeks on a PowerPoint presentation that described how she, like Grace, could be anything if she put her mind to it. She also became known as the person in class who could read Jacqueline Woodson's (2001) *The Other Side* in a way that sounded like poetry. She eventually gave in to her classmates' pleas to read it aloud, just one more time.

Risë and I searched for children's literature that connected with Rachel's life experiences and the experiences of other students in the class. Two books seemed especially relevant to us. The first, *The Circuit: Stories from the Life of a Migrant Child* (Jiménez, 1998), was not only a compelling tale about the plight of migrant farm workers, poor immigrants, and racism but also detailed how older children had to look after younger siblings in a large family where parents had many responsibilities. The second book, *Just Juice* (Hesse, 1998), portrays 9-year-old Juice as the middle child in her Appalachian family of eight (with a pregnant mother). Juice loves taking care of younger siblings, and Hesse juxtaposes this with Juice's academic problems including difficulty in learning to read and completing schoolwork.

One day, Rachel mentioned the commonalties she saw between herself and the main character in *Just Juice*: "She [Juice] took care of her brothers and sisters a lot and helped out her mom. She told things about her mom, like whenever a guest comes over she brings out the sugar cubes and things and she describes her sisters and how they are, like she knows them. She helped her mom when she was going through birth."

Rachel knew about birth, children, and caring for others. During a piano recital at school, Risë and I noticed her sitting beside her third-grade sister while holding her kindergarten brother, lulling him to sleep in her arms. In Room 4, Rachel became regarded as someone who knew a lot about young children, and she became a respected resource. As Risë introduced the invitation (i.e., learning center) titled "Birth and Pregnancy," Rachel clarified classmates' misconceptions and became an important teacher whom peers turned to when needing more information.

As the year progressed, Rachel assessed her school experiences as being much better than in previous years—noting that her friends were better, that she got things done, and that she was now an interested learner—even though everything was not always easy. She began to talk about her classroom as a place where "we like work together on things .... [People] know what they're supposed to be working on, and really it is that they respect you."

What Can We Learn from Sara and Rachel's Experience in Room 4?

In the 1980s, a group of educators studied how the theories that we hold about learning and teaching are often implicit, unconscious, and not readily open to examination (Lester & Mayher, 1987; Lester & Onore, 1986; Peterson & Clark, 1986; Schön, 1987; Smyth, 1989; Tom, 1985; Zeichner, 1983). They argued that, by becoming more aware of our implicit assumptions about life in the classroom, we are more likely to perceive and to examine the beliefs we hold about learning, teaching, and curriculum, thus enabling us to become more skilled and effective educators. This reflective stance has been described as distancing oneself from an engagement, taking a new perspective on what occurred, seeing alternatives, and developing new understandings (Short & Burke, 1989).

We strongly believe that a conscious awareness of the theories that influence our teaching enables us to be more reflective about our practice. What were the underlying assumptions that guided the curriculum Sara and Rachel experienced in Room 4? This curriculum did not happen by accident. Risë and Katie held a specific set of beliefs about learning, teaching, and curriculum that guided their actions in the classroom. After a close reading of Katie's narrative, we found three important theories that informed how curriculum was enacted in Room 4.

Theory 1: Since all students are capable and bring a wide range of experiential, cultural, and linguistic resources to the classroom, our job as teachers is to figure out ways to regularly use these resources and to give them a place of prominence in what counts in our classrooms.

The students in Room 4, especially immigrant youngsters like Sara, experience school in ways that are qualitatively different from many of their peers across the country. In this class, Sara is viewed as a capable, knowledgeable student who is admired for her knowledge of Berber, French, and Arabic. She is not perceived as deficient because she does not speak English. Sara is able to participate with other students in writer's workshop by composing in Arabic—a language neither Katie nor Risë reads or understands. They both have a remarkable level of trust that Sara is doing appropriate schoolwork in her writer's notebook. This level of trust is unusual and stands in stark contrast to more traditional models of English as a second language (ESL) instruction where it is important to know exactly what each student is producing—usually having the students work exclusively in English. During writing time in a more traditional ESL classroom, we might see Sara copying the alphabet or short texts in English from the board or from books. It is important to note that Sara does participate in regular ESL instruction, but there is no pressure for her to abandon the complicated stories she writes in Arabic to quickly move into English writing. Even as she becomes proficient in English, we see Sara using the Arabic writing in her notebook as a text from which to speak in English to her classmates about the differences in schooling and life in Algeria and the United States.

The way Risë and Katie encourage Sara to write in Arabic for writer's workshop relates to a concept developed by Thomson (2002) called the *virtual school bag*. Thomson describes how children enter school with a virtual school bag full of all of the things they have learned at home, their languages, abilities, and past experiences. Some students' school bags are more valued in classrooms and metaphorically opened daily, whereas other, less privileged children are rarely allowed to open their bags and use the cultural resources they have acquired at home. These closed bags position many students as disadvantaged. Sara is fortunate in being able to open her virtual school bag daily in Room 4.

TABLE 2.1

Virtual school bag observations

Virtual School Bag Observations	
Student:	
Abilities, knowledge, and experiences that get unpacked regularly in the classroom.	Abilities, knowledge, and experiences that remain in the bag

What I am going to try to unpack:
How will that happen?

How did it work?

Invitation for Disruption 2:

Home Visits

- It is important that curriculum build connections between the outside world and school.
- Try to visit the homes of some of your students during the school year.
- How would you design a curriculum to build on the funds of knowledge you witness in students' homes?
- How could parents become a part of your curriculum without positioning them as deficient or needing to do something different with their children?

Thomson (2002) came up with the idea of virtual school bags by drawing on Bourdieu's (1986) notion of *cultural capital*. In a school setting, cultural capital is the knowledge, resources, ways of thinking, and dispositions that are valued in classrooms and can be used to successfully accomplish school tasks. These are the things that count in school. Normally, we might think of Sara as lacking in cultural capital because she cannot speak English, but in Room 4, where differences are perceived as valuable assets rather than obstacles to be overcome, Sara is encouraged to use her ability to speak and write in a language other than English as cultural capital. From this example, we see that the teacher is in a powerful position—one of being able to *expand* or *restrict* the types of cultural capital that is valued in the classroom. Risë and Katie's strong belief in the benefits of using a wide range of experiential resources in the classroom makes Room 4 a place that invites students from all types of backgrounds into the literacy club (Smith, 1981) rather than restricting membership to only those who come from homes where certain languages and literacy practices are used.

Theory 2: To be relevant to students' interests and knowledge, we build curriculum by creating connections between the classroom and life outside of school.

Room 4 is a place where home-school connections are the norm, not the exception or special event where parents come to school for a performance or other celebration. Students like Rachel benefit from being in a classroom where curriculum is intimately tied to students' lives outside of school. During writer's workshop, Rachel was able to write about what she was interested in and good at—being a very responsible and knowledgeable older sister and part-time caretaker to five younger siblings. Risë and Katie used Rachel's notebook entries as a way to find out more about what was on Rachel's mind. Although many kids come to school with experiences and interests similar to Rachel's, it is not very often that children's lives become a central part of the classroom curriculum. In this instance, Risë and Katie sought out children's books that dovetailed with Rachel's interests.

Bringing children's concerns from outside of school into the classroom is often seen as negative—too child centered, not rigorous enough, not geared to state standards. But the inclusion of the real world into the curriculum in Room 4 did wonders for Rachel academically. She was no longer positioned as a kid who does not do well in school and often made to feel like she has to catch up on uncompleted work. She was trying on the identity of a capable student with lots to offer others—someone who could do anything she puts her mind to.

Rachel's knowledge of child rearing, babies, and family life is what Moll et al. (1992, p. 133) refer to as *funds of knowledge*, which include the "… historically accumulated and culturally developed bodies of knowledge and skills essential for household or individual functioning and well being." Rachel has a vast store of skills and abilities that were learned as she interacted with members of a complex social network—her immediate family, relatives, and neighbors. She drew on the knowledge and resources of many people as she became the competent young woman we see today. It is easy to imagine contrasting the productive learning environment in Room 4 with so many classrooms that often seem encapsulated or isolated from the rich home and community resources that children have access to outside of school (Moll et al., 1992, p. 134). In Room 4, writer's notebook served as a vehicle for Rachel to draw on the extensive funds of knowledge that she used outside of school. Her notebook was a place where Rachel could "do school" in a way that valued who she is and what she knows.

Theory 3: People must see themselves in literacy to become literate, which involves starting with the personal and moving to the social.

To become literate, children and adults must have the belief that they are already literate. For someone who thinks that literacy is something that other people have, the barriers to becoming literate are huge. Rogers (2001), in her research on family literacy practices, describes Vicky, an African American sixth-grade girl whose experiences are somewhat parallel to Rachel's. Vicky, like Rachel, had an affectionate relationship with her siblings and often took on the roles of caretaker and babysitter for her younger sisters and brother (Rogers, 2001, p. 101). But there is one huge difference in the girls' stories. Rachel was in a classroom where her home experiences and literacies were valued, and Vicky was not. In Vicky's case, home and school literacies never converged, and even though she demonstrated high levels of literacy competence at home, she described herself as "the lowest reader in the class" and was identified as learning disabled by her school (Rogers, 2001, p. 102). Neither Vicky nor her teachers saw the literacy practices she used at home as being connected to reading or writing at school.

Britton, Burgess, Martin, McLeod, & Rosen (1975) believe that although personal (i.e., expressive) and school (i.e., transactional) language should never be separated, instruction in writing should begin with the personal. This is something that Rachel regularly experienced in her classroom and Vicky did not. They argue, "What children write in the early years should be a form of written-down expressive speech" (p. 82), but they do not think writing should stay in the personal. Freisinger (1982) noted that Britton, et al. described genuine written communication as an organic interaction between personal and informative writing. By using the expressive mode, "students have the chance to discover what they think before they try to convey their ideas to others" (Freisinger, 1982, p. 10).

Invitation for Disruption 3:

Beliefs About Learning and Teaching

- Jot down two statements that you strongly believe about learning and teaching.
- Try to think of a time when a specific child—or a specific situation—did not seem to fit with one of your statements. How did this anomaly contradict your theory and cause tension?
- Expand what you know about learning and teaching by rethinking your theory and revising it.

Rachel, in contrast to Vicky, was in a classroom where her teacher believed that she was already literate and that the knowledge she brought from home was valuable. What Rachel knew about family life became her entrée into literacy in Room 4. She was clearly the expert on taking care of younger siblings in a classroom where other students were also awaiting new brothers or sisters. Rachel's knowledge, first demonstrated by personal narrative entries in her writer's notebook, gradually became the basis for building a new unit of study in the classroom. In response to Rachel's interest and that of other students, Risë created an invitation (i.e., learning center) about birth and pregnancy. Rachel went to this center often and, at times, added to and corrected information found in the books present at the center. She saw herself and was recognized by others as a competent member of the classroom community. Rachel moved a long way from the beginning of the year when she was questioning her academic abilities.

Even though curriculum often begins with students' interests in Room 4, Risë encouraged her class to look at the larger social issues that stem from their personal experiences. Focusing back on Sara, the girl from Algeria, provides another example of how this move from the personal to the social happens. Sara did lots of writing in Arabic at the beginning of the year about her strange new life in the United States. It was as if she came from another planet—everything was different and strange, especially her classroom. Her writer's notebook served as a tool to explore this strangeness—this being the "other." Eventually, she brought her understandings of otherness into a public forum by writing the poem "The Lonely Fish." By writing a fictional piece based on a real-life issue—social narrative writing (Heffernan, 2004; Heffernan & Lewison, 2003)—Sara did not just call attention to herself but rather also to the larger problem of being different and an outsider. This opened the door for Risë to have students discuss the multiple ways in which they and groups in American society have been viewed as the other and why some groups are more likely to be treated this way.

It is important that kids' issues do not just stay in the personal. As Kamler (2001) points out, meaning is never individual or private; it always has social and cultural dimensions. If we are enacting a critical curriculum, it is never enough to leave a personal interest or grievance in the personal. By moving from the personal to the social, students are able to explore how historical practices, power relationships, and cultural systems of meaning all are at play in daily life. It is through this awareness—by in-depth interrogation of real-life issues—that we and the students in our classrooms have the potential for making schools more humane communities.

TABLE 2.2
How Critical Literacy was Enacted in Room 4

Cultural Resources	Critical Practices Enacted	How the Teachers Took Up a Critical Stance
Students' immigrant experience	Interrogated difference in everyday life between the United States and Algeria	Expanded what counts as cultural capital for students
Languages other than English	Valued diverse literacies, experiences, and ways of knowing	Inquired into who Sara is and what she knows
Social issues books—The Circuit and Just Juice	Provided critical classroom resources that make difference visible	Used Rachel's experience to reposition the curriculum so that voices that might traditionally be marginalized are heard
Students' out-of-school knowledge and abilities	Moved beyond the students' personal knowledge to focus on larger social issues—in Rachel's case, birth and pregnancy	Understood the importance of creating an invitation based on students' interest, thus entered into a risky space where the outcomes of curriculum are uncertain
Writer's notebook entries	Built solidarity between diverse groups of students by having them share writer's notebook entries	Was cognizant of how to expand ways students can respond to and contribute to curriculum planning

How Was Critical Literacy Enacted in Room 4?

Table 2.2 highlights the ways we see the critical literacy instructional model being realized in the vignette about Sara and Rachel at the beginning of this chapter.

In addition, we can map how Risë moved curriculum between the personal and the social with Sara and Rachel (Figure 2.1).

In both cases we see how Risë used writer's notebook as a tool for helping children express their personal interests, concerns, and expertise. She used a number of strategies that made it safe for students to make their writer's notebook entries public. Risë then incorporated some of the content of the notebooks into the classroom curriculum, often building on this content to include wider social or political issues.

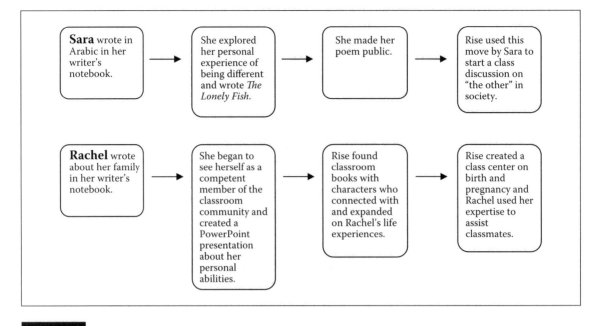

FIGURE 2.1
How Risë moved curriculum between the personal and the social.

Jerry Harste's thought piece on uncertainty relates directly to what happened in Room 4. Risë did not preplan the curriculum assuming she knew exactly what students needed. Instead, she let the students teach her. Building reading and writing activities on students' interests and observed needs always infuses a level of uncertainty into the curriculum. You can never predict what will be going on in class next month, much less next week. Yet by taking cues from students, we allow ourselves to outgrow our current understandings of teaching and learning, providing the potential to become better educators.

Lingering Questions

■ What are strategies that would be useful in turning your students' home experiences and resources into cultural capital in the classroom?

■ What are some ways we can help our students perceive themselves as already being literate?

■ How can we make teacher research a regular part of our daily teaching activities?

Uncertainty and the Teaching of Reading and Writing

Jerome C. Harste

There is probably nothing more dangerous than someone who thinks he or she knows everything there is to know about the teaching of reading, whether that person is a phonics advocate, a firm believer in a skill and drill model of reading instruction, or a whole language teacher. Once people think they know all there is to know about the teaching of reading, they are a danger both to themselves and the profession.

This may go counter to what you were hoping. You were hoping you would become an expert—the one who knows all the little tricks there are to know about the teaching of reading and writing.

We often extol certainty as a good thing and associate it with action, with decisiveness, with getting things done. And indeed it can be a source of action. It takes a very certain individual to mandate a particular reading program for everyone, to fly a plane into the World Trade Center, to organize a school shooting. We do not call all these acts of terrorism, but we should. Extremes are natural products of certitude. If I am absolutely certain I am right, then it will appear to me that I am justified in anything I do.

Teachers, more than most, desperately need a way of seeing in the dark. We naturally feel the need to be certain that what we do is right. We value experience because with it we are sure will come knowledge. But if experience were the infallible teacher, the more seasoned members of our profession would always be better able to cope rather than, as all too often happens, leave the profession in despair.

This is not to dismiss the importance of experience. As we experience more and more of the world, our internal models of the world get pretty good. This is why we can make so many accurate predictions, whether our decision is when we should cross the street or what we might do to help a learner who someone perceives as in trouble. As we see more and more students who need our support in learning to read and write, we get better and better at hypothesizing what their problem might be and how to support them in overcoming it. This is as it should be. But it is important to remember that our prediction is only a guess, a hypothesis, not a formula or a fact.

If we treat what we know as fact, we are in effect saying we have nothing to learn. Even worse, we have arrested our own learning process. This is why good learners—no matter how developed their internal theory of the world is or how much experience they have had—have to believe that at least one tenet in their existing theory is wrong. Believing most of what we know to be right allows us to act, but knowing one tenet is wrong and not being sure of which tenet it is allows us to learn.

Someone once said that teaching was like sailing a faulty ship on the high seas. We need to be constantly repairing the thing, but we can only do it one plank at a time. If we dismantle the whole ship, we cannot teach come Monday morning.

The state of uncertainty is not one of indifference. It leads, MacGinitie (1983, p. 679) says, "to the stonier path of tolerance." To be genuinely uncertain is to care. Good teachers must have doubts. Good teachers know that there is always much to learn. Good teachers understand that it is the lack of certainty that opens up that space wherein they just might discover effectiveness. Only an uncertain person can learn. Only an uncertain person can demonstrate how learning occurs. Whether spectator or participant, this truly is the power of uncertainty.

What Does Uncertainty Mean for Teaching Generally and Literacy Teaching Specifically?

One of the problems with teaching is that it is easy to forget the child, to see ourselves—the teachers—as foremost and central. In a keynote address, Combs (1971) tells the story of how he was hired by the University of Florida to create a demonstration school. He said they had unlimited resources. Importantly, he got to select what teachers he wanted. Then, not only did they design the school, but they also selected what furniture they wanted—tables instead of desks, walls that doubled as bulletin boards and whiteboards rather than wasted space. Instead of mandated textbooks they were able to select the instructional materials they wanted. They even, he reported, had the whole summer, on full salary, to plan the curriculum. "The problem," he said, "is we opened in the fall and they sent us the wrong damn children."

Though this comment is humorous in some ways, I argue that the problem Combs (1971) points to is more universal than it may appear on first blush. Mandating a particular reading program for everyone puts programs over people (Smith, 1983). So does instituting a standardized test, running children through a prepackaged set of curricular units, covering all the skills listed in the state's curricular guide, or teaching children everything we currently know about language simply because we know it. This is not just a problem with new teachers; it is a problem with all teachers.

MacGinitie (1983, p. 682) says this more cogently: "When we literacy teachers rely too much on the past, we think too little in the present." Said differently, curriculum should not be built from memory—what we think we remember about something—but from research.

I see this programs-over-people mentality as a professional hazard, and, even more alarming, it seems to be growing. In lieu of this mindlessness, I argue that there is just one way to be successful with learners. Clay (1993) calls it *working in the known*. Rather than assume we know what is wrong and how it is we might fix a language learner, it is first necessary to find out what the child already knows and is doing. Without exception, effective instruction starts from this base, not from what we think we know about language. Just because we know something about language, this fact in itself does not give us a right to teach it. Why, you might ask? The answer is simple: The child may not need it.

One of the errors I have seen way too often is that teachers plan a child's instructional programs based on what they think they know about language and language learning without first finding out what the child already knows and understands. Before we teach something we need to have reason to believe it is needed. I am not denying that knowledge about language is not important. I am just denying that whatever we know or think we may have learned from experience is not where effective teaching starts. It starts in the known, in our knowledge of a specific child. This is why teachers have to be researchers and why it is only when we operate as teacher–researchers that we have the right to see ourselves as professionals. Being a puppet for someone else's program is not teaching, despite what pundits would like us to believe.

What Does Working in the Known Entail?

For very young children, it means finding out what it is they can read before adopting *Hooked on Phonics* or some other sequenced set of reading materials. But before we go there, working in the known is not just something we do for young readers. It is something we do for all learners. Before we begin any focused study, it is important that we build from what students already know.

I am not negating planning. I am just saying that step 1 in planning has to include finding out what it is the children already know about the topic and building curricular invitations from that base.

With more proficient readers and writers, it means asking children to find a book, listening to them read it, and having a conversation about what was read afterward. It means giving them a sheet of paper and asking them to write—their name, any other words they can write, a "what is on my mind" piece, a personal letter to someone, a story, a poem, a content piece. It also means having an extended conversation with children about what kinds of things they like to do, both in school and out of school, what literacies they engage in, what their interests are, as well as their history, hopes, and aspirations.

One of the benefits of working in the known is that we tap into the child's culture and the child's way of knowing. In the process we garner data about how we might best approach instruction. Unless what we teach fits into the mental structures children already have formed, no real learning takes place. That is what is wrong with thinking about teaching as teaching. To be effective we need to think about teaching as "studenting," by which I mean getting in touch with the learner.

In closing, let me try to say this differently. Good teaching is always up close and personal. Unless children can see themselves in literacy, they will always remain illiterate. As teachers, our first job is to help the children see how they and their cultures are represented in the literacy practices which we are about to teach. There is no certain path to doing this other than building from the known.

In some ways uncertainty is both frightening and liberating. Though we teachers often link uncertainty with fear, its foundation is really hope. Hope for a better tomorrow. Hope that someday we will be able to reach all learners. Hope that over time we will continue to outgrow our current selves. And hope is not a bad foundation on which to build a much-needed new set of instructional practices for this profession.

Cultural Resources
Using Popular Culture to Promote Critical Practice

Vignette

The Great Bratz Debate

Kate Kuonen-Bakhtiary

"Ms. K, we don't play with Barbies. They're out of style. We play with Bratz." This was the unexpected response I received when I probed my fourth graders to find out if this cultural icon might be a topic they would like to explore. The discovery about Barbie's demise occurred during my second year of teaching when my attempts to get the kids engaged in debates were falling far short of what I had experienced with the previous year's class. I was not sure why the responses of the two groups were so different, but I suspected that it had something to do with the fact that kids in my first classroom had high levels of emotional energy and loved to argue about everything. They also seemed to be very committed to the pursuit of truth and justice and would eagerly pursue questions relating to what was fair in any situation. They were not content with easy answers and thrived on classroom debates that gave them opportunities to argue.

My second year brought a move to a different urban school, and I quickly learned that high emotional energy was not the norm with these kids. In addition, I was now part of a team and was responsible for teaching writing to the entire fourth grade—all three classes—in 45-minute blocks. At first, the relatively calm demeanor of the new group was refreshing. Students rolled into the classroom and seemed to need a nap. I had little time to get them engaged in anything.

I immediately introduced the idea of involving them in debates since they had been so successful the year before. But after a short time I realized that debates were not generating the same level of enthusiasm with this new group. These kids seemed to see themselves as too cool for arguing with each other. They did not seem to have a strong sense of social or personal justice, no boiling pursuit of the truth. Apathy and eye rolls seemed to be the most frequent reaction to the topics I offered for organizing debates.

At that point it occurred to me that maybe the real issue was that I was the one choosing the topics. They were important to me, but maybe not so important to my students. I knew that I needed more information, so I started listening carefully to students' conversations. And sure enough, day after day I noticed that discussion in the fourth grade focused on issues of popular culture and media, including music videos, magazines, toys, and television shows. I discovered that *American Idol* was very popular with my students. This TV show, which had been around for several years, provided opportunities for new stars to be discovered. My usually apathetic kids became quite animated when voicing their opinions about various aspects of the show—and how, for example, one contestant stared at the camera when he sang. They also seemed to enjoy hearing—and sometimes disagreeing with—the opinions of their peers. I had planned to focus the next debate on whether products should be tested on animals but decided to follow their lead and go with something more closely related to popular culture. Some of the conversations I overheard related to body image and focused on the concerns of kids who were worried about being fat. I knew where they were coming from since I had personally experienced eating disorders as an adolescent. So I asked them to think about how people are portrayed in music videos, magazines, and toys like Barbie dolls. What do they look like? The kids immediately informed me of Barbie's fall from superstardom and were eager to introduce me to her heir apparent, a collection of dolls called Bratz.

What are Bratz? A Google search turned up a whole list of websites that focus exclusively on this popular toy. I quickly learned that http://www.bratzpack.com is "the Official Bratz Website" and that "Bratz and all related characters, names, and trademarks are owned by MGA Entertainment." Visiting this website was an experience in itself. There were images of various Bratz characters with links to locations like Fashion Mall, Pretty 'n' Punk, and Slumber Party. I concluded that these dolls were quite different from good old Barbie. Their bodies were even more stylized and featured oversized heads, oversized hair, and oversized eyes. They had tiny torsos, skinny arms and legs, and no noses. (The kids showed me later that they also have no feet and that their legs simply slip onto their shoes or boots.) The website also introduced me to other Bratz spin-offs like Bratz Babyz, Bratz Boyz, and Bratz Petz. They all lacked the look of brainless sweetness that Barbie seemed to exude. Instead, there was something reminiscent of anger or defiance in these faces. A closer look made me realize that part of the impression of defiance might be emanating from their clothing. Skirts were shorter than normal, pants were tighter than normal, and heels were impossibly high. The dolls seemed to be daring viewers to chastise them for dressing inappropriately. I could see why kids might be fascinated with them. They seemed to represent a counterculture of sorts, maybe Barbie's evil twin coming back in a different form to challenge the status quo.

Our inquiry began with a bubble map. The words *music videos*, *Bratz*, and *magazines* were written on the board and subsequently surrounded by student descriptions of what people looked like in these different contexts. Kids shared their ideas with excitement and certainty. Every hand was waving in the air. They could not seem to talk fast enough or loud enough. This was quite a change from their near-comatose response to my earlier efforts. To capitalize

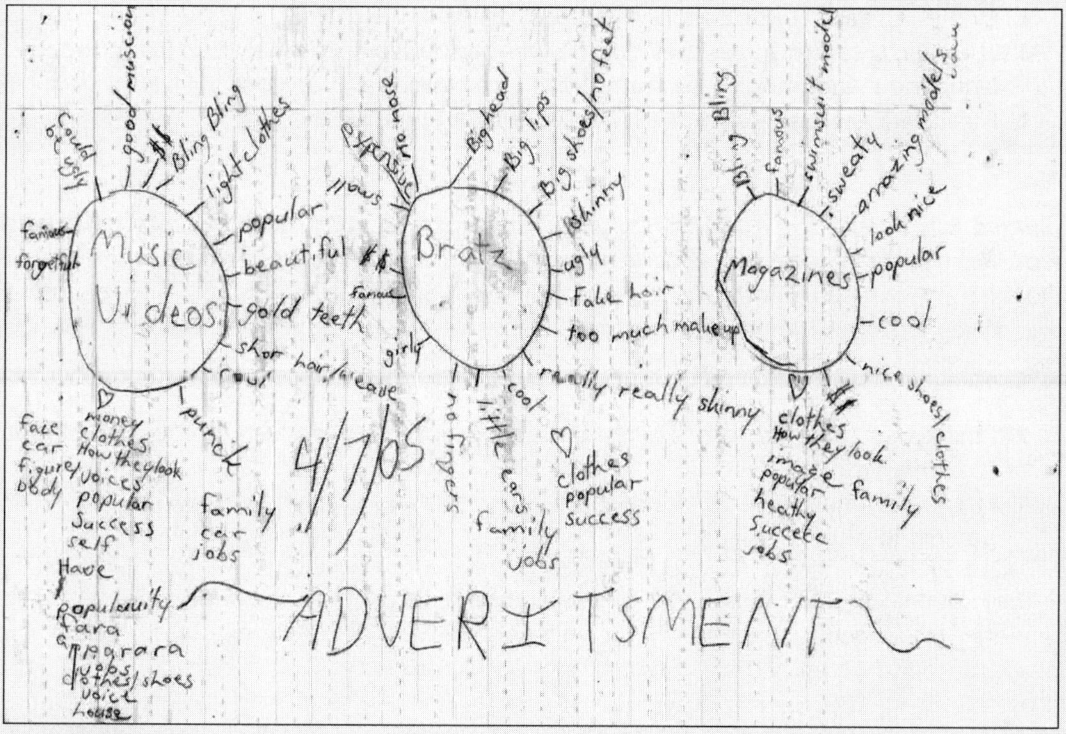

FIGURE 3.1
Sample bubble map

on this excitement as much as possible, I advised them to discuss these topics with their families that evening so that they would have more ideas to add the next time we met.

I also used our meetings as an opportunity to talk more formally about some of the concepts they were raising. For example, when someone brought up the point that all three media types made kids think they just had to have specific items, I wrote *manipulate* on the board, and we talked about how advertisers try make people believe certain things that might not be true. We also talked about words like *consumerism* and *exploit;* each of the three different fourth-grade classes that I met with each day for writing added to the collaboratively authored list that remained on the chalkboard all week. Whenever these concepts came up in discussions in any of the classes, I went back to the list and demonstrated how to use the words in different contexts.

After a while the students started noticing how different topics were connecting to each other. Words like *popular, beautiful, cool clothes, money, fame, cars, houses, good bodies, image, self, family,* and *success* were found on almost every map. Students also decided that it was important to write the word *advertisements* across all of the topics since all three media outlets served as a way to advertise products. Figure 3.1 shows a sample map. On the second day of this exploration I saved the last 15 minutes of each period for writing in response to the following questions: How are you similar to and different from either Bratz, people in music videos or in magazines? What is most interesting or impressive about them? Do you want to be like them? Why? The majority of kids, both male and female, wrote about Bratz. And many girls reported that they wanted to be like Bratz.

- One thing I like about Bratz is that they have money.
- They can wear whatever they want. I want to be really, really skinny, I want popularity and I want money. I want to have nice clothes and be cool.
- I like Bratz because they have style and they are really cool.

The next day we made another bubble map. *Bratz* was written in the middle with the words *parents, kids,* and *choices* along with several critical questions: Why do companies make them look like this? What values do *Bratz* teach kids? What do companies get from selling *Bratz*? Do the companies care about kids? The children added other critical questions as we discussed and shared our ideas. Fifteen minutes of writing followed. It was clear that many of the kids had discussed this topic with their parents.

- I think some parents do not tolerate Bratz because they are fast. All they care about is themselves.
- I think they make Bratz look like this to draw attention. Maybe girls will beg their parents for them.

The next day I brought up the idea of planning for a debate that would focus on Bratz. This time they responded with enthusiasm; it seemed they were not too cool to argue about this particular topic. We formed small groups and decided who would defend and who would prosecute Bratz. Then each group made a list of for and against points that focused on the question, "Should kids (or their parents) buy Bratz?" Working collaboratively, they added questions and statements to a very large pro and con list that stretched across the entire chalkboard. The room was bustling. Students used every resource available, including adults in the room and each other.

It did not take long for our room to become filled with all things Bratz. We had about 25 dolls—girls and boys—10 miniatures from McDonald's, a pillowcase, traveling cart, jewelry box, watch, notebook, and stickers. Children scrutinized everything about the dolls and accessories. The small debate groups were aware of everything that other groups added to the collaborative list and thought quickly of rebuttals. They were lined up and wrapped around the desks, eager to add their individual ideas. Everyone was excited and focused.

At one point in the discussion we talked about where Bratz were made. A student suggested we look for the tag. We did and discovered that Bratz were made in Sri Lanka. This brought up the tsunami disaster in December 2004. The kids in favor of buying Bratz decided that kids in Sri Lanka needed Bratz to play with, too. They wanted to send dolls to tsunami victims. Those against decided that kids should donate their money to tsunami relief instead of wasting it on Bratz. At that point, I mentioned that child labor existed in countries like Sri Lanka, although I did not know for sure whether Bratz were made using child labor. The kids were visibly shocked to learn that child labor even existed. A seed was planted in their minds. I had no idea how large the tree would grow.

- Pro Bratz
  - Bratz are cute. Look at this outfit. It's cool and hip. Kids want to be cool and hip.
  - Kids work hard and they deserve Bratz. They are like friends to kids.
- Con Bratz
  - We have to put up signs that say, "NO MORE BRATZ!" Probably that's why girls be so skinny.

- Bratz are too expensive. Maybe their mom doesn't have enough money to eat and buy Bratz.

With evidence gathered, knowledge built and arguments developed, it was time for the debate. Desks were arranged in two groups that faced each other. The dolls were positioned as handy visual aids. Some students had made pro and con posters that added to the décor. The debate went back and forth. Some kids spoke like born lawyers, and some struggled to speak at all. At the end of three days of debating, kids were ready to write how they really felt about Bratz. We took the entire 45 minutes the next day to write responses to the question, "Should parents buy Bratz for their kids?" Kids started writing immediately and wrote furiously. Several asked for more paper after only 15 minutes. They used the resources that were plastered all over the room. It was a quiet time, but I suspected that inside the students' minds it was anything but quiet.

> After you hear everyone's opinions and your brain is thinking so hard and you are thinking yes Bratz are good, no Bratz are bad, your mind feels like it is going to explode because you have so much to say.

Some students considered future social action. Many showed a healthy new distrust for the companies that make Bratz and other toys.

- I feel so manipulated.
- Everything about child labor reminds me of slavery.
- Child labor is really made of little kids my age. They make different things, things for companies, companies that care only about the money.
- I never thought about the people that made them. I was just brainwashed.
- Companies act like they care, but all they care about is money.

When I had a chance to look through all of the work collected during this inquiry, I realized two things: (1) My goal of getting these kids emotionally involved in their learning had been achieved; and (2) my goal of getting them to interrogate the cultural model of "thin = beautiful" had been only partially achieved. Though there were some signs that kids were rethinking this idea, it clearly had been trumped by their interest in child labor practices.

A partial victory at this point was fine with me. It was a good start, and we had come a long way in a short period of time. Further, the children had already identified the next inquiry, child labor practices. Although I realized they were seeing this issue too simplistically and were not considering the role that many children play in providing economic stability for their families, I knew that complications like this would arise as they researched the topic. For now, the kids had taken a big step toward developing an identity as people who care about the welfare of others. I started this project worrying about their welfare—and how body image negatively impacts many teens—and they had moved beyond my concern for them into their own concern for children they did not know on the other side of the world. Though I was pleased with the literacy skills they demonstrated during this project, I was even more pleased with their development as caring global citizens.

What Can We Learn from Kate's Experience?

In some ways, Kate's story offers hope for any teacher who feels like she or he is drowning in standards, mandated curriculum, and apathetic students. Anyone who can carve out time for kids to write during the school day can use that time to address students' interests and to integrate the language arts as she did. It is true that Kate's students did more than write during writing time: They also read, listened, and spoke as preparation for writing. And after all of the reading, listening, and speaking they had a lot to write about. No students sat with blank paper in front of them and said they could not think of anything to say. At the same time, Kate was meeting the standards of her district and the School Improvement Plan for her failing (according to the "No Child Left Behind" definition) school. In this case, as in most curriculum scope and sequence documents that we have seen, skills that must be taught were clearly listed, but the choice of how to teach writing skills was left to the teacher. Kate used this margin of choice to engage her students in topics that were current and interesting to them—while teaching mandated skills within a meaningful context. Her vignette demonstrates not only a way to work within the system without compromising our beliefs but also some larger theories that can inform our teaching.

Theory 1: Literacy keeps changing and is often linked to popular culture.

"Ms. K, we don't play with Barbies. They're out of style. We play with Bratz." The words of Kate's fourth graders remind us that change might be the only constant we can count on when we think about popular culture and media in the classroom. Most of us are only momentarily surprised to learn that Barbie has been replaced. After all, this doll has been a cultural icon for many years—decades even—and it seems reasonable to assume that she will someday end up on the shelf with other toys whose heyday has passed. Change is also a major factor in how literacy is defined and used. In his book *Literacy in the New Media Age*, Kress (2003) notes that image is replacing writing as the dominant form of making meaning and that the screen is becoming just as important as the page. This, he suggests, is because *the world told* is vastly different from *the world shown* (p. 1, italics in original). That difference was verified for Kate when she went to the Internet and found a site that showed what the new "Barbie replacement" dolls look like. Indeed, a student's explanation that Bratz were "sort of like Barbies, but cooler" was completely inadequate to prepare her for the image that instantaneously appeared on the screen. Kress explains the difference as follows: "Images are plain full with meaning, whereas words wait to be filled" (p. 4). The words "sort of like Barbies, but cooler" might be waiting to be filled, but one look at the images on the screen verifies that they are indeed plain full with meaning. The dolls' bodies, clothing, and makeup spoke volumes about current notions of what it takes to be cool.

In addition to noting the effects of change in the nature of text and the speed with which texts of all types are delivered, increased globalization is another important factor impacting what people buy. Popular culture produces texts, artifacts, and practices that are frequently mass produced on a global scale and that therefore have the potential to be attractive to large numbers of children. "These goods are frequently linked by common themes, so that 'tie-in' goods are related to popular television or film characters and narratives" (Marsh, 2005, p. 2). In the case of Barbie and Bratz dolls, tie-in goods include a wide array of merchandise. Kate was amazed to see that the fourth graders in the three classrooms she worked with brought in a total of 32 Bratz dolls over the course of a week, some of which were miniature versions from McDonald's Happy Meals. She also discovered other Bratz merchandise: a jewelry box, a pillowcase, a Bratz watch. Evans (2004, p. 101) explains how this happens: Due to the efforts of multinational companies, consumers are carefully guided into wanting what everyone else has—"a slice of the same good lifestyle cake." The process of globalization ensures that everyone gets the same message regardless of his or her culture or ethnic background.

In case anyone thinks that fourth grade is too early to start talking about consumer literacy and the effects of globalization, it is good to remember that researchers are documenting earlier and earlier attention to popular culture by young children. Merchant (2005, p. 192), for example, describes a 3-year-old child named Melody who introduced herself by announcing, "I've got my Barbie jeans on today." When Merchant acknowledged the Barbie jeans, Melody called his attention to a matching bag with a picture of Barbie stitched on the front. When Merchant invited Melody to write on a laptop computer, she first wrote her name and then wrote Barbie. As she watched other children and realized that screen color could be changed, she requested a pink background and pink writing. Although her pink-on-pink idea did not work out and she had to choose another color to make the writing show up on the screen, Melody's interest in having everything pink shows the strength of her attraction to the Barbie theme. At age 3, this child had taken on Barbie as part of her gendered identity. And at age 3 she had "already stepped aboard the ever-expanding, continually moving youth market conveyer belt" that would inevitably lead to her "being commercially exploited by the big multinationals" (Evans, 2004, p. 98).

It is hard to deny that literacy and popular culture have many connections—and equally hard to deny that they are both in a state of constant flux. What is not so readily acceptable is the idea that literacy instruction should help students develop new frames for talking about consumerism. When the dominant discourse relating to literacy instruction is centered on topics like phonemic awareness, there is

Invitation for Disruption 1:

Educators as Consumers

- Collect brochures and advertisements for educational programs over a period of time.
- Get together with a group of colleagues to talk about the language used in these texts to describe the products. For example, are there numerous claims that materials are easy to use or time saving?
- Analyze the subtle messages about educators that are present in the promotional materials. For example, if *easy to use* is a recurrent theme, what does this imply about educators?
- How might educators begin to talk back to discourse that positions them negatively?

Chapter Three
Cultural Resources

little motivation for teachers to design literacy curricula that focus more broadly on issues like helping kids see how they are positioned in the world both as consumers—with the power to buy or not buy something—and as victims of consumerist trends that deny their identity and turn them into walking advertisements.

Theory 2: School can provide a site for interrogating cultural texts and repositioning oneself.

Kate had a personal interest in helping her students see how all of us are positioned by implicit cultural messages that define how we should look, act, and be. She was particularly concerned with images that link definitions of beauty with expectations of extreme thinness and wanted her students to have ways to respond to the endless parade of ultrathin models—on television, in magazines, and even in toys—that she knew they would experience. To bring this body image subtext into the open, she treated various artifacts of popular culture as texts that could be brought into the literacy curriculum and studied. Once there, the underlying messages could be unpacked and examined by the students as part of their regular academic work.

The body image inquiry was introduced by inviting students to think about what they already knew. Using a graphic organizer, Kate invited them to consider what people look like in three different contexts: music videos, Bratz dolls, and magazines. Children were able to identify patterns among the topics that appeared on the extensive lists generated by this activity. They noted that certain words like *popular, beautiful, good bodies, cool clothes, money,* and *fame* appeared consistently in most students' work. After encouraging students to share these findings with family members and to discuss the same topics at home, Kate used a writing assignment to help them connect the different images of people with how they saw themselves. Did they want to be like Bratz dolls or any of the people shown in magazines or music videos? The answer was an enthusiastic "yes!" Most of her students—both girls and boys—chose to write about Bratz dolls and characterized them as *beautiful* and *perfect.* Many of the girls articulated a desire to look like, and be like, these dolls. Kate interpreted these responses as evidence of the children's interest in this aspect of popular culture and decided to pursue it further as a debate topic.

Researchers like Pearce (1999) might agree with Kate's decision to help children interrogate the ideals of beauty and perfection embodied in *Bratz.* In discussing an ad for a watch that featured a very thin model, he noted that this text was strongly dependent on the presence of an "'anorexia' discourse" (p. 84). This discourse was apparent in the model's "blank, apathetic or lethargic expression" and the way her eyes were "heavily made up, partially closed and appearing sunken" (p. 84). In addition, the paleness of the model's face and the way her gaze seemed to avoid engaging with the viewer left "a connotation of both physical and mental frailty" (p. 84). The same descriptors can easily apply to Bratz dolls. It is reasonable to conclude that seeing lots of images like this without stopping to talk about them could lead people, especially children, to see what they portray as normal rather than problematic.

"Beauty is in the eye of the beholder" resonates with many of us as a familiar cliché. What one person sees as beautiful might be totally unattractive to someone else. The age-old discussion about the relationship between body type and beauty is a good example of what Gee (1999, p. 34) refers to as a "big C Conversation (Table 3.1)." This is a historic conversation that crosses discourses and involves more than individual people. Typically, Conversations involve controversy and the idea of taking sides as well as values and symbolic objects and institutions. In this case, we would not be surprised to find some disagreement about what criteria we use to decide what makes a person—especially a woman—too fat or too thin. The question might be answered differently by people in various cultural groups as well as by, for example, people with more or less education or older or younger people. Values that need to be negotiated include beliefs about the relationship between body type and general health as well as what looks good to someone.

Kate's curricular decision to frame the body image discussion as a Conversation challenged her students to think across different themes, or discourses, as they gathered evidence to support the side of the controversy assigned to them. Her simple question, "Should kids play with Bratz?" invited them to think broadly about issues relating to health, freedom of choice, morality, and safety.

Table 3.2 documents representative discourses articulated by students. The debate sparked controversy and appeared to cause some kids to change their minds about Bratz. Although most of them ended up taking the view that these dolls are "bad news" and should be boycotted, there were a few who steadfastly defended this toy. One 10-year-old girl put it this way: "I know that I'm being manipulated and the toy company makes tons of money from selling Bratz, but I still like them and I'm going to keep playing with them."

Discourses in Bratz Discussions

Discourse	Example
Health	Bratz might make you want to be too skinny, and you could get sick or die.
Freedom of Choice	Kids should play with whatever toys they like best.
Morality	Do you want a doll showing that much skin in your house?
Safety	If kids dress like that, they might get snatched.

In the vignette that frames this chapter, we can see how a teacher provided opportunities for kids to interrogate cultural texts and to reposition themselves. Though a few never did change their minds about Bratz or body image, many did. And no matter what they believed at the end of the study, it is easy argue that they were highly engaged in the work they were doing. Indeed, their willing participation in the process of interrogating something that they had previously taken for granted might be the most significant aspect of the story. We can imagine them asking similar questions about other toys, other advertisements, and other discourses in the future.

Theory 3: Children need to develop the language of critique to be truly literate in the 21st century.

According to Shannon (1995, p. 118), we all need to "talk back" to people and views that try to position us in ways that benefit their interests but not ours. This talking back usually occurs as the result of participating in dialogues and raising questions about the topic at hand. "Dialogues must be informed by texts and data that participants gather and bring to the exchanges. Through the actions necessary to gather that information and the information itself, participants help each other to clarify their thoughts and positions by probing contradictions and inconsistencies" (Shannon, 1995, p. 106). When she invited her students to interrogate a cultural text, Kate realized that she also had to give them tools to research and talk about this topic. As a result of her previous work with debate, she knew that her students would do a better job if she assisted them in learning the language of critique. Informal team discussions before the actual debates provided opportunities for Kate's students to gather information for their own arguments and to see how they could also challenge, or talk back to, the arguments being formulated by others. This provided a different frame for examining some social issues that were highly relevant to the students' lives.

In addition, Kate taught the vocabulary they needed to be articulate in their critiques. As different topics came up in the dialogue, she helped to name the concepts that were being highlighted. For example, when children talked about how toy companies want them to think they have to get a certain toy, she introduced words like *consumerism*, *manipulate*, and *exploit* and discussed what the words might mean in different contexts. All new words were left on the board so that she could refer back to them and so that kids could easily access them in writing their arguments. In addition, Kate hoped her students would take ownership of both the vocabulary and the concepts they represented: "They're your words and we spent a lot of time talking about them—so use them in your arguments," she reminded them.

Kate's example shows that critical literacy is not about avoiding tough issues. Rather, it is about helping people learn how to use language effectively to get their perspectives heard. It is about giving people opportunities to challenge the cultural pressures that influence every aspect of their lives. Comber (2001, p. 1) reminds us that teachers do not need to start from scratch in developing the language of critique: "Children begin school with ideas about what's fair and what's not, gleaned from five years of experience with family and community life." They have been critiquing things for a long time and can tell us what they see as good, bad, cool, or not cool. From this foundation teachers can continue to build the language of critique and the language of possibility.

According to Giroux (1991, p. 52) a language of possibility "is capable of thinking risky thoughts … enlarges a project of hope, and points to the horizon of the 'not yet.'" Kate did not teach her students the term *neoliberalism* as part of this study—not yet, at least. But it is easy to imagine that word appearing on the board when the class moves into the next inquiry—one they specifically requested to learn more about child labor issues around the world. Hade and Edmondson (2003, p. 136) define *neoliberalism* as "a political ideology that emphasizes capitalistic, or so-called 'free market' principles in all areas of social, political, and business life." They go on to say that the current grip of neoliberal ideology has led to "a whittling away of the social safety nets for the poor and disadvantaged" (p. 136). If all aspects of society are left to the wisdom of the market and profits end up as the end goal, then it does not matter how we get them. In this context, practices like child labor can easily become more widespread. "The search for cheap labor, the powerlessness of children, and the 120 million children who are born poor each year create fertile conditions for multinational corporations to profit by hiring children, largely in developing countries. The International Labor Office estimates that 120 million children between the ages of 5 and 14 are compelled to work full-time, often under harsh and inhumane conditions" (Giroux & Giroux, 2004, p. 77).

When the topic of child labor was raised, Kate's students reacted first with disbelief and then with indignation. They were more upset by the thought of children in other countries working for pennies

---

Invitation for Disruption 3:

Thinking About Neoliberalism

- According to Giroux and Giroux (2004), neoliberal philosophy discourages governmental support of anything public. This includes public schools, public libraries, public transportation, and entities like public television and public radio. What potential effects will this philosophy have if it is translated into policy?
- Name three examples of neoliberal philosophy in action.
- Who benefits and who loses in the examples you identified?
- How does neoliberal philosophy fit with your notion of democracy?

a day to sew clothing for Bratz dolls than by the thought that they themselves might develop poor eating habits as the result of playing with these toys. They generated risky thoughts about how to talk back to this form of oppression. Whereas it fell to social reformers in the 19th century to challenge conditions that put industrial profits above the welfare of working children, it might be individuals who experienced critical literacy with teachers like Kate who step forward to take similar social action for children in Sri Lanka—or wherever—in the future. It is easy to imagine at least a few of them becoming allies (Christensen, 2000, p. 82), people who can use the language of critique to speak up for others with less power. At the same time, it is also important to help children see that issues like child labor are complex and multifaceted. Simply stopping child labor is not necessarily a good outcome because many families depend on this income for their survival. Putting children in danger of starvation might not be any better for them than continuing to work.

How Critical Literacy Was Enacted in Kate's Classroom

Table 3.3 summarizes how a critical literacy instructional model was enacted in Kate's fourth-grade writing classes. In addition, we can map how Kate moved her students between the personal and the social through their collaborative work on the debates (Figure 3.2). The flow-chart shows how Kate began with the goal of getting her students more actively involved in the debates that she used as a large part of her language arts curriculum. After realizing they were interested in topics relating to popular culture, she took a risk and invited them to look critically at commonplace objects like videos, magazines, and toys. As she noticed that most of her students wanted to talk about Bratz dolls, she designed an inquiry activity that addressed this topic by incorporating reading, writing, and speaking in purposeful ways.

What Kate's experience makes clear is that none of us—including Kate and the students in her classroom—may be consciously aware of how visual literacy and consumer culture are impacting us. When examined closely, Kate and her students found that Bratz dolls were affecting their reading of themselves, others, beauty, and what it means to be in style. All of this is a bit scary. Bratz dolls represent only one instance of popular culture, and Kate's vignette explores only one instance of how popular culture impacts our lives and the lives of the children we teach. The thought piece that follows makes a case for why now, more than ever, we need to support children in becoming critically literate by explicitly teaching them how to read images as well as words.

TABLE 3.3
How critical literacy was enacted in Kate's classroom

Personal and Cultural Resources	Critical Practices Enacted	How the Teacher Took Up a Critical Stance
Class discussion to find out kids' interests, which included music videos, magazines, and Bratz dolls	Challenged commonplace views about curriculum and what is appropriate for children to study	Took kids' lead and encouraged inquiry into new topic
Discussions with family members about how people are portrayed in popular culture	Interrogated multiple perspectives about how people should look and act	Moved children beyond initial understandings
Information kids collected about Bratz	Debated an issue not commonly addressed in schools: Should kids play with Bratz? Engaged in critical language study of words and concepts like manipulate, exploit, and consumerism	Supported students in framing things differently and trying on alternate ways of being
Kids' interest in child labor issues	Used students' desires to plan curriculum that focused on socio-political issues	Demonstrated reflexivity by giving up her agenda relating to body image and moving to address students' interest in child labor

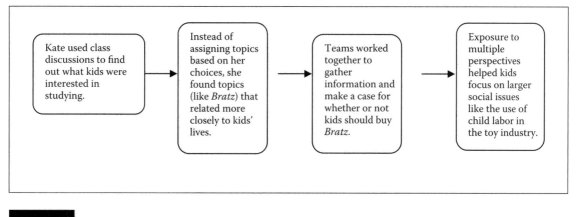

FIGURE 3.2
How Kate moved curriculum between the personal and the social.

Lingering Questions

▮ How should we respond to claims that involving children in interrogating icons of popular culture ruins the innocence of childhood?

▮ Current legislation restricts some advertisers (e.g., tobacco and liquor companies) but not others, even though an argument can be made that their products (e.g., fast food) are not healthy and potentially harmful. Do advertisers have a moral and ethical obligation when it comes to marketing these products to children? If so, what policies would you recommend?

Thought Piece

Visual Literacy

Jerome C. Harste

One of the hard things about creating a critical curriculum is that few of us have had the opportunity to actually live such a curriculum. For the most part we have been taught consumer literacy rather than critical literacy. By this I mean we have taught the skills needed to acquire goods or services for direct use or ownership rather than the skills needed to critique what is being sold in terms of how such goods position us and who is or is not being served by our consumerism.

I want to argue that our goal for the next generation should to be to have children become agents of text rather than victims of text. Though we have argued for critical literacy, we have not argued for visual literacy as an important component of critical literacy. Today's children are spending more time reading online than they are spending time reading books and other print-based materials. Kress (2003) and a variety of media studies people (Leu, Kinzer, Coiro, & Cammack, 2005) argue that as a result, not only is literacy changing but so are literacy practices, including how we process text—broadly defined—to read and comprehend. Since a large part of what are being called the *new literacies* (New London Group, 2000) is pictorially based, a strong case has been made for why we should teach children something about how to read visual images in schools.

The Grammar of Visual Design

To introduce people to the notion of visual literacy I typically focus attention on counternarrative artists and their art, by which I mean art and artists that speak back or fight against what are dominant interpretations, themes, or stories running through the culture. Counternarrative art and artists offer new perspectives on taken-for-granted, dominant motifs.

African American artist Jacob Lawrence is a case in point. His work is representative of a group of artists now being credited with having played a major role in bringing to conscious awareness the Black experience in America. The paintings in his collection can be seen as counternarratives, as a form of social action, as a demonstration of how the efforts of a collective have enhanced and enlightened the thinking of a community.

I begin by showing a lot of Lawrence's art and then ask participants to copy, juxtapose, and transform one of Lawrence's paintings into "a message about something you believe

FIGURE 3.3
Literacy as counternarrative (student work done in the style of Jacob Lawrence).

about literacy and/or the direction you believe literacy should be taking." For the most part participants select individuals depicted in Lawrence's painting, attempt to replicate them as best they can and then fill in what they see as an appropriate context given their message to the world.

Figure 3.3 is a Lawrence-esque picture that a participant in one of my workshops created. Using a framework that Kress and van Leeuwen developed (1998) for reading visual images, I will walk you through the reading of this painting. First, however, it is important to understand that one of the assumptions Kress and van Leeuwen make about art is that all signs—in this case markings—are motivated. By this they mean that there is nothing random in art; what is there was done for a purpose.

Kress and van Leeuwen (1998) also say that we often think of art as abstract and language as concrete. Using a very young child's rendering of an elephant—in this case I use my own daughter's elephant, which she made at age 3 (Figure 3.4)—Kress and van Leeuwen make it clear that a child saying, "This is an elephant," is a lot more abstract than is a picture of an elephant drawn by the same child. Typically we think of language as concrete and art as

FIGURE 3.4
Drawing of an elephant (Alison, age 3).

abstract. Said the other way around, we know a lot more about what the child thinks an elephant is from the picture than we do from her statement.

Kress and van Leeuwen's (1998) system invites the user to analyze a text systematically, whether that text is all art or a mixture of various semiotic systems, like language, music, or art. Figure 3.5 juxtaposes Kress and van Leeuwen's framework on the Lawrence-esque drawing shown in Figure 3.3.

▮ **Top and bottom.** The top of a picture, Kress and van Leeuwen (1998) argue, is "the ideal," the bottom, "the real." In Figure 3.5 the top of the picture is a blue sky, which metaphorically we might read as open or full of unlimited possibilities. The bottom is green grass, which metaphorically we read as a stabilizing force, an anchor.

▮ **Left and right.** The left side of the picture, Kress and van Leeuwen (1998) say, is "the given," the right side, "the new." In Figure 3.5 the two sides are pretty much the same, with the exception of the top right-hand corner. What is new here is the figure expressing herself in multiple literacies.

▮ **Center.** The center of the picture provides a focus. In this case an African American girl is sitting in a chair rather rigidly—hands at her side, feet squarely on the ground—while her voice rises to the heavens. Since her chair and feet fall in the bottom part of the picture (i.e., the real), we read the figure as fixed, immobile, and trapped. What is new and ideal are her voice and the multiple forms of expression symbolized in the wedge of her voice rising.

▮ **Vectors.** Kress and van Leeuwen (1998) argue that vectors are important. One vector in this picture is the line separating the grass from the sky, the real from the ideal. Another vector is created by the speech bubble, from the girl's head to the top right corner of the page, which we read as positive, or in the direction from the real to the ideal and the given to the new. It is these vectors that give us confidence in our reading of the picture. They, in a sense, confirm our other interpretations.

Margin
Ideal
Given

Margin
Ideal
New

Center

Margin
Real
Given

Margin
Real
New

ABC

FIGURE 3.5
Kress & van Leeuwen (1998) framework juxtaposed on Jacob Lawrence painting.

▌ **Colors.** Whereas Figure 3.5 is rendered in black and white, the original was in color. Further, there was something fairly optimistic about this artist's use of blues, greens, and yellows in the picture. The use of these bright colors suggests something positive or hopeful.

▌ **Gaze.** The character in the picture is looking away from the viewer. In this instance her head is up, and she appears to be looking off the page, in the direction of the new and the ideal. Her gaze suggests she is focused on the future rather than on the here and now.

▌ **Exaggeration.** Kress and van Leeuwen are (1998) also very interested in exaggeration. Lawrence, for example, often exaggerates the hands in his paintings to honor manual labor and to remind us of the hard work that African Americans performed in serving their masters and in building this society. In this picture, the artist has drawn the hands out of proportion to the rest of the figure. They are weak hands, adding credence to our reading of her as being trapped, a bit helpless or weak.

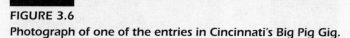

FIGURE 3.6
Photograph of one of the entries in Cincinnati's Big Pig Gig.

■ **Interpretation.** Kress and van Leeuwen (1998) see understanding as a search for unity across all available signs. The following statements seem to capture the overall message this picture conveys. Though there clearly are differences in these statements, the similarities in meaning made by four readers of this text are striking:

- We need an expanded definition of literacy that includes multiple ways of knowing.
- For literacy to give voice to all learners, multiple ways of knowing need to be advocated.
- Individuals are trapped with old notions of literacy rather than with multiple ways of knowing.
- Multiple sign systems provide access to literacy for minority learners.

To confirm what the author-artist had in mind, I asked participants to write a reflection on their experience. Here is what this artist-author had to say about her work and what she was hoping to say:

> This is a representation of a Jacob Lawrence postcard. The girl here is representing all learners and all sign systems: dance, language, drama, science, visual art, and movement. I hope this work demonstrates how educators can honor all learners and multiple ways of knowing. As I was painting, I was remembering a line of poetry, "I'll tear those words from your throat and shout them into the hot night for all the world to hear."

The readings that four readers gave to this picture as well as the author's reflection on what it was she was attempting to say add credence to the use of Kress and van Leeuwen's (1998) grammar of visual design for raising consciousness as well as interrogating new forms of literacy.

FIGURE 3.7
"Red, Blond, Black, & Olive," Bloomington (Artist: Jean Paul Darriau, 1980).

Using Kress and van Leeuwen's (1998) Framework to Read Everyday Texts

Everyday texts are defined as "those spoken and written texts that are part of people's daily lives, both public and personal" (Luke & Watson, 1994, p. 9). Simpson and Comber (1995, p. 2) argue, "Because these texts are so common, they are almost invisible and we are, therefore, likely to be less aware of the kinds of messages about our world which they convey." Because children learn to read not only from books but also from McDonald's signs and Coke bottles, it is important that they understand how such texts construct them. If we take a Post cereal box, for example, and apply Kress and van Leeuwen's (1998) framework, the work that cereal box is doing becomes more apparent. In the center of the cover is a spoonful of cereal over a red heart, thereby suggesting that this cereal is good for them. This is the central message, and it is reinforced by a banner that runs on the bottom of the package ("the given" in Kress and van Leeuwen's framework) stating, "Helps *REDUCE* the risk of *HEART DISEASE* because it is rich in whole grain." In "the new" area of the cover is the Post logo with a banner underneath saying "Healthy Classic," thereby establishing, or attempting to establish, Post as one of the good guys with classic tradition on its side. Though the side of the box advertises other rich whole-grain cereals available from Post, the fact that sugar is a dominant ingredient in many of these cereals is totally ignored. To add credence to the healthy heart message, the back of the box cites the American Medical Association by stating, "Did you know? 9 out of 10 Americans do not get the recommended three or more daily servings of whole grains." This is followed by the invitation, "So go ahead, have another bowl of whole grain Post Grape-Nuts." This invitation ignores the fact that a single serving is listed as half a bowl and contains 47 grams of carbohydrates. So anyone taking the advice to refill their bowl will end up getting far fewer than the 16 servings per container stated on the box. If we read carefully, we find out that Post is a division of Kraft Foods and that Kraft Foods is a proud sponsor of the American Diabetes Association, whose motto is "Cure, Care, Commitment."

Though work in studying the grammar of visual design is just beginning, Kress and van Leeuwen's (1998) framework works surprising well for studying advertisements, public sculptures, scenes in movies, as well as some forms of graffiti. Art, like language, for Halliday (1985)—on whose theories of language Kress and van Leeuwen base their work—is a semiotic, or meaning-centered, system. Regardless of the complexity of the form of the message, to interpret that message we simultaneously have to attend to the field (i.e., the setting, the content of the message, as well as what is happening) the mode (i.e., the various sign systems involved and what messages each carry) and the tenor (i.e., the relationship depicted between and among people including how we as readers of this text are positioned and what identity we are asked to take on).

Following Chicago's success with cows, Cincinnati sponsored "The Big Pig Gig" in which local artists were commissioned to decorate pigs under corporate sponsorship. Although we could discuss this sculpture at length—as well as the other 75 some pigs in this gala event—what is clear is that pigs (Figure 3.6) are somehow being aligned with what it means to be American. A cynic might read this text as representing pork barrel economics in which the interests of a specialized group are cast as being in the interest of the whole country. Given the positioning of the flag on the pig we might see the tail (i.e., corporate America) as metaphorically wagging the dog. A historian would note that Cincinnati came into creation because of pigs and its loca-tion at the crossroads of America. Pigs, in this sense, are as American as apple pie or Campbell's soup. Noting that this piece mimics Andy Warhol's work as an artist, which pointedly addresses the politics of culture, only reinforces our reading of this work. The question remains, however, "Is this a narrative posing as a counter narrative or a counter narrative in and of itself?" We let you decide.

In our town we have a sculpture called "Red, Blond, Black, & Olive" created by Jean Paul Darriau for the City of Bloomington in 1980. The statue is very popular and is often read as speaking to the multicultural nature of the city and its tolerance for various races, ethnici-ties, and nationalities. What makes the statue particularly striking is the fact that as one walks around—and through—it, all of the major racial groups in the world are depicted. What is not told, however, is all the racial tensions that have erupted in Bloomington over the period of this statue's existence, from 1980 when it was commissioned to now. Even further, central Indiana was for years the home of the Ku Klux Klan, hardly the paragon of racial virtue depicted by this historical marker. Though it might have been in the city's interest to project an image of racial tolerance, it takes an inquiring critical mind to unpack this and other images that bombard us daily (for more on the topic of what lies historical markers often tell, see Loewen, 1999).

I close with these examples of art to demonstrate that Kress and van Leeuwen's (1998) grammar of visual design is almost as useful in analyzing statutes as it is in analyzing pictures.

As literacy keeps changing, we need to continue to develop better and better analytic tools. There is a sense of urgency about this as schools are important sites for supporting children in developing the language of critique as well as in supporting our citizenry in moving beyond consumer literacy to critical literacy.

Cultural Resources Using Children's Literature to Get Started with Critical Literacy

Vignette

How Critical Picture Books Changed a First-Grade Classroom[*]

Christine H. Leland and Kim Huber

When Kim Huber finally decided to read *The Lady in the Box* (McGovern, 1997) to her first graders, she was not convinced that they would get much out of a book about homelessness. She wondered what they would think about the main character, a woman attempting to survive the winter living in a cardboard box. Kim had been teaching first grade for five years when she was introduced to critical literacy in a graduate class. She had never considered the idea of reading books about tough social issues in her classroom and was intrigued—but not convinced that she wanted to discuss what might be seen as controversial topics with children. Two years later, as she considered topics for her master's thesis, she was still interested and wanted to explore the idea further. At the recommendation of a faculty advisor, she joined with teachers who were already investigating critical literacy as part of a professional development study group.

Teachers and university researchers in this study group came together each month to share their investigations of critical literacy in K–8 classrooms. Participants had access to a library of critical picture books and adolescent novels that they could take back to their classrooms. These

---

[*] Adapted from C. Leland & J. Harste J. with K. Huber. Out of the box: Critical literacy in a first grade classroom. *Language Arts.* Copyright 2005 by the National Council of Teachers of English. Reprinted with permission.

books typically focused on difficult social issues and involved situations where characters were marginalized in some way as a result of the existing systems of power. Though the stories rarely had happy endings where all of the problems got solved, they all left readers thinking about fairness and what could or should be done differently in the future. The study group Kim joined consisted mainly of urban teachers, and she initially felt out of place since she taught in a rural setting and had no racial diversity in her classroom. Many of the books being explored by the urban teachers focused on racism, and Kim wondered if her White students would be able to connect to these stories.

As it turned out, Kim was in for some surprises. Though she initially worried that her students would not be able to make personal connections to stories that addressed subjects like home-lessness, racism, and war, what she discovered was that they made stronger connections to these books than to the "normal, happy books" she usually read. And even though she was not surprised that their awareness of social issues showed considerable growth when she started to read books that focused on these topics, she did not expect to find that the children would start to treat each other with more compassion and understanding. She was also surprised to find that they put considerably more effort into their written and artistic responses, took on multiple perspectives, and made lots of intertextual connections when they were reacting to these books. Since she did not have any plausible explanation for what she was observing, Kim made this her personal inquiry project. She had many questions to consider: Why did books like *The Lady in the Box* seem to have such a different effect on her children? Could it be that her classroom became a different place when she started sharing the social issues books at story time? These questions and many others fueled Kim's inquiry into the role that critical literacy might be playing in the evolving culture of her classroom.

One of the first patterns Kim noticed was an increase in the children's awareness of social issues. She described how her school had been collecting items for the local food pantry since just after Thanksgiving. She observed that the emphasis seemed to be put on collecting more than other schools in the district so that the school could retain the title of being the most responsive to the needs of others. The children heard reminders each morning and right before going home for the day. There was even a contest set up to see which class could bring in the most items. Kim noted that her children had been bringing in items since that first day and would often mention they thought they would win. When they made these statements, she countered with comments that had to do with how many people they would help with the food, but she felt that her message was not getting through to the children. During the final week of the project, several children announced that their parents said they could not bring in anything else. Then she read *The Lady in the Box*. The very next day, the children came in loaded down with more items. No one made a comment about winning, but instead they talked of how the food would be used by people who did not have enough to eat. What really amazed Kim was that it had taken 15 days to collect 90 items, but in just three days, the children went on to collect a total of 205 items. What was even more impressive to her was the change in the children's attitudes. Instead of looking to win, they now seemed to begin focusing on helping others.

Kim noticed further evidence of the children's growing awareness of social issues after reading *Fly Away Home* (Bunting, 1991) to the class. This is another book about homelessness and tells the story of a father and son who live in an airport. On the 100th day of school, Kim assigned the writing topic that she always assigns on this day: "If I had one hundred dollars, I would..." About two thirds of the class wrote the usual responses such as, "If I had $100, I would biu me a hors. I alwas wuntit a hors" and "If I had $100, I would by a Voltswagin jetu. Win I groe up

I would praktis driving it." At the same time, however, Kim was surprised to discover was that the issue of homelessness popped up in one third of the children's responses. For example, one child wrote, "If I had $100, I would give pepele mony to by a hause. I wont to be nise to other pepel that don't have homes." Another wrote, "If I had $100 I would give the homelis pepol my mone because I like to give." A third child wrote, "If I had $100, I would by them stuff for the homeless people."

In addition to expressing a desire to help homeless people like the ones in the books Kim had shared with them, the children also began to ask questions about why these people were homeless in the first place. They noted that the characters in both books used to have homes but that in each case, something happened to change this situation. Dorrie from *The Lady in the Box* lost her home when she lost her job, and the boy in the airport in *Fly Away Home* lost his home when his mother died. Many of the children were surprised and indignant to learn that people could lose their homes for something that was not their fault. Some made connections to times in their own lives when someone lost a job or a working family member died or moved away. One child argued eloquently that people need to have homes while they are looking for new or better jobs, and another asked why other people did not help them find homes. Phrases like "it's not fair" and "how are people supposed to live?" came up many times during the discussions of these books.

Further discussions about fairness came up after Kim shared the book *So Far from the Sea* (Bunting, 1998) with her students. This is a story about Japanese American citizens who were forced to live in internment camps after the attack on Pearl Harbor. In this case, Kim gave the children time to talk about the story and the vivid illustrations before inviting them to respond through art as well. She was surprised to see how much attention they put into recreating many unpleasant details of the camp. The children's depictions of high guard towers, barbed wire, and guns might have reflected the shock of discovering that kids their own age were taken from their homes and sent far away. Kim noted that though her students would usually "slap any old thing down" to complete a drawing assignment, this one generated a level of energy and concern that she had not observed previously. In this case many children waited patiently to look at the book and took the time and effort to erase and redraw until they were satisfied with their pictures.

By the end of the year, Kim saw many changes in her children's level of critical awareness. She wrote in her journal:

> In my wildest dreams, I would never have thought my students would have come so far in just one school year. At the beginning of the year, they simply saw a book as being for their enjoyment, like a Disney experience. They now look critically at texts, looking for clues into the meaning the author intended. They have examined books for hidden assumptions and have looked at how the readers are being positioned through these texts.

Kim also considered the role that books about racism had played in acquainting her rural children with issues of diversity that often seemed invisible in their monocultural setting. "Without exposure to race, how would my children ever get past the differences to see what is similar? And in a small, white town, they might be adults before they know someone who is not white. By that time, after going so long, it will be hard to tear down the fences of mistrust of someone who looks different. How much more important it becomes in a rural area like this to expose the children to other groups."

What Can We Learn from Kim's Experience?

When Kim first joined the study group, she had many doubts and fears. She worried that focusing on critical literacy might not be appropriate for her children, and she did not know how she would fit yet another instructional area into an already crowded first-grade curriculum. As the year went on, she realized that critical literacy is appropriate for all children, and she found ways to include critical conversations in her daily routine without making any major program changes. Instead, she was able to make subtle changes in her own practice that opened up spaces for discussing books and social issues. We want to suggest that Kim's professional growth resulted from her willingness to challenge two traditional views that tend to be dominant discourses in both schools and the larger culture. First, she challenged the view that literacy is only a question of decoding and making meaning. She continued to teach phonics and comprehension with the reading program mandated by her district, but she also started asking questions that encouraged critical thinking: "Whose story is this? Whose voice is heard? Whose voice isn't heard? What do you think the author wants you to think?" Second, she challenged what many teachers and parents perceive as common sense regarding appropriate subject matter for story time. This view positions children as needing protection from complexity and unpleasant topics. As a result, the common-sense approach leads teachers and parents to choose stories that have simple plot lines and happily-ever-after endings. In making a conscious effort to read books and to engage children in conversations that did not follow the common-sense philosophy, Kim demonstrated how individual teachers can outgrow their former selves. Despite the wall of commercial programs that surrounded her, she was able to use the time-honored institution of reading aloud to children to make a crack in that wall. She could still select books to read at story time and discuss them with the children. The topics of these books could be revisited through writing and art. As the year went on, Kim and her children began to question the assumptions that drove what went on in their classroom, their school, and their community. Without causing much of a stir, critical literacy began to seep into the culture of their classroom. Three underlying theories in Kim's story can help to explain how and why this happened.

Theory 1: Teachers don't have to work alone.

Much has been written about the benefits of teacher study groups (Birchak, et al., 1998; Lewison, 1995; Lewison, Flint, & Van Sluys, 2002). These authors offer wonderful examples of teacher study groups at work and provide evidence for the claim that professional development should not attend to the goal of "filling teachers' heads with new and innovative ideas that may come and go" but should instead "aim to enhance teachers'

TABLE 4.1

Guidelines for Identifying Critical Books

On several occasions during the past few years, we have worked with a study group of our colleagues to explore new books that address social issues and to articulate guidelines for identifying books that can easily be used to begin critical conversations. In two instances, these efforts led to chapters focusing on critical literacy that were subsequently published in *Adventuring with Books* (Harste, et al., 2000; Leland, et al., 2002). These chapters provide annotations for many picture books and chapter books that our study group judged as meeting at least one of the following criteria.

(1) They do not make difference invisible but rather explore how differences can actually make a difference. In this case, the differences noted might relate to culture, language, history, class, gender, race, age, or disability.

(2) They enrich our understanding of history and life by giving voice to those who have traditionally been silenced of marginalized. We call them the *indignant ones*.

(3) They show how people can begin to take action on important social issues.

(4) They explore dominant systems of meaning that operate in our society to position individuals and groups.

(5) They help us to question why certain groups are positioned as others.

Of course we did not always agree on whether a book met one of these criteria and our differences of opinion came out in a number of heated discussions. But as usual, tension served to drive the learning process, and though we never reached consensus on some issues, we did develop a deeper understanding of the multiple perspectives that were at play.

Source: From J. Harste, A. Breau, C. Leland, M. Lewison, A Ociepka & V. Vasquez. Critical literacy. In K.M. Pierce (Ed.), *Adventuring with Books* (12th ed.). Copyright 2000 by the National Council of Teachers of English. Reprinted with permission.

Invitation for Disruption 1:

Investigate Students' Conversations About Books

- Make a list of the social issues you hear your students discussing. This might include topics like divorce, disability, gangs, homophobia, and poverty.
- Choose one topic, and pull together a text set of at least three books that address it. Choose at least one book that is a risky text for you.
- Read the books aloud, and help students to identify common themes as well as differences that are reflected in the books.
- What surprised, bothered, or pleased you about the students' conversations that followed after reading this text set? How did students respond to the risky text?

---

intellectual activity" (Nieto, 2003, p. 18). Participation in an inquiry or study group entails a lot of intellectual activity. Researchers have also discussed the power of collaboration more generally without using the *study group* or *inquiry group* designation. Sach (2003, p. 117) talks about collaborative action "as a strategy to interrupt and 'take stock' of what is happening in schools and classrooms." In a meta-analysis of studies on professional development, Borko (2004, p. 6) concludes, "strong professional communities can foster teacher learning."

In Kim's case, joining a teacher study group gave her access to both materials and a community of fellow teachers who shared many of her interests. The books they discussed at study group meetings (Table 4.1) gave her a place to begin her own investigation. She simply started reading some of these books aloud at story time and encouraged her students to talk about what was going on in them. Since all of the books focused on complex social issues, the children were almost always anxious to participate in discussions, and she never had to work very hard to keep

**Invitation for
Disruption 2:**

**Learning What
Happens When
Students Linger
in Text**

▪ Read aloud a single
picture book about a
tough social issue
three times. Jot down
field notes after each
reading.
▪ After the first reading,
encourage the
students to make
personal connections
to the text.
▪ After the second
reading, invite students
to ask questions about
the text.
▪ After the third reading,
have the class discuss
how this text connects
to larger issues in the
community or culture.
▪ Review your field
notes. What insights
did you gain about
your students during
each of the readings?

the conversation going. She also noted that the topics of the books kept coming up again and again. In addition to the books provided by the study group, Kim also had the benefit of collaborating with colleagues who were engaged in similar investigations. When she reported back on new strategies she tried, the study group audience always gave her helpful and supportive feedback. Colleagues who had more experience with critical literacy provided models from their own classrooms while acknowledging the impressive progress Kim was making in hers. When something did not go well, other teachers offered suggestions for what to try the next time.

Theory 2: Lingering in text is important.

In *Why Reading Literature in School Still Matters*, Sumara (2002, p. 19) offers numerous examples that show how discussing, rereading, and annotating a common text "generates surprising and purposeful insights." Sumara defines a common text as one that has been read and revisited by two or more people. In this sense, any text read aloud and discussed with a child or group of children is a common text for the reader and all of the listeners. But reading (or hearing) a story is not enough. It also takes some lingering in the text to get to the kinds of insights Sumara discovered. This lingering can occur in discussion forums that provide opportunities for individuals to offer (and hear) different perspectives. Each contribution helps to expand other participants' understandings while also offering new questions to ponder.

Lingering also takes place when we reread texts, write about them, and transmediate (Short, Harste, & Burke, 1996) what they mean to us. The process of transmediation challenges a reader (or listener) to articulate the underlying meaning of a story and present it through an alternate sign system. For example, Kim knew that her students were surprised and angry to see pictures of the Japanese internment camps in *So Far from the Sea*, so she invited them to linger in the text and to respond to it through art and writing. The end result of this activity was that it helped the children to identify and unpack aspects of the story that were hard for them to understand and accept. Drawing pictures of the barbed wire and writing captions like, "It was not fair that they locked some people up" gave them a chance to share their opinion about this chapter in American history with others. This was not the only instance where lingering in text proved to be helpful. As part of her work with the critical literacy study group, Kim read many books that front-loaded various difficult social issues like poverty, racism, or war. But she did not just read the books and then drop the subject. She made time for the children to talk about them, write about them, act them out, and draw pictures of what they meant.

Lingering in text is important because it gives us a chance to see things differently. Some books that we have never looked at critically might turn out to have more issues than we expected. For example, many of us recognize "Once there was a tree and she loved a little boy" as the first line from *The Giving Tree* (Silverstein, 1964). Our teacher education students smile indulgently and say, "Oh, I love that book," when we read it to them. Seen through a noncritical lens, it is a cute story that they have heard many times. However, when we follow immediately by reading *Piggybook* (Browne, 1986), the conversations get more intense. *Piggybook* tells the story of a mother who got so sick of waiting on her husband and sons that she walked out on them and did not come home until they agreed to share the work. Almost immediately, we hear our students—who are mostly women—saying things like, "Oh! I never noticed that the tree was a she. And now I see that this is like the story of my life—give, give, give. There's nothing left of me once everyone else in the family is satisfied! I never saw that in *The Giving Tree* before." After a few comments like this, the men—always an underrepresented group—begin to feel victimized. Usually one of them will say that *Piggybook* is unfair because it makes men look bad and "some of us really do help out around the house." Often there is someone in the group who reacts negatively to *Piggybook* for yet another reason and argues that a mother should never walk out on her family. Someone else will immediately ask why it is any worse for a mother to do that than a father. Statements like, "Maybe there's a double standard going on here that we need to talk about" keep the conversation going and invite more people to get involved in it. There is often a great deal of tension that accompanies these conversations, and sometimes people get involved because they vehemently disagree with either the book or someone's response to the book. This brings us to the last theory we want to address.

Theory 3: Tension drives the learning process.

The common-sense notion of tension is negative in our consensus-driven culture. It is often seen as something to be avoided at any cost. To us, tension is a plus that goes hand in hand with diversity and difference and opens up spaces for more voices to be heard. There is never a shortage of tension in our teacher education classes when we read picture books like *Sister Anne's Hands* (Lorbiecki, 1998), *White Socks Only* (Coleman, 1996), and *Freedom Summer* (Wiles, 2001). These stories recount ugly racist incidents that stop all of us in our tracks. When we read these books to children, as Kim did, they are often puzzled as to why some people would be so mean. They see this treatment as not fair and conclude that these things should not happen. But with adults we often get complaints that the books are unfair because they make White people look bad. This reaction is almost always followed by someone on the other side of the issue asking if blaming the victim is really very productive, and the conversation continues. We suspect that this is the first time many of our adult students have ever been asked to think about—or talk about—

Invitation for Disruption 3:

Transmediation

- Read aloud a single picture book about a tough social issue three times. Jot down field notes after each reading.
- After each reading, invite students to respond to the story through the use of a different sign system—for example, drama, art, music, or mathematics.
- Share transmediations with the whole group, and discuss how the meaning potential of the story was expanded or constrained through this process.
- Review your field notes. What new understandings about learning through transmediation were developed?

TABLE 4.2

How Critical Literacy was Enacted in Kim's Classroom

Resources	Critical Practices Enacted	How the Teacher Took Up a Critical Stance
Books about homelessness: The Lady in the Box (McGovern, 1997); Fly Away Home (Bunting, 1991)	Discussed how people are positioned by homelessness and the resulting stereotype	Consciously chose an alternate way to enact storytime to focus on a difficult social issue
Teacher study group	Worked collaboratively with others to change practice and take social action	Took a risk to inquire into the use of social issues texts
Books about racism: Sister Anne's Hands (Lorbiecki, 1998); Freedom Summer (Wiles, 2001); White Socks Only (Coleman, 1996)	Interrogated multiple perspectives by telling the stories of different people who experience discrimination	Developed new instructional approaches as a result of being cognizant of options in interpretation, response, and action
School food drive	Problematized a commonplace practice (i.e., food drive) to show another perspective	Moved children from personal experiences to larger social issues
Class discussions about controversial topics like homelessness and why some Japanese people were put into internment camps	Asked difficult new questions about why these things (i.e., homelessness, internment camps) happened in the first place	Focused on issues of power and equity with young children

racism. Not everyone is thrilled with the experience. Having one's mind opened can be a painful experience, but we do not see that as a reason to let our future teachers—or anyone else, for that matter—off the hook.

How Was Critical Literacy Enacted in Kim's Classroom?

Table 4.2 summarizes how a critical literacy instructional model was enacted in Kim's first-grade classroom. In addition, we can map how Kim moved between the personal and the social with her interest in learning more about critical literacy (Figure 4.1). The flowchart shows how Kim began with a personal inquiry and then invited her children

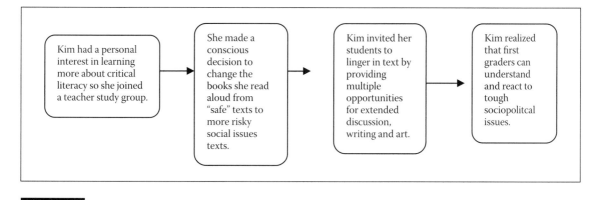

FIGURE 4.1
How Kate moved curriculum between the personal and the social.

to become coresearchers with her. Taking the initial risk to feature a different kind of book at story time allowed her to open up new topics of conversation. In addition, she began using some of the instructional strategies that were shared by teachers in her study group. These strategies provided opportunities for children to linger in text and to respond to the social issues books through a variety of sign systems. The more Kim incorporated different social issues into her reading and writing curriculum, the more interest her students displayed in investigating these issues further. Her initial hesitancy to use risky texts gradually turned into enthusiasm as she saw how engaging they were for her students. In the thought piece that follows, Jerry Harste debunks some reasons for avoiding these books and challenges us to come face to face with our position on censorship.

Lingering Questions

▪ At the present time, critical literacy exists outside of the officially sanctioned school literacy curriculum. How can teachers and university researchers start to get things turned around so that it becomes an essential part of the curriculum rather than an optional add-on?

▪ Are any issues too controversial to discuss with children? How should we respond to censorship? There is an increasing set of books that focuses on issues related to individuals and groups who identify themselves as gay, lesbian, bisexual, transgendered, or questioning (GLBTQ). This set includes both picture books and adolescent fiction (Table 4.3). Some parents have registered concerns about books that address homosexual themes. What can be done to invite parent input without diminishing teachers' ability to address topics that many of their students are already facing?

Chapter Four
Cultural Resources Using
Children's Literature
to Get Started with
Critical Literacy

Books That Address GLBTQ Topics

Daddy's Roommate (Willhoite, 1990)

[a]*From the Notebooks of Melanin Sun* (Woodson, 1995)

[a]*Ironman* (Crutcher, 2004).

Max (Isadora, 1984)

Molly's Family (Garden, 2004)

Oliver Button is a Sissy (De Paola, 1979

Heather Has Two Mommies (Newman, 2000)

Holly's Secret (Garden, 2000)

[a]*Split Image* (Glenn, 2002)

[a]*The Brimstone Journals* (Koertge, 2001)

The Sissy Ducking (Fierstein, 2002)

[a] Books for adolescent or young adult readers.

Thought Piece

Risky Texts

Jerome C. Harste

Teacher Comments:

■ Jules Lester's *From Slave Ship to Freedom Road* (1998): "This book is not age appropriate for the children I teach."

■ Virginia Walker's *Making Up Megaboy* (1998): "I don't think the children I teach would understand this book. It's way beyond their instructional level."

■ Peter Hautman's *Godless* (2003): "If I think a book is controversial, I don't use it. Who needs it? I have found contemporary novels, too often, deal with drugs, premarital sex, alcoholism, divorce, school shootings, high school gangs, school dropouts, racism, violence, and sensuality. Any one of these topics would get the parents in my district up in arms."

■ Ntozaki Shange's *White Wash* (1997): "I think this book makes White people look bad."

As is evident from these oral and written comments by teachers, there are lots of ways to censor books. Teachers are particularly good at it. Oh, they do not call it censorship. They call it selecting, but it is censorship nevertheless, plain and simple. In "selecting" books for reading, teachers will tell you they consider the contribution that the work will make to the topic under study, its aesthetic value, its honesty, its readability, and its appeal to the children they teach. "All that sounds fine," you might say. "It's what professionals should do."

And, to some extent I agree. But when the net result is safe texts that are not worth talking about, I have to take issue. In fact, I would argue that most of the reasons you may be thinking of not using a particular text in your classroom should be reconsidered. Your reasons are probably the very reasons you should not only be using it, but using it with a vengeance!

First things first: It is the right of every individual not just to read but to read whatever he or she wants to read. This is absolutely basic to a democratic society. Second, this right is based on an assumption that educated people can be trusted to make their own decisions because they understand consequences, can make judgments, and are knowledgeable and informed. Third, the first and second reasons are not only what schooling is all about but why we absolutely need to use risky texts if we really do our jobs. It is also why banning particular books in our classrooms is a very bad idea even when we think we have some pretty good reasons.

It is bad enough that we have narrow-minded, anti-intellectual, ultramoral, and ultrapolitical groups against freedom of speech and of the press. I argue that we should not inadvertently join them or support their cause by avoiding risky texts. If we do, we are in effect preparing the children we teach to think like them.

Keep in mind these two facts: (1) When asked, teachers will say they abhor censorship; and (2) more teachers ban more books than any censorship group has ever managed to ban. Said differently, neither of the following reasons holds water:

It's Not at Their Instructional Level

What does this really mean? The book has hard words in it? The book contains too many hard words? Too often, we are taught that if a child reads a page of text and comes to five unknown words on one page, the book is too hard; it is not at that child's instructional level. Teachers who have been taught this belief often teach children to censor books themselves by holding up one figure for every word they cannot read on a page, with the message being that if they get all the fingers on one hand held up, they should choose a different book.

The problem is this might be a topic that the child is really interested in. Would it not be a lot better to say, "I know you might not be able to read every word in this text, but just read as much of it as you can because you are going to love this book."

I knew all of the words in some of the hardest books I have ever read—books like Dewey's (1916) *Democracy and Education*. I am still trying to figure out all of the relationships he saw between democracy and how we educate. And one of the most meaningful books I ever read is one in which I still cannot pronounce all the words: Bakhtin's (1983) *The Dialogic Imagination*.

It is an instructional problem when we try to make reading safe. Most basal reading programs have teachers introduce all of the new words in a story prior to inviting children to read the story. But this is crazy. We have a right to run into a new word every now and then.

We read to learn things. This is what drives the learning process. It is only in schools that we read to practice reading. We call it *reading instruction*, and kids mistake reading instruction for reading. No wonder we create what Huck (1966) calls *aliterate literates*: citizens who know how to read but do not. So censoring books because they have hard words in them is not a good idea.

Nor is readiness. We are never ready for the stuff we learn. If we are ready, we probably already know it and it is not new. I would say the same about scaffolding. I think we overscaffold in the name of good teaching and in the process make learning dull and prosaic. Think of it this way: Risky texts can help us put an edge to learning.

It's too Controversial

Too often we want to play it safe. Few of us got into teaching because we were rabble rousers. We are nice people. We like to talk about nice things. We study things like clowns and magnets, not condoms and race riots.

Former teacher, now novelist, White (1994) tells the story of teaching a particularly hard group of third-grade nonreaders to read. She says she was reading about the sinking of the Titanic at home one night and was struck with the horror of the sinking, the death, the destruction, the ugliness of the affair. She decided to bring the book into class to read the next day. She reports, "Once those children found out that reading could be about things this ugly, this bloody, this brutal, I had no trouble teaching them to read, nor keeping their interest either!"

Teachers often complain to me that they cannot get good literature discussions going in their classrooms. They want to know the secret. The secret is, "Read a book worth talking about." I am not talking about reading politically correct controversial texts. Read some politically incorrect ones. Read some books you know they will never get in Sunday school or at home.

My recommendation is that you put together text sets that represent lots of divergent views. If *war* is the focused study, put together books that question war as well as books that describe our latest military machinery. Do not say goodbye to *Babar* (de Brunhoff, 2000) or decide that there will be no more *Adventures of Huckleberry Finn* (Twain, 1981) just because these story lines are not in vogue anymore. Juxtapose these texts with texts that send a different message. The tension is what guarantees a grand conversation (Peterson & Eeds, 1999).

Contemporary children's books and adolescent novels talk about life experiences that are relevant to contemporary readers. This is what makes them good and worth reading. They talk about the very issues that students are talking about and need to think through. Better to talk about premarital sex or homosexuality than be faced with a sixth grader who is pregnant or has committed suicide.

Sometimes districts have policies about what topics can and cannot be talked about in school. More frequently, we censor ourselves, thinking we need permission to talk about certain topics like sexuality. It is interesting that many teachers can talk about race but feel they need to send a note home before talking about sexuality. This is most unfortunate since sexuality is a very important topic to people at all ages. Kindergarten children already have notions of what girls can do and what boys can do. There is a lot about sexuality to work through. It is better to be conscious of the decisions we make and their consequence to us and to others than to hold positions unknowingly. It is easy to feel weird or to be positioned as odd. We know a lot about sexuality and are learning more daily. Most parents are probably not going to talk with their kids in an open manner. And if learning about sex back behind the barn worked, we would not be in the mess we are. What better place than in the classroom?

I end this essay with a quote from Justice William O. Douglas of the U.S. Supreme Court (*Adler v. Board of Education,* 1951):

> Where suspicion fills the air and holds scholars in line for fear of their jobs, there can be no exercise of free intellect.... A problem can no longer be pursued with impunity to its edges. Fear stalks the classroom. The teacher is no longer a stimulant to adventurous thinking; she becomes instead a pipe line for safe and sound information. A deadening dogma takes the place of free inquiry. Instruction tends to become sterile; pursuit of knowledge is discouraged; discussion often leaves off where it should begin.

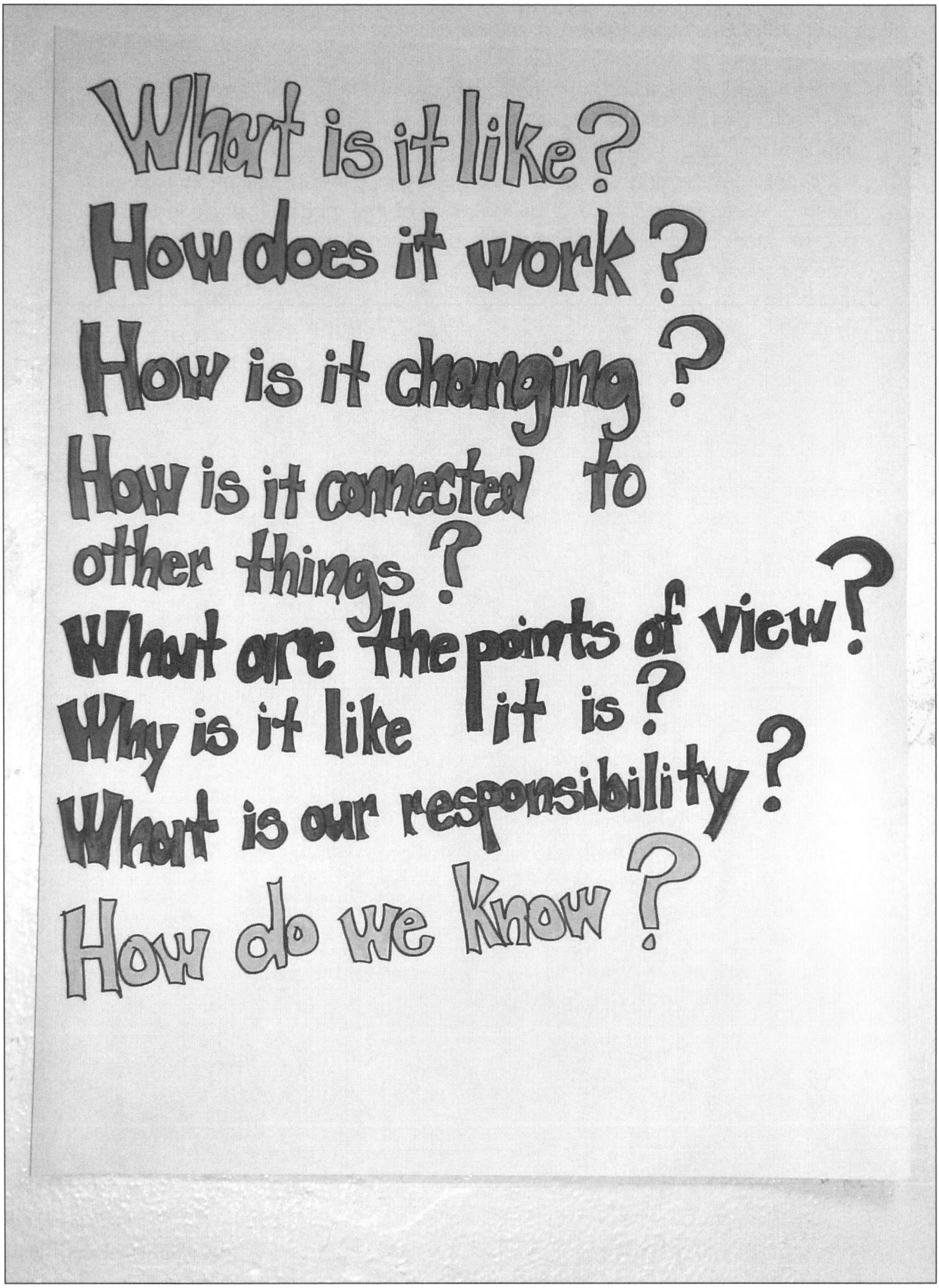
What is it like?
How does it work?
How is it changing?
How is it connected to other things?
What are the points of view?
Why is it like it is?
What is our responsibility?
How do we know?

Critical Social Practices
Disrupting the Commonplace Through Critical Language Study

Vignette

Unpacking the Everyday: Americans at War

Christine H. Leland and Jerome C. Harste

Gee (1999, p. 25) describes the label on an aspirin bottle as seeming to embody two different voices. He notes that one voice sounds like an experienced lawyer who is poised to protect the company if consumers decide to use the product in an unauthorized way and end up hurting themselves or their children as a result. This voice seems to be saying, "Don't bother suing us if you don't follow our directions—you have been warned." The second voice is still authoritative and knowledgeable in explaining the importance of using the product responsibly, but it sounds friendlier and seems to be reassuring consumers that aspirin is no more dangerous than other over-the-counter medications. This voice seems to be saying, "Hey, taking aspirin is no big deal, but we want to make sure that you don't have any problems because we really care about you."

Gee's (1999) analysis of the text on a medicine bottle echoed in our heads as we visited the Smithsonian National Museum of American History in Washington, D.C. Large banners across the building's exterior facade announced a new exhibit called "The Price of Freedom: Americans at War." We discussed the title. The term *price* implied something that had to be paid and that someone had to do the paying. Having personally lived through, participated in, and protested the Vietnam War, we knew the price was real in the sense of both human lives and human emotions.

The entrance to the gallery housing the exhibit featured continuous video clips of war scenes. Words like *sacrifice, bravery, brotherhood,* and *courage* flashed intermittently across the screen in the spaces between the clips. The exhibit itself was set up as a chronological journey through the various wars in which Americans have played a role. The first panel, "Rivalry in North America," referred to a time before the nation existed:

> Wars erupted frequently in North America in the 1600s and 1700s as rival groups clashed with each other and with the resident Indians. Spain, France, and Britain established colonies around the world to enrich their economies, enhance their prestige, and increase their power. All three countries laid claim to portions of North America already settled by Indians. They waged war with Indian nations to establish footholds in America. And they fought with each other to advance colonial interests or to gain the upper hand in European-centered power struggles.

The phrase *wars erupted* caught our attention. The "who is doing what" here was not clear, in that there was no agent—no one doing the action. Volcanoes erupt. We typically associate the word *erupt* with natural or out-of-control causes. Volcanoes erupt because of natural causes. We wondered whether the person—or persons—who put this exhibit together wanted viewers to conclude that war is natural, something that just happens.

The sequence of wars in the exhibit was predictable. There were separate spaces for the American Revolution ("to gain independence from Britain"), the Civil War ("to preserve the union"), the Wars of Expansion, and the World Wars. Although a theme of defending our freedom did run through the World War I and II exhibits, a conflicting theme—one of greed— ran through the section dedicated to the Wars of Expansion, which, we learned, began in 1812 and ended in 1902, a span of 90 years. This section, which included information on wars with various Indian nations, Mexico, and Spain, was summarized by the caption "Americans fought in North America and overseas to expand the nation's territory." The placards spoke directly to our nation's not-so-noble intentions in these instances:

- In the 1830s, the U.S. government forced eastern Indian tribes to resettle in the West.
- During the Spanish–American War, the United States entered an era of overseas expansion.
- As the 20th century approached, the United States was becoming a world power with expansionist ambitions.
- Instead of liberating the Philippines from Spanish domination, the United States chose to annex the islands and begin building an American empire.
- Following the fall of Cuba, the army seized Puerto Rico. Samoa, Guam, and Wake Island also came into American possession, followed by Hawaii.

Again, the language, or discourse, was interesting. The U.S. government had "forced" Indian tribes to move, "annexed" the Philippines instead of "liberating" them, started "building an empire," and "seized" Puerto Rico. Despite aggressive language of this sort, the final panel claimed innocuously that "Samoa, Guam, Wake Island, and the Hawaiian Islands came into American possession." The no-agent pattern was repeated. Apparently these events just happened.

Both the Korean and Vietnam Wars were characterized as wars to "contain Communist expansion." Given all of the details in the exhibit about Americans' multiple efforts to expand their territories through war, we had to wonder why anyone going through the exhibit would not question why expansion was fine for us but not for the Communists. This issue was not addressed.

After focusing on the fall of the Berlin Wall and the breakup of the former Soviet Union, a new discourse appeared: "In 1991, the United States became the world's only superpower and began redefining its global role." What specifically the new role for the United States as a superpower might be was never defined. A snippet dealing with Afghanistan explained that the United States had to take action after the attacks of 9/11. This was followed by statements about Iraq made in February 2003 by Howard Dean and Condoleezza Rice:

> Dean: I believe that Iraq does have chemical and biological weapons, and they are a threat to their many nations in the region, but not to the United States. Therefore, in my view, the United States ought not to attack unilaterally. The United Nations should disarm Saddam [Hussein], and we should be a part of that effort.

> Rice: When democracies wait too long to confront tyranny more people die. That's why after 9/11 we're not prepared to let this cancer continue to grow. It is why the president … if Saddam Hussein does not disarm, will discharge his responsibilities with a coalition of the willing to disarm Saddam Hussein by force.

Although both Dean and Rice can arguably be categorized as embodying politicians' voices, the more interesting question is this: Who selected these quotes and juxtaposed them in this particular way? What was the intent? Was someone attempting to get readers to believe that Dean was just as fooled by the infamous threat of weapons of mass destruction as his opponents were? And what about Rice's contention that democracies need to confront tyranny quickly? Was this voice arguing that democracies need to play a global law enforcement role whenever and wherever oppression occurs? Rice also connected the events of 9/11 with the cancer of the Iraqi regime even though that was—and still is—a questionable, if not false, connection.

Dean and Rice's comments were followed by a placard on the war in Iraq in which the rhetoric of our current times was clearly featured: "In March 2003, the United States, Great Britain and other coalition forces attacked and overthrew Saddam Hussein's brutal regime in Iraq."

The next panel described air strikes of unprecedented precision and ground attacks that were fewer, faster, and more flexible than those of the 1991 Gulf War. As if to temper this technological endorsement for why the war was important, the final panel closed with this statement: "Major combat operations took less than two months, but coalition units remained entangled in a controversial effort to establish an Iraqi democracy."

We wondered about teenagers going through this exhibit. Can getting "entangled" compete with "air strikes of unprecedented precision" in terms of getting attention?

The war in Iraq was not the end of this exhibit. The last stop was a gallery where a continuous video played. This video emphasized patriotism and the honorable role of giving service to one's country. It included both printed and spoken statements:

▌ Heroes are made by what lies within the heart.
▌ This country is safe because people have fought for it.
▌ We resolve that the dead shall not have died in vain.

- Democracy is worth saving.
- Freedom is worth saving.
- This country is worth saving.
- We have unfinished work.

The last statement echoes Lakoff's (2004, p. 68, emphasis in original) dire prediction: "With no definition of victory and no exit strategy, we may be entering a state of *perpetual war* (emphasis in original)." Although the exhibit contained multiple—and at times competing—messages, it was clear that the dominant and overriding message people exiting the exhibit were to walk away with was, "War is a natural state of being that never ends." This conclusion left us with many new questions. Who had chosen this focus for the new exhibit? Who provided the money for its construction? We knew that we had more research to do on our own and were anxious to start digging around on the Internet when we got home.

What Can We Learn from the Museum Experience?

Although critical thinking skills are frequently listed in commercial and district curriculum documents, a closer examination reveals that they are often synonymous with concepts like finding the main idea, making inferences, and sequencing details. There is seldom any emphasis on figuring out how a text positions different people or what worldview a text is advocating. As a result, it is not surprising that most of us have work to do in this area. The museum vignette offers an example of our conscious and deliberate attempt to challenge the conventional notion of critical thinking and to flip the script, so to speak, about what it really means to think critically in the deeper sense. The decision to approach the museum in this way was guided by several underlying theories about language and learning.

Theory 1: No text is neutral.

We might not expect what we see in a museum to be controversial. Unfortunately, most of us have grown up thinking that history is just a bunch of facts. It is disconcerting to realize that these so-called facts come from someone's perspective and that these facts are chosen and displayed purposefully for some effect. It is important to understand that someone is always attempting to position us in a specific way. We can follow along docilely, or we can bring up other perspectives and challenge what is being presented.

Lensmire (2000, p. 64) reminds us that this is what critical literacy is all about:

> Dominant groups determine dominant meanings, but not without a struggle, and never once and for all. In fact, the larger educational and political project of critical pedagogy is exactly to empower stu-

dents to engage in this struggle over meaning—in solidarity with the wretched of the earth; in the name of social justice, equality, and democratic community; and in preparation for and as part of transformative social action.

One way to help children understand that no text is neutral is to begin with blatant examples of nonneutral texts: the advertisements that bombard us on a daily basis. We can invite children to analyze ads and to categorize them according to the techniques they use. Is there an expert with numbers and charts telling us to buy something? Or are plain folks like us shown to be enjoying a product? Is there a catchy rhyme or slogan that might stay in our heads? Is someone trying to get us to believe that our lives will be better if we use a certain kind of shampoo or eat in a certain restaurant? Advertisements construct and deliver specific messages about products just like the museum exhibit constructed and delivered a specific message about war, but they are much more obvious, and the analysis is easier. Kids can also see quickly that companies want us to buy their products so that they will make more money. Engaging in this kind of analysis helps them understand how they are being positioned to think that they need or want something that they really do not need or want at all. (See "Critiquing Consumer Culture" and "Unpacking Appealing Ads" in the Invitations section.)

Interrogating illustrations is another way to help children see that no text is neutral. Political cartoons provide good examples of how art can be used to sway people's thinking. The person doing the drawing wants us to believe something about the characters. For example, the cartoon by Mick Stevens in Figure 5.1 shows a man sitting at a desk while he talks with three other men. What catches our attentions in this picture is that they are sitting in what appears to be rising water. The caption reads, "Gentlemen, it's time we gave some serious thought to the effects of global warming." Conversations with students about this text might first focus on where the cartoon is taking place, who the men in the picture could be, and why they are flooded. Once students come to the conclusion that it is probably taking place in Washington, D.C., and the men are high governmental officials—maybe even the president and his advisors—they can talk about the flooding and the reference to global warming. At this point, questions like, "What does this cartoonist want us to believe?" and "Why?" can be posed. (See "Political Cartoons" in the Invitations section.)

Children can also be invited to analyze the illustrations in books and to hypothesize about what the artist wants them to believe. Kim Huber's first graders were able to study the illustrations in *The Other Side* (Woodson, 2001) and to conclude that the author wanted them to think that the main character, a black girl, was "strong and powerful" (Leland, Harste, & Huber, 2005, p. 265). The students also concluded that the

Invitations for Disruption 1:

Advertising in Public Spaces

▪ Jot down your thoughts about businesses using public spaces (e.g., schools, museums) to advertise.

▪ The commonplace wisdom is that such advertising is no big deal and that it is a good way for underfunded institutions to get additional resources. How does your perspective align with this view?

▪ Whether you agree or disagree that it is no big deal, what are some potential consequences of this practice that you might not have thought of? How does hidden advertising position students? How can we help students become more savvy consumers?

▪ What strategies can be used to begin interrogating this practice in a public way?

'Gentlemen, it's time we gave some serious thought
to the effects of global warming.'

two mothers in the story—one Black, one White—were wearing very similar clothing when they passed by each other in town because the author wanted them to see how similar they were: "If she wanted us to think that they were really different, she wouldn't have done that" (p. 265).

Theory 2: Critical language study needs to be an integral part of the curriculum.

Critical language study focuses on the actual words in a text and how those words are used to create an overall image or to make a point. Lakoff (2004) uses the term *framing* to describe how groups use specific words in deliberate ways to build a view of the world that is sympathetic to their beliefs and interests. Using Lakoff's framing lens, we can see how Rice's quote equated Hussein's regime to tyranny and a form of cancer that would continue to grow if left unchecked. Clearly she was attempting to frame the Iraq war as one of self-defense for Americans— and therefore a just war. Using the framing lens again, we can see that Dean's quote was carefully chosen to support the same view of Hussein—and by association, Iraq—that Rice was suggesting. Dean's opening sentence, "I believe that Iraq does have chemical and biological weapons," positioned him as seeing Iraq as dangerous—maybe not a cancer, but dangerous. The rest of his statement regarding his belief that Iraq did not pose a threat to the United States carried little weight after the part about chemical and biological weapons. The frame was already established, and "frames once entrenched are hard to dispel" (Lakoff, 2004, p. 73).

Children and adults both need to learn how to recognize framing. We often bring in new versions of old fairy tales to introduce critical language study. For example, everyone seems to love the updated version of the original Cinderella story that adds a trendy new neighbor named Cinder Edna (Jackson, 1994) to the story. According to this text, the traditional Cinderella "sat among the cinders to keep warm, thinking about all her troubles" when her housework was finished each day. The more assertive and creative Cinder Edna decided that sitting in the cinders was "a silly way to spend time" so "she kept warm by mowing the lawn and cleaning parrot cages for the neighbors for $1.50 an hour." Whereas Cinderella approached her problem of needing a dress for the ball by wishing she had "a fairy godmother "who could change her rags into a beautiful gown, Cinder Edna "used her cage-cleaning money to put a dress on layaway." When Cinderella rode to the ball in "an elegant coach"—also supplied by the fairy godmother—Cinder Edna "took the bus." The book ends with Cinderella marrying the handsome, but deadly dull, prince and Cinder Edna marrying his goofy-looking, but definitely more fun, brother. Readers are invited to "Guess who lived happily ever after." Everyone is smiling happily until we ask how both the original and the new version frame women. It takes a few minutes for students—both children and adults—to work through this question. They would rather dwell on all the stereotypes that the new version challenged. But they eventually have to conclude that even the modern version makes sure the heroine gets married off at the end. It is hard to dispute that both women are framed as finding happiness through their marriage to men. Other fairy tales are equally useful for learning to recognize framing. Invite kids to think about how the story of Little Red Riding Hood frames little girls, grandmothers, men, and wolves.

The idea of framing is reminiscent of Fairclough's (1989, p. 94) claim that "the meaning of a single word depends very much on the relationship of that word to others. So instead of the vocabulary of a language consisting of an unordered list of isolated words each with its own meaning, it consists of clusters of words associated with meaning systems." A cluster for the traditional Cinderella story includes words like *cinders, fairy godmother,* and *elegant carriage.* A cluster for the more modern Cinder Edna includes words like *strong, spunky, layaway,* and taking the *bus* to the ball. Clearly the two characters were portrayed as being very different. Yet both clusters can also include some of the same words: *cruel stepmother* and *wicked stepsisters,* which they both had, and *were married* and *lived happily ever after,* which they both ended up doing. So in this case, the meaning system for the new modern woman

---

Invitations for Disruption 2:

Perks for Patrons?

- Jot down your thoughts about how people who give lots of money to some institution (e.g., school, library, museum) should be positioned as a result of having made this donation.
- Should any special treatment or perks be given to those who make large donations? If so, what type of perk would be appropriate? Which type would not be appropriate?
- How can public institutions keep a balance between the wishes of patrons and the wishes of the larger public? How can communication between the two groups be optimized?

- The next time you are reading a newspaper article related to education or listening to a story about education on the radio or television, pay special attention to how the issue is being framed. For example, an article about how a state legislature is cutting school funding to help achieve a balanced budget might frame the issue in terms of, "This is what has to be done to achieve fiscal responsibility. It's hard, but someone has to do it."

- What are the implications of this framing? In this example, do the legislators who are voting to cut school funding look like they are the strong adults? Do the ones voting against it look like children who need more guidance on how to spend responsibly?

- Who benefits from the perspectives highlighted by the framing you identify? Who loses? How is this political?

- Think about your own state. How are your legislators framing educational issues?

seems to have passively absorbed the dominant cultural sense that she too should achieve happiness by getting married.

Meaning systems were at work in the museum as well. We thought that *freedom* would be defined as a nation's ability to rule itself without foreign interference, but analysis of the text in the exhibit made us realize that the meaning system had changed. What we saw as common sense turned out to be cultural sense and exemplified what Fairclough (1989, p. 94) labels as "something of an ideological sleight of hand." Without fanfare, the meaning system for freedom was altered to include global superpower and a distinctly humanitarian, if not Christian, responsibility to confront tyranny wherever it exists. Fairclough calls this type of change "an effect of power" (p. 95)—an occurrence indicating that one side in the struggle between meaning systems has gained dominance, at least for the time being.

Theory 3: Curriculum should support the development of counternarratives.

Counternarratives are important because they empower us to see other possible realities. They encourage people to challenge the unquestioning acceptance of cultural norms that have become more or less invisible over time. Sumara and Davis (1999, p. 191) argue that "curriculum has an obligation to interrupt heteronormative thinking—not only to promote social justice, but to broaden possibilities for perceiving, interpreting, and representing experience." After reading *Cinder Edna* and discussing how the story frames women, we can invite students to write counternarratives that challenge the dominant cultural beliefs underpinning this story and many others. Similarly, after visiting the museum, we might invite kids to write counternarratives for how war was presented in this exhibit. Noddings (2004, p. 490) argues that schools should provide opportunities for all students to think critically about war and their attitudes to it:

> A question that needs closest examination is the one usually avoided: What makes war so attractive? It is not honest to cover this over with layers of propaganda extolling the virtues of "our heroes" who sacrifice willingly for "our freedom." Such sacrifice is indeed part of the story, and should not be denied or mocked. But simply acknowledging sacrifice does not face up to the fact that many people—both soldiers and civilians—are excited by war.

It is not hard to imagine children and adolescents getting excited about war as a result of viewing this exhibit. After all, what young person does not wish to be thought of as courageous or patriotic? Clearly, other perspectives on what might look glamorous and inviting are needed. Noddings (2004, p. 490) suggests that any discussion of what makes war attractive should also lead to a critical examination of gender and violence since "rape and brutality seem to be part of a faulty vision of masculinity, one that supports both war and a 'rape culture.'"

Peace education can provide a framework for developing counternarratives to the glamorous portrayal of war. Some components of peace education include learning about conflict resolution, studying the causes of war, developing appreciation for diverse human cultures and all forms of life, learning about global issues, and becoming aware of universal human rights (Joseph & Efron, 2005, p. 528). Fortunately, some picture books provide opportunities for discussing war and other tough social issues with children. For example, *Sami and the Time of Troubles* (Heide & Gilliland, 1992) and *The Cello of Mr. O.* (Cutler, 1999) depict the deadly reality of what daily life is like for children living in war zones. Stories like *Feathers and Fools* (Fox, 1989) and *The Butter Battle Book* (Seuss, 1984) challenge the idea that safety can come from possessing weapons. And books like *So Far from the Sea* (Bunting, 1998) and *Gleam and Glow* (Bunting, 2001) make the suffering of people who are forced out of their homes by war painfully clear. These books provide a powerful counternarrative for more glamorous views of war. Yet it seems that books like these are not easy to get into print. For example, Judith Gilliland (cited in Lewison, Leland, Flint, & Moller, 2002) reports that publishers worried her book *Sami and the Time of Troubles* might be seen as too political by some parents. We agree that books about war are political, but we see the museum exhibit and how the news is reported on television every night as equally political. Experience with counternarratives can help students become adept at identifying political themes in texts that have been culturally framed as apolitical or neutral.

Developing counternarratives can also help children understand that patriotic behavior can be defined in many different ways. Noddings (2004, p. 491) notes how the impressive opposition to the war in Iraq was in effect neutralized by the deeply socialized admonition to "support our troops." Since this slogan has proven to be enormously powerful, she advocates encouraging students to analyze its effects on patriotism, on conformity, and on the preservation of traditional attitudes toward war and warriors. She asks a series of questions relating to the support-our-troops initiative. "Can a person be against the war and still support the troops? Must patriots provide such support? What else is supported when we give way to this pressure?" (p. 491) Her questions are reminiscent of Fairclough's (1989) meaning systems and Lakoff's (2004) frames as we realize that patriotism has now been linked to supporting the troops—and, in effect, to supporting the war. To help children construct counternarratives for definitions of patriotism that connect directly to supporting war, we suggest using Noddings's questions as the basis for inquiry projects. What better way for kids to learn about different perspectives on what it takes to be a patriot than to let them ask lots of people how they define this term?

We exited the museum talking about two statements from the video at the end: "We resolve that the dead shall not have died in vain"; and "We have unfinished work." It seemed that both of those statements were offering reasons to fight more wars. But a counternarrative might use the same statements as reasons to stop fighting wars when our freedom is not at risk. Maybe the best way to make sure that dead soldiers did not die in vain is to think more carefully in the present and future about how we define the kind of freedom we are willing to die for. A counternarrative can also be constructed for the statement about having unfinished work. Maybe the work ahead is to figure out how to help people see that Americans have not always given their lives to protect our freedom. In some cases, wars were fought so that some people could get rich—or richer. Neil Postman and Charles Weingartner (cited in Noddings, 2004, p. 492) refer to this particular kind of critical thinking as "'crap detecting'—uncovering 'misconceptions, faulty assumptions, superstitions, and even outright lies.'" For example, we would like to think that high school students could call on some well-developed crap-detecting skills to help them interrogate advertisements that focus on the benefits of enlisting in the armed services. Unless they can see beyond the positive images in the ads and connect them to images of war that are not being shown, they will not have a full and informed picture of what their decision means.

As readers and viewers of the museum and other everyday texts, we are ultimately "responsible for bringing all these contentious assumptions into the process of interpretation" (Fairclough, 1989, p. 83). It is up to us to accept the underlying assumptions or to subject them to further interrogation and possible rejection. We can encourage our students to analyze, evaluate, and rewrite texts like those we encountered in the museum. We might even encourage them to come up with a better exhibit to replace—or at least to stand in contrast to—the one on display in Washington, D.C. "The Price of Freedom: Americans Thinking Critically" comes to mind as a title, but the possibilities are endless.

Why bother? What is to be gained from picking a fight with the National Museum of American History? Freire (1970, p. 33) reminds us that "it is impossible to humanly exist without assuming the right and the duty to opt, to decide, to struggle, to be political …. In other words, though I know that things can get worse, I also know that I am able to intervene to improve them." Not intervening means the dominant voice gets louder and louder. There is more than one way to be courageous, and there is more than one battlefield where courage can emerge. We do not have to accept the frame that patriotism equals blind allegiance to policies contradicting the values of fairness that served as the ethical foundation of this nation. If the dominant discourse frames patriotism

TABLE 5.1

How Chris and Jerry Adopted a Critical Perspective at the Museum

Personal and Cultural Resources	Critical Practices Enacted	How Participants Took Up a Critical Stance
Predictions made about the exhibit before viewing it	Considered systems of meaning that might be operating	Paid attention to the language used in the exhibit
Museum texts	Asked questions about how the museum texts worked	Were consciously engaged in critical language study
Analysis of underlying messages in museum texts	Disrupted commonplace notions about accepting texts at face value	Entertained alternate ways of being by composing counter narratives
Internet searches to find outmore about the exhibit	Took responsibility to inquire by conducting research on issues of social and political importance	Used inquiry as the foundation for challenging the status quo

with defending these values, then a "reading, writing, and rising up" (Christensen, 2000) approach becomes our civic duty as literacy teachers. Lakoff's (2004, p. 34) advice is to "practice reframing, every day, on every issue …. Use your frames, not their frames." Let us take busloads of kids through this exhibit and use the experience as an exercise in critical thinking and reframing. After all, many of them will almost certainly be called on to fight in some war. Finn (1999) talks about the need to educate working-class children in their own self-interest; when this happens, students develop "literacy with an attitude," as the title of his book suggests. Judging whether they will be risking their lives to preserve national freedom or to build someone else's wealth and power seems like an important skill to develop before they hurry off to enlist. In this case, literacy with an attitude might literally save lives.

How Was Critical Literacy Enacted During the Visit to the Museum?

Table 5.1 summarizes how Chris and Jerry adopted a critical perspective as they worked through the museum exhibit.

In addition, we can map out how they moved between the personal and the social in terms of developing an understanding of the exhibit and its underlying intent (Figure 5.2).

Perhaps the most memorable learning from this experience was the realization that the words we use make a big difference. This is as true in a museum as anyplace else. Not being aware of this does not make it

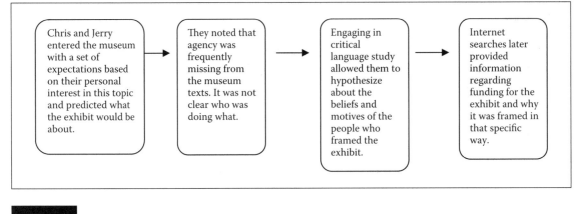

FIGURE 5.2
How Chris and Jerry moved from the personal to the social.

less significant; it just means that we are less apt to figure out how we are being positioned and what someone else wants us to believe. If we pay attention to language, we can make a conscious decision about its intent and what our response should be. In some cases we might decide to talk back to the commonplace knowledge that we used to take for granted. In the thought piece that follows, Jerry challenges us to think critically about the language we use with our students and how it makes a difference.

Lingering Questions

▍ How should we respond to parents or members of the community who do not think it is appropriate for children to develop a critical perspective?
▍ How can we keep the conversation going when school knowledge and ways of thinking contradict family or religious knowledge and ways of thinking?

Thought Piece

Critical Choices

Jerome C. Harste

Teacher Talk:

I have been interested in collecting examples of what critical theorists and teachers attempting to develop a critical stance in their classroom say to children. What kinds of questions do they ask? What kinds of follow-up to children's responses do they make? How do teachers, through their talk, support children in taking on a critical stance?

The teachers Chris and I worked with in creating the Center for Inquiry in Indianapolis became interested in teacher talk because we noticed that, when trying to implement an inquiry-based curriculum, even too much talk caused problems. Sometimes the problems resulted from giving lengthy directions. Too many directions seem to thwart the students in developing agency. Students came to think of themselves as the kind of people who cannot figure things out on their own. From an inquiry perspective, they became passive recipients of knowledge rather than researchers who had the resources and strategies to verify facts, to figure things out on their own, and to make informed judgments. And it is important to remember that we meant well. We all firmly saw education as inquiry and inquiry as education. It was our mouths that did not seem to be cooperating.

A review of the research on teacher talk turned up some interesting findings. Edwards and Westgate (1987), for example, discovered that school language was very different from out-of-school language.

- **Instance 1:**
  - Speaker A: What time is it?
  - Speaker B: 3:30.
  - Speaker A: Thank you.
- **Instance 2:**
  - Speaker A: What time is it?
  - Speaker B: 3:30.
  - Speaker A: Very good, Sarah.

Language creates identity as well as positions language users one to another. In Instance 2, Speaker A is clearly the person in authority. He or she is not only asking the questions but also is evaluating the quality of the response. Speaker B is clearly the underling. In Instance 1 both speakers are on equal footing. Speaker A has a question. Speaker B answers that question. Speaker A, in return, is thankful. The relationship is reciprocal rather than hierarchical.

The most common pattern of interaction between teachers and students in school is what Edwards & Westgate (1987) call an Initiative action–Response–Evaluation of the response (IRE) pattern. Outside of school, if someone were to evaluate the quality of the answer to the question of what time it was with "Very good, Jerry," my first reaction—providing it was not a friend just trying to be clever—would be one of irritation with the person as well as with myself: I read the question being asked as a legitimate inquiry, not as an instance of evaluation; the other person apparently read me either as not very bright or as so unsure of myself that I needed some type of affirmation.

Johnston (2004), after audiotaping a wide range of classrooms and analyzing the results, maintains that one qualitative difference between high- and low-performing classrooms is the kind of teacher talk that takes place in them. Johnston goes on to argue that teacher talk influences what gets noticed, what and how things get named, what identities both teacher and student take on, whether the student will develop a sense of agency, how strategic a learner the student will become, as well as how flexible the student will become in terms of his or her thinking. Although Johnston was interested in studying teacher talk that supported the development of a quality reading and writing curriculum, my language study was geared to finding out what kinds of teacher talk support the development of a critically literate citizenry.

I have organized many of the powerful things I have found researchers recommending and teachers saying to children around the social practices we see making up a critical stance on literacy. What makes each of these instances of teacher talk powerful is that they support children in taking a critical stance by making them more consciously aware of what might otherwise be just taken for granted. Even further, they are expected to take the stance of an inquirer, invited to entertain alternate ways of being and to use themselves and others to outgrow their current self.

Disrupting the Commonplace

- What does the author want us to believe? What parts of the text gave you clues?
- What assumptions is the author making about us as readers? Are we comfortable being positioned this way?
- Let's read this again, but this time let's think about all of the things that do not ring quite true.
- What message did the author of this magazine advertisement want readers to walk away believing? As researchers, rather than just accept the advertiser's statements, how could we go about checking their accuracy?
- What questions would you like to ask the person who created this piece?
- How could we check what is being reported here? Let's have some volunteers go to the Internet to see what they can find.
- Any surprises? Any others?

Considering Multiple Viewpoints

- What are you thinking as you are reading? Stop, talk to your neighbor, and compare your thoughts.
- How do you think the main character is feeling right about now? Let's act out some different possibilities. Let's also act out what things were like the day before this story began. What do you think things are like now that the story is over?
- I wonder how this story might have been different if it had been written by someone of the opposite gender, different religion, or different ethnic group.
- Instead of the person being depicted in this illustration, think of members of different ethnic being the focus. How, then, does the message change? How does thinking about the picture in this way clarify the message originally being sent?
- Go home tonight and interview your parents and a couple of your neighbors about the issues in this text. We will talk about them again tomorrow.

Focusing on the Sociopolitical

- That was brilliant thinking. Walk us through how you came to just the opposite conclusion of the author.
- What are the economic issues that underlie this part of the text?
- What are some parts of this text that really bother you politically? How else might these have been written?
- What frame is the author using? How else could this issue be framed? For example, in this instance, taxes were framed as a burden rather than as an investment in our future.
- What would a piece written from a different frame look and sound like?
- Given the way the author has written this text, who benefits? Who does not benefit?

Taking Action to Promote Social Justice

- How would this text change if it reflected what you believe?
- How could we talk about this differently? What would happen if we changed our talk? Let's role play some possibilities after reading a social issues book.
- What could we do that would call attention to this issue both in school and out of school?
- Now, there's a dinner conversation for you to have at home.
- We cannot just leave this topic. We have to do something. Let's explore various alternatives and possibilities.

Becoming critically literate means building the identity of a person who does some things and not others. It comes about as a result of trying on what it is like to be a certain kind of person in a certain kind of social space. What we as teachers say can support children in the taking on of a critical perspective on literacy. By hearing how other teachers talk, we too can learn to mind the gap between what we believe and what comes out of our mouths. Though it is hard to think of our mouths as a strategy lesson, in the final analysis what we say may make all the difference.

Chapter 6

Critical Social Practices
Interrogating Multiple Perspectives

Vignette

Seeing Differently

Christine Leland and Amy Wackerly

Amy Wackerly teaches in a multi-age second-and-third-grade classroom at the Center for Inquiry in downtown Indianapolis. About 55% of the students who attend this public magnet school are African American, and another 5% are Latino. Helping her students to understand and appreciate diverse perspectives is a major goal for Amy, but she does not treat diversity as a separate topic or an add-on. Instead, she and her colleagues have developed a literature-based literacy program that integrates reading, writing and seeing differently within a context of critical awareness. Observations of Amy's teaching provide numerous examples of how this approach affects every aspect of life in her classroom.

One book that Amy uses to begin conversations about seeing differently is *Voices in the Park* (Browne, 1998). This story features four gorilla characters that dress and act like humans. The author used a different font for each character and structured the text so that each speaks from the first person in telling his or her version of what transpired in the park one day. This is a story about social class; it recounts the interactions of two families when they were in the park at the same time. One family consists of a bossy, wealthy mother and her rather shy son. The other is a despondent out-of-work father and his outgoing young daughter. Before reading the book a second time, Amy asked each student to focus on the role of one of the four characters as she read the book again. She told them that they would be "retelling the story from your character's point of view" during the next activity. After the second reading, she put them into groups that contained representatives of all four characters and invited them to assume the role of their assigned personality as they talked through the story without reading the actual text. Field notes gathered during this segment showed how the children worked together to try to figure out why the characters acted as they did. For example, there were conversations about the "mean mother" in several of the groups observed. Amy then asked all the children playing the same role to take turns dramatizing what they thought their character was thinking during the story. Their examples included many different perspectives.

1. The wealthy mother was thinking:
   - My son Charles is too nice to be hanging around with someone who [looks like she] just got out of a trashcan!
   - These people look like they don't have a home.
   - That man is a bum. He might rob me.
2. The unemployed father was thinking:
   - Rich people are not friendly.
   - I'm happy that Smudge made a new friend.
3. The shy son (Charles/Charlie) was thinking:
   - I am glad to have a new friend.
   - I wish my mother would stop acting so mean to Smudge.
4. The outgoing daughter (Smudge) was thinking:
   - I still love my father even if he doesn't have a job because he tries his best to take care of me.
   - Charlie is nice but he is scared to talk to me.

Their insights into what the characters were thinking document an understanding that four people who experienced the same events could come away with very different perceptions. To do this, they had to challenge the common-sense notion that there is only one way to see the facts of any event.

Amy also provided opportunities for her students to inquire into the multiple perspectives that influenced their interactions with each other. After receiving several complaints from children about the amount of name calling that was going on, she called a town meeting to discuss this issue. She began by asking the children to think about whether name calling was a form of bullying. When they concluded that it was, she wrote, "A bully is someone who …" on a dry-erase board and listed the students' responses as they worked through this topic (Table 6.1).

During their discussion, Amy noticed that children always seemed to use the pronoun *he* when referring to bullies, so she asked them if bullies were always boys or men. Several children immediately stated that girls and women could be bullies, too, and one student noted the importance of saying *he or she* in the future.

Amy then invited her students to think about why bullies might be doing those kinds of things on the list in the first place. She talked about how she does not think of herself as a bully, yet sometimes she finds herself acting in a mean or bossy way at home. She explained that this does not happen very often, but it might happen when she is tired or not feeling well. She challenged the students to put themselves into someone else's shoes and think about what might be going on in that person's life to make him or her act like a bully. Why is it that people who are usually nice sometimes turn into bullies? Table 6.2 shows the list of ideas the children shared.

TABLE 6.1

Bully Chart Made by Amy's Class

Statement	Student Responses
A bully is someone who …	… is a rule breaker.
	… is mean.
	… picks on people.
	… is bossy.
	… might not have good parents.
	… likes to cause trouble.
	… threatens people.
	… lies.
	… is rude.

TABLE 6.2

Why People Become Bullies

Question	Student Responses
Why does someone become a bully?	Maybe somebody hit him or her earlier.
	People said mean things to him or her.
	People threatened or scared him or her.
	She or he is disappointed or sad about something.
	School hasn't been a safe place for him or her in the past and she or her was bullied by others.
	She or he is worried about problems at home and takes it out on other people.
	People stole things from him or her, and that caused anger.
	She or he is having parent problems.
	She or he has built-up anger and takes it out on others.
	Other kids got them in trouble, and now it's time for payback.

Amy took both lists home and created three scenarios for the children to dramatize in small groups the following day.

■ Scenario 1: Sheila lives with her mother and her sister Anna. Her mom is not at home very often, but when she is, she yells at Sheila and her sister. Sheila feels lonely and angry. When she is at school, she acts mean to other students.

- Scenario 2: At home Michael's dad tells him that his mom is in the hospital. Michael is worried and upset and takes his anger out on Bill and other friends at school.
- Scenario 3: Allison was picked on by Jevonna at her old school. At her new school she is mean to Tammy and other students before they can be mean to her.

Amy divided the class into groups and gave each group a card with one of the scenarios and a list of characters needed for creating a dramatization. The children eagerly claimed the parts they wanted to play and began to plan their skits. The bully role appeared to be the one in greatest demand.

A group working on scenario 1 spent some time trying to figure out what was going on with Sheila's mom to make her yell all the time. They decided that she probably had a stressful job and had to work late every night and on weekends. They talked about how the mother's problems might be connected to Sheila's problems and decided that Sheila was probably stressed out from her mother's yelling. "So she takes it out on the kids at school." One child admitted, "Yeah—I do that too."

In a group working on scenario 2, DeShawn quickly claimed the bully role. Anton, another boy in this group, said that was appropriate since the exact same thing had happened the year before when DeShawn's mother was in the hospital. He reminded everyone of how mean DeShawn had been until his mom came home again. At first DeShawn denied this connection, but after hearing testimonials from several peers who had been with him the previous year, he agreed that maybe it was "sorta true." He admitted that he yelled at people and said it happened because he was upset and worried about his mother. When this skit was performed, it was interesting to note that the children included a scene where Anton confronted DeShawn (playing the role of Michael the bully) and told him that he did not like being picked on. The skit ended with the bully apologizing to his friend and the two boys shaking hands and smiling at each other.

In a follow-up writing activity the next day, Amy used a strategy developed by Kim Huber (Leland, Harste, & Huber, 2005) to help children identify multiple perspectives. She demonstrated how to divide a large piece of unlined paper into three columns and to write the names of three characters from the scenario they worked on at the top of each column. Under each character's name, they were asked to write an "I statement" showing what that person might have been thinking during the dramatized scene. Examples for scenario 1 illustrate the children's efforts to put themselves into the shoes of Sheila, her mother, and one of Sheila's friends.

- Sheila:
  - My mom came home and yelled at me. I was too scared to yell back. I started to yell at the students in the class.
  - I'm mad at my mom. I'm so lonely. She is always yelling at me. I really don't know why. It might be work or Daddy. I take it out on my friends because of my mom. I'm pretty sure something is wrong, wrong about her work.
- Sheila's mother:
  - Today my boss told me I had to come to work on Sundays to get my project done. And if they [Sheila and Anna] keep missing the bus and I have to get to work late, I will get fired soon. They must be doing it on purpose.
  - I'm stressed almost every day. They [Sheila and Anna] don't understand that I'm cooking, working and raising them. Sometimes it's hard for me.
- Sheila's friends:
  - I was being nice but she [Sheila] kept yelling at me. And I wanted to talk it over because that's what friends do. But I just left her alone.

FIGURE 6.1
Hussein.

Hussien

the soldeir's werent
very nice. And I
had To change my
name into Harry. I
was very sad.

FIGURE 6.2
Soldier.

Soiders

When I came to bulgaria
noone went out side. I
Knocked on this man's Door.
he changed his name to
selim. I felt sad for
them.

FIGURE 6.3
Father.

Father

I couldn't go to
the mosque.
Hussien went with
me. but the mosque was
closed. I was very sad.

- I thought Sheila was our friend. Now she's so mean to us. I was just saying hello and she got mad. Now I don't want to be her friend anymore because she's so mean.

Both the drama and the writing activities encouraged the children to go beyond the simplistic assertion that Sheila and her mom were just mean. It required them to imagine they were someone else and consider what might be going on in that person's life. Amy hypothesized that taking on the role of a bully might provide some insights for the children into why bullies act as they do. She hoped that this might be the first step in minimizing the bullying behavior the children had observed.

Finally, Amy also used specific picture books to help her children understand that bullying and power struggles in general can take many different forms. These books addressed difficult social issues like racism and war. They provided firsthand examples of people dealing with the horrific effects of institutionalized bullying, as documented by stories of the Nazi holocaust, Japanese internment camps during World War II, and racial desegregation in the American South. Amy frequently read one of these books aloud, led a discussion about it, and then used writing, drama or art to provide a space for children to express their varied reactions and interpretations. Figures 6.1–6.3 show examples of how the "I statement" activity worked in another classroom with the book *My Name Was Hussein* (Kyuchukov & Kyuchukov, 2004). This book tells the story of a Muslim boy in Bulgaria who was forced by the government to adopt a Christian name.

Invitation for Disruption 1:

Parents' Night

▪ Plan a short program for parents' night that focuses on multiple perspectives.

▪ Share a text set that highlights a marginalized group.

▪ Engage parents in a discussion of the text set.

▪ Invite parent input on the issue of controversial topics.

▪ Take notes on the parent responses. How can they be categorized? Which type of response is the most and least prevalent? How does this fit—or not fit— with what you expected to find?

What Can We Learn from Amy's Teaching?

It is difficult to focus on difference when the dominant cultural milieu seems to be firmly fixed on standardization and consensus. In discussing the legacy of the landmark Supreme Court case *Brown v. the Board of Education* during the past 50 years, Ladson-Billings (2004, p. 11) argues that "real education is impossible in isolation from diverse and critical perspectives." She goes on to describe the challenge educators face as more than a deceivingly simple Black versus White issue and urges them to see this as an opportunity "to examine not just the mis-education of children of color and the poor but also that of White, middle-class children whose limited perspectives severely hamper their ability to function in a global community" (p. 11). What we see going on in Amy's teaching is a genuine effort to open minds and too enlarge the scope of classroom conversations. This is not a random occurrence. Rather, it happens when teachers have specific theories and beliefs about teaching. We have identified three underlying theories that appear to inform Amy's teaching decisions.

Theory 1: Multiple perspectives complicate what we already know.
Commonplace wisdom suggests that none of us—including teachers— should ever try to make anything more complicated than it already is. Amy's willingness to challenge this dominant view demonstrates her understanding that simplistic responses to complex issues rarely help to solve problems. Instead of giving her students an answer to the bullying problem or telling them to ignore it, she invited them to inquire into the underlying causes of this kind of behavior. She used extended conversation (e.g., town meeting), drama, and writing as vehicles for complicating the children's stereotypical notion of bullies as bad people. Even though students initially categorized both Sheila and her mother from the first vignette as mean, the activities Amy introduced required them to contextualize, and complicate, their understanding of what was going on. As a result, they began to see links between how people are treated and how they subsequently treat others.

The importance of this type of complication is supported by a number of theorists. For example, Delgado and Stefancic (2001, p. 55) see a focus on multiple perspectives as a way to avoid stereotypical thinking: "The insistence on examining how things look from the perspective of individual actors … can enable us to frame agendas and strategies that will do justice to a broader range of people and avoid oversimplifying human experience." This is especially important given the multiple roles that all of us take on at various times. Gee (1999) uses the term *Discourse* (with a capital D) to describe a kind of identity kit that defines someone in a specific group. This kit includes ways of talking, ways of interacting, gestures, clothing, and objects used as tools (p. 7). For example, we might see a man who is registered in one of our teacher education classes simplistically as a student. He dresses a certain way (e.g., in jeans), carries specific tools (e.g., paper, books, snacks), and says things like, "I have some questions about the article we read for today." If we extend our interaction with him, however, we might find out that he is also a father, a part-time bartender, and a trumpet player in a band. What it takes to make this happen is the inclusion of his voice. Without it, we can only make guesses about the multiple perspectives he might bring to any conversation. Of course, this adds complexity and complicates our understanding of him. We might learn something about him that bothers us—like a political position he holds that we do not agree with or membership in a group we find offensive. Even so, we will still end up with a better understanding of him as a person than if we simply walked away with the deceivingly simplistic student role in mind. In addition, complicating things offers an opportunity to work toward a just and equitable solution to what we might have originally perceived as irreparable differences. (See "What Differences Make a Difference?" in the Invitations section.)

Theory 2: A focus on multiple perspectives involves the representation of people who have traditionally not been prominent in school curricula.

Amy engaged her students in activities that highlighted multiple perspectives and the stories of people who have been silenced. The drama activities with *Voices in the Park* and the bullying inquiry invited students to explore multiple roles and to see the world from different points of view. Like *Voices in the Park*, many of the picture books she shared belonged to the critical literacy text set we identified as focusing on tough social issues (Harste, et al., 2000; Leland & Harste, 2002). Books Amy used that specifically addressed racism, for example, included *Sister Anne's Hands* (Lorbiecki, 1998), *White Socks Only* (Coleman, 1996), *The Other Side* (Woodson, 2001), and *Freedom Summer* (Wiles, 2001). As a result, her students did not develop an understanding of the history of racism in terms of a single event but as many related events that combine to make it a pernicious social force. Since many of Amy's students were African American, she felt it was important to acquaint them with history—especially the knowledge that their ancestors had challenged racism and ended up changing their world. At the same time, however, she also wanted to acknowledge that more change is still needed.

Some of the work that remains to be done relates to the way the stories of various ethnic groups are told—or not told—in mainstream texts. *Lies My Teacher Told Me: Everything Your American History Textbook Got Wrong* (Loewen, 1995) describes a number of events from American history in ways that challenge what has been the dominant discourse. We are sure that some readers will brand Loewen's book as unpatriotic because it critiques icons of American history like

Invitation for Disruption 2:

Seeing Through Different Eyes

- Think of two students who are struggling in your classroom.
- Create a description of each student from three different perspectives: the teacher (you), the child, and the child's parent.
- Analyze and summarize any differences you see.
- Why does the same child appear differently to the three of you?
- What can you learn by trying to look through the child's eyes? What can you learn by trying to look through the parent's eyes?

Christopher Columbus, the Pilgrims, and the notion of America as the *land of opportunity*. Indeed, Loewen joins Ladson-Billings (2004, p. 3) in challenging "a view of America as a nation endowed with inherent 'goodness.'" Without hearing from forced minorities who found America to be more of a prison than a land of opportunity, potentially enlightening conversations about altruism versus economic self-interest in American history may never take place.

Our understanding of history is further complicated by claims about the overrepresentation of white men and the exclusion of women and people of color in various documents that describe our nation's beginnings. For example, Larson and Ovando (2001, p. 111) present the following argument:

> The logic of privileged White men has been not only documented, sanctioned, and sedimented in the history we have inherited, but in the knowledge we have derived through religion, literature, medicine, law, and science as well. As a result, the lives, experiences, and counter narratives of women and men of color have been historically silenced and expunged from the stories we pass from one generation to the next. These glaring omissions of other people's perspectives have resulted in the uncritical portrayal and overrepresentation of white men in our curriculum.

Presenting the dominant view of history (i.e., the story of White men) to children as unproblematic and factual is both arrogant and misguided. If we want future citizens to challenge a past and present that has sometimes rewarded privilege and ignored fairness, then we need to get them seeing differently at an early age. Amy's use of activities and books that frontload other people's perspectives is one way to begin new conversations about voice and power. (See "Multiple Perspectives" in the Invitations section.)

Theory 3: It is important to weave diversity and seeing differently into the fabric of curriculum.

Although we are great supporters of ensuring that all children learn about Black history, the idea of Black History Month every February has always seemed problematic to us. First, there is an implication that it is possible to cover black history in a month. This reductionist mindset leads to superficial activities that do little to build an understanding of multicultural education as a form of social activism. In this instance, students rarely get past topics like food, music, and art. We believe that Black history—and diversity in general—should be an integral part of the curriculum, not an add-on that gets highlighted for one month each year. Amy's approach to diversity was very different. Themes of social justice (e.g., What is fair? How do people take action to achieve fairness?) were embedded in the everyday events of her classroom. These themes were included in—but not limited to—the literacy curriculum.

In addition, Amy constantly encouraged her students to attempt to see through the eyes of other people. Christensen (2000, p. 5) refers to "a curriculum of empathy" and describes it as a way of putting students "inside the lives of others" (p. 6). This is no simple accomplishment since childhood is more often marked by selfish instincts than by empathy for others. We suspect that attempting to see the world through someone else's eyes is an acquired skill, not something that children should be expected to pick up on their own. Amy used drama and writing activities from the bullying inquiry and *Voices in the Park* to give her students opportunities to step metaphorically into someone else's shoes.

Voices in the Park is an example of what we have come to call multiview books (Lewison, Leland, & Harste, 2000). Instead of relying on a narrator to tell the story, books with this structure allow the various characters to speak for themselves. Other elementary-level books that feature multiple perspectives (i.e., characters speaking for themselves) include *Seedfolks* (Fleishman, 1997), *Bat 6* (Wolff, 2000), and *From Slave Ship to Freedom Road* (Lester, 1998). (For other multiple-perspectives books that are appropriate for adolescent and young adult readers, see Thomas, 1997; Frost, 2003; Hesse, 2001; Walter, 1998 in the resource list.) Amy used drama with *Voices in the Park* to help her children explore the multiple perspectives that the four characters might bring to the story. Since they were already reading the different characters' words, it was not a huge stretch to extend those words beyond the text and to expand the characters' perspectives. For example, even though the book never said that the rich mother was afraid that the man on the park bench might try to steal her money or kidnap her son, the children were able to see that these fears might have been driving her unfriendly behavior. Sometimes it is unpleasant to put ourselves in another person's shoes, especially if we do not approve of that person's actions. But this might be where understanding and tolerance begin. At the same time, it is also important to remember that even in a multiple-perspectives book, not all possible perspectives are ever offered. For example, *Voices in the Park* would motivate distinctly different conversations if the unemployed father had been "angry and leading a labor protest in the park, calling on businesses and corporations to hire local citizens rather than farm out jobs overseas" (Damico, Campano, & Harste, 2005, p. 4) rather than sitting dejectedly on a bench. In the existing story, the father seems to be accepting unemployment as his lot in life, whereas in an alternate version he could be actively attempting to achieve change. (See "Multiview Books" in the Invitations section and Table 6.3.)

TABLE 6.3
Multiple Perspective Books for Adolescent/Young Adult Readers

Thomas, Rob. (1997). *Slave Day*. New York: Simon & Schuster.

Through a series of short first-person narratives, readers follow the thoughts and actions of seven students and a teacher as they experience "Slave Day" at their high school. While the stated purpose of this long-standing annual event is to raise money for student activities, Keene, an African American student condemns the idea as racist and demeaning. When he invites others to join him in some type of action (like a boycott), his calls are emphatically rejected by Shawn, a basketball star and the first African American president of the Student Council. Despite Shawn's refusal to see the problem, Keene finally succeeds in raising everyone's awareness of racial issues. Other characters in the book provide a context for considering issues relating to gender, institutional power, and social class.

Frost, Helen. (2003). *Keesha's House*. Farrar, Straus & Giroux.

Keesha and six other teenagers in trouble have found a safe place to live while they try to face their issues and get their lives back on track. Through the use of traditional poetic forms, each of the teens tells his or her story. Readers hear from a pregnant girl, the confused father of the baby, an abused girl, a boy whose parents have disowned him because he's gay, a boy whose parents are in prison, a girl arrested for drunk driving, and a girl who is angry at her mother and stepfather.

Hesse, Karen. (2001). *Witness*. New York: Hyperion Books.

Residents of a small town in Vermont provide their individual accounts of what happened in 1924 when the Ku Klux Klan moved in. They illustrate how people can gain power through working together as a community with a shared vision.

Walter, V. (1998). *Making up Megaboy*. New York: DK Publishers.

This powerful book is as stark and shocking as an unexpected news headline. It tells the story of a quiet boy named Robbie Jones who, on his 13th birthday, took a gun from his father's bureau drawer and shot the elderly Korean man who owned a local liquor store. The story unfolds through a series of first person narratives supplied by people who knew— or thought they knew—this boy as well as from people who were drawn into the case through their roles as witnesses, corrections officers, police officers, and new reporters. The only conclusion that comes through is a picture of a boy who never really fit in, either in school or at home.

How Was Critical Literacy Enacted in Amy's Classroom?

Table 6.4 summarizes how Amy made curriculum critical and helped her students expand their perspectives.

In addition, we can map out how Amy moved her students from the personal to the social in terms of understanding how people's actions

TABLE 6.4
How Critical Literacy Was Enacted in Amy's Classroom

Personal and Cultural Resources	Critical Practices Enacted	How the Teacher Took a Critical Stance
Students' concerns about Name calling	Engaged in inquiry to research social issues	Generated curriculum from learners' questions
Dramatizations for bullying scenarios	Understood the multimodal nature of literacy	Encouraged children to try out alternate ways of being
Story of herself as someone who has been a bully	Critiqued herself as someone who is not innocent	Demonstrated reflexivity
Voices in the Park	Disrupted the commonplace wisdom that there is just one right way to see a situation	Was cognizant of her options and consciously engaged in expanding students' perceptions of bullies
Writing from different characters' points of view	Challenged children to consider how different characters might see things differently	Asked children to identify alternate ways of thinking and being

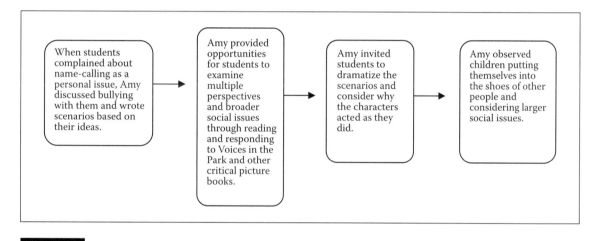

FIGURE 6.4
How Amy moved curriculum between the personal and the social.

and their treatment of others relate to the experiences they have had (Figure 6.4).

Amy used the children's own experiences as a basis for talking about larger social issues. The bullying activity she created was a direct response to what was going on in her classroom and on the playground. Through participating in the dramatizations that Amy created for them, children were able to use their personal knowledge of bullying to construct theories that helped to explain its possible causes. Their responses greatly expanded both the texts and the options for taking social action. This increases the likelihood that they will be more conscious of their own bullying actions in the future and might someday intervene to help a bully understand and modify his or her destructive behavior. Similarly, asking her students to explain how the characters in *Voices in the Park* saw the same events so differently helped to establish a model of seeing differently as acceptable and normal. If they later apply this concept in their interactions with others, they might well become agents of positive social change. Although multiple perspectives and seeing differently might generally helpful, however, that does not mean that they cannot also be problematic at times. In the thought piece that follows, Jerry Harste puts an edge on this topic by reminding us that complex issues never lend themselves to simplistic explanations.

Lingering Questions

▮ How should we respond to perspectives that might appear to be potentially hurtful to some children? For example, what if a child brings up the perspective that the mother in *Voices in the Park* did not want her son to play with the other child because she was dirty and smelled bad? What if other children in the class have similar issues?

▮ Are any perspectives too hot to handle in the classroom? Should any be silenced?

Thought Piece

Understanding Reading—Multiple Perspectives, Multiple Insights

Jerome C. Harste

One of the problems with advocating for multiple perspectives is that it sounds too liberal, too politically correct. Everyone believes there are at least two sides to an issue, do they not? What critical educator in his or her right mind would present things as if they were the gospel truth? I argue that even if we buy into the notion of multiple perspectives, it is important—probably even more so—to ask, Why do I hold this belief? Where do I think multiple perspectives get us that single perspectives do not? Advocating for multiple perspectives is not unproblematic even for those of us who believe in it. Without a doubt, multiple perspectives complicate what we know and thus complicate curriculum. To explain what I mean, I use a review of the insights gained from reading research over the last 40 years as an example.

Insights into Reading

Table 6.5 summarizes, by the various disciplines involved, what I see as major insights into reading. I reference each insight with the name of at least one key researcher. Readers who wish to learn more about these insights and the history of reading can go to my website (http://php. indiana.edu/~harste/wrkprg/) for an expanded version of Table 6.5 in article form.

Because the discussion of multiple perspectives that follows rests on your familiarity with the content of Table 6.4, my suggestion is that you make yourself a "stapleless little book" (see "Touchstone Texts" in the Invitations section), and as you read through it, use the pages in your little journal to note:

- One connection
- One observation
- One question
- One surprise

Jennifer Story, a middle school teacher at Dole Middle School in Hawaii, developed "One connection, one observation, one question, one surprise" as an instructional strategy. Several other teachers have expanded on this strategy by asking students to record other things like, "Name something you wish to remember for always" or "List topics that you could write about now that you have read this piece." Should you be fortunate enough to be reading this thought piece with other people, my further suggestion is that once you have completed your "little books," you take time to talk about the connections, observations, questions, and surprises you each had. Then, given the fact that you have just experienced how your reading of Table 6.5 benefited from multiple perspectives—in that each of you has different connections, observations, questions and surprises—you might wish to take some time to discuss what you see as the relationship between multiple perspectives and literacy before reading on.

Multiple Perspectives: Some Benefits

From my perspective, this list of insights into reading leaves little doubt that we as a profession have benefited greatly from the multiple perspectives that researchers have brought to the study of reading. Although there is more to learn, what we already know is substantial. That having been said, however, there seems to be a commonly held perception that multiple perspectives are inherently good, that all perspectives are valid, that somehow looking at things from all sides characterizes the educated person from the uneducated one.

Although this review does little to refute any of these views, it does verify that as new perspectives have been brought to bear on reading, old ideas often have had to give way. Though competing perspectives may seem equally valid when first proposed, over the long haul some perspectives prove more robust. Some take on increased significance as we continue to learn more and think more deeply about reading. Booth (1988) explains this phenomenon by arguing that literacy and ultimate readings are finally always a matter of ethics. One argument that can be made for why multiple perspectives are important, then, is that over time multiple perspectives become a self-correcting device.

Also apparent from reading through this list is the fact that not all perspectives are equal. Some are clearly more powerful than others in that they are more robust; they explain more of what constitutes our ever-changing and more complex insights into reading. Though everyone may have a right to his or her own opinion, multiple perspectives invite people to continue to grapple with fundamental issues, thus disrupting the tendency to provide easy answers to complex problems.

A third benefit of multiple perspectives, and the one I personally think is the most powerful, is that implicit in the notion of multiple perspectives is the expectation that no matter what is

■■■■■■■

TABLE 6.5

Key Insights into Reading: Perspectives from Different Disciplines

Perspective	Key Insights
Linguistic	• The systems of language (i.e., graphophonemics, syntax, semantics, pragmatics) provide a powerful conceptual framework for thinking about the complexity of language (Fries, 1963). • Reading is only incidentally visual (Smith, 1971). More proficient readers rely on less visual information than less proficient readers. • Our intuitive sense of syntax is one of the most powerful cueing systems in language (Chomsky, 1965).
Psycholinguistic	• The greater the difference between a text's surface structure (i.e., what is written) and its deep structure (i.e., what is meant), the more difficult it is to process (Chomsky, 1965). • Language learning is rule governed and occurs in distinct stages (Brown, 1970). • Children do not learn language through imitation but rather by being active participants in a language community (Brown, 1970; Halliday, 1975). • Language users and language learners are agents in language learning rather than passive recipients of language (Brown, 1970; Halliday, 1975). • Language is not acquired so much as invented from the inside out (Halliday, 1975). • Any language event provides language learners the opportunity to learn language, learn about language, and learn through language (Halliday, 1982). • Learners attend to specific demonstrations in written language events according to their interest and experience rather than according to their age or presumed cognitive stage (Harste, Woodward, & Burke, 1984; Smith, 1971). • Meaning making in reading and writing involves the orchestration and allocation of meaning across multiple sign systems (Harste, Woodward, & Burke, 1984). • Because reading, like the other expressions of language (i.e., speaking, listening, writing) is first and foremost an instance of language, anything that can be said about language should hold true for what can be said about reading (Goodman, 1967). • When readers encounter words in the context of a story as opposed to isolated on a list, they recognize and read many more correctly (Goodman, 1965). • The very complexity of the reading supports the reading process (Burke, 1969). • Meaning is central to language learning (Smith, 1971). • Reading is not something one is taught but rather something one learns through exposure to written language in meaningful situations (Smith, 1971). • Most of what we know about language is learned from being in the presence of others (Wells, 1986). • When readers depend too heavily on the visual information in the text, the reading process breaks down (Chomsky, 1972).
Cognitive	• The structure of idea units in a text provides a key insight into how the comprehension process works (Kintsch, 1974; Rumelhart, 1980; Stein & Glenn, 1979). • Though the structural elements in a text are important, what a teacher emphasizes as important during instruction dramatically alters which propositions or idea units students retain (Schallert & Tierney, 1982).

TABLE 6.5 (continued)
Key Insights into Reading: Perspectives from Different Disciplines

Perspective	Key Insights
Cognitive	• For something to be learned it has to be tied into a particular schema, and it is this linkage that makes it accessible and memorable—in short, learned (Anderson & Pearson, 1984). • Comprehension of a text occurs when we are able to find slots within particular schemata to place all of the bits and pieces we encounter in a text (Rumelhart, 1980).
Reader Response	• The coming together of a reader and a text results in a new text or, metaphorically, a poem (Rosenblatt, 1938, 1987). • For the reading process to work, readers need to understand that the stance they take up is dependent in part on the nature of the text (Eco, 1970). • A search for a coherent meaning drives the reading process (Iser, 1980). • Reading—and literacy, more generally—is a matter of morality and ethics in that our values determine the ultimate readings we make (Booth, 1988). • To understand reading is to understand the lived-through experiences of the reader (Rosenblatt, 1987). • Even though great books complicate our lives, our lives ought to complicate great books in turn (Bleich, 1979).
Sociolinguistic	• Dialects are not inferior or bastardized forms of the mother tongue but rather just as organized and predictable as standard English (Baratz & Shuy, 1969; Labov, 1972). • Rather than rewrite stories into dialect—which dialect speakers often find confusing—teachers need to stop correcting dialect-induced miscues and get on with the business of teaching reading (Sims-Bishop, 1982). • Context includes not only the words on the page but also the child's instructional history as well as the kinds of instructional and noninstructional interactions that take place among students and teachers in the classroom (Bloome & Green, 1984; Harste & Burke, 1977). • Language did not come into existence because of one language user but because of two who wanted to communicate to get things done (Halliday, 1973). • Semantics and pragmatics, rather than graphophonemics and syntax, are the key systems of language to study if the goal is to understand language and language learning (Halliday, 1973). • Literacy is a cultural construction (Heath, 1983; Street, 1995). • What constitutes literacy in one community differs from what constitutes literacy in another community (Heath, 1983).
Critical	• There is not one literacy but multiple literacies (Street, 1995). • Literacy is always situated and maintained by the social practices that are operating in a particular culture or context of situation (Luke & Freebody, 1997). • Reading is first and foremost a social and cultural event in which one has to read the world to read the word (Freire, 1985). • Rather than talk about language in terms of letters, words, sentences, or texts, we ought to talk about language in terms of discourse to signal the fact that all language is ideological or motivated in favor of someone's interest to get something done (Gee, 1999).

TABLE 6.5 (continued)
Key Insights into Reading: Perspectives from Different Disciplines

Perspective	Key Insights
Critical	• Because discourse is never neutral, readers need to become text analysts who understand the relationship between language and power (Luke & Freebody, 1997). • Language is always about power (Lankshear, 1997). • To be literate is to understand how you as a reader are positioned by text (including the identity you are being asked to take on) as well as to understand how texts do the work they do (Comber, 2001). • In the 21st century children need to learn how to be agents of texts rather than victims of text (Janks,1999).

known there is still yet another perspective from which to grow. I like to think of this "yet another perspective" as a potential: something yet to be, the hope that someday we will understand.

Multiple Perspectives: Some Caveats

Given these benefits of multiple perspectives, my advice is that rather than seeing any of the insights in Table 6.5 as fact, it is best to see them as hypotheses in need of further testing. Peirce (1931–58), one of America's greatest philosophers, characterized facts as beliefs at rest. By this he meant that things often only look like facts until someone gets up the gumption to study them closely.

This review of what we know about reading lends credence to Peirce's (1931–58) assertion. As new disciplines have turned their attention to reading, older notions about reading (e.g., seeing it as largely a perceptual process) have needed to be rethought.

My second caveat is that by ordering this review chronologically, readers should be aware that I have reified and conflated the twin notions of multiple perspectives and progress. This is problematic as it suggests that these two lenses are inherently linked. Though both *progress* and *multiple perspectives* might be nice metaphors to believe in, rest assured that not every step taken—even in the history of thought about reading—has been forward. This is, in fact, what is wrong with this review of literature specifically, as well as all reviews of literature more generally. Reviews sand off all of the edges and give the sense that there has been a straight line of progress from there to here. Gone are all the catfights and with them the stories and often sagas of how new ideas came to be. Reviews of literature are often dead, if not deadly, whereas the history of ideas and the politics of scholarship are alive, and often quite lively.

The issues of evolution versus creationism and No Child Left Behind legislation are cases at hand. Both movements disregard much of what is currently known. Rather than being new perspectives they seem disruptive—an attempt to revive earlier beliefs. Though it is hard to see these movements as progress, they are, nonetheless, good examples of the relationship that always exists between language and power. Critical educators, for example, have seen these issues as an opportunity to study larger social forces at play and how these get shaped into educational policy regardless of what scientifically is known (see, e.g., Coles, 2003; Garan, 2004; Goodman, Shannon, Goodman, & Rapoport, 2004; Garan, 2004). As a result of this work not only have such phrases as *the politics of literacy* taken on new significance, but science and scientists are no longer seen as neutral observers, above reproach. They, too, have theoretical and political agendas even when they are not cognizant of them or try to make us believe they are neutral.

My last caveat relative to multiple perspectives is that even though they might add to our understanding of reading, this does not mean that either the actual teaching of reading or the actual process of learning to read has changed. This gap between rationalizing and doing is what is called the scholar's fallacy (Ketner, 1976). It refers to the belief that because some new insight has been explicated and articulated, a real change in the world has occurred. Think about what we know about reading and the dominant mode of instruction being advocated under No Child Left Behind legislation, for example. Strong sociopolitical forces seem to be able to trump knowledge. So, though multiple perspectives might be valuable, we need to keep asking ourselves whether multiple insights have really made a practical difference in the lives of teachers and children. This is, of course, where you come in and why the social practices you put in place in your classroom make a difference.

So, let me end by saying that even for insights that have both stood the test of time and are influencing practice in significant ways, what is important to remember is that they are just beliefs at rest. If we really play our cards right, someday—say another 40 years from now—when someone updates this review of reading, all the insights we currently hold to be true will have been found, if not wanting, at least hopefully sharpened. There within, it seems to me, lies the precariousness as well as the promise of multiple perspectives.

Critical Social Practices
Focusing on the Sociopolitical

Vignette

The Sociopolitics of Hunger

Emily McCord

I consider myself a socially informed citizen and a social activist. I want the students I teach to be socially informed too, as well as willing to act on their convictions. As the world continues to shrink, it is important that we all get involved. The war in Iraq, the Israeli–Palestinian conflict, genocide in Rwanda, internally displaced persons in Sudan, death on the border of Kashmir, environmental catastrophes touching every part of the globe, child labor, Africa's HIV/AIDS epidemic, and countless other global tragedies affect all of us. As tomorrow's leaders, our students need to understand these issues in terms of both their complexity and what it is that they as individuals and we as a country can do about them.

Because of these beliefs and this interest, I registered for a summer program at Indiana University called the International Studies Summer Institute (ISSI). Offered through Indiana University's Center for Global Change, ISSI brings teachers from around the world together for two weeks of intensive study regarding teaching in and for an increasingly interconnected, global world. This institute not only reinforced my beliefs about teaching but also helped me turn these beliefs into a sociopolitical, problems-centered curriculum for my students.

I applied what I learned at ISSI in many ways in my instructional practices. Here, I explain only one of them. At ISSI, I worked with a group of teachers to explore the idea of *systems thinking*. The foundation for this type of thinking is the idea that there are multiple, interconnected factors

---

that work together to cause any given event or problem. This is very different from standard, cause-and-effect logic. What I found promising about systems thinking was the underlying hypothesis that given multiple interconnected causes of a world problem, for example hunger, our actions can have a positive impact by working at the site of merely one of these multiple causes. Systems thinking maintains that problems are sort of in limbo, held in place by a web of causes. Change any one vector in this web, and the entire web changes.

Seen globally, systems thinking challenges the seemingly insurmountable nature of many problems as it gives individuals multiple ways to make a positive impact. It was in systems thinking, then, that I discovered the hope I wanted to deliver to my students: the sense that their individual actions truly can and do make a difference not only locally but globally.

As a result of what I learned about systems thinking in this institute, I developed a project to pilot with one of my seventh-grade classes. I called it the "Hunger Project" and began with an exploration of Bearak's (2003) article, "Why Famine Persists." The focus of this article is famine in Malawi. What is powerful about the article is the detailed description it provides of the myriad interconnected causes of famine in this single country.

I used Bearak's (2003) article to introduce my students to systems thinking. To make sure that they had a firm understanding of the concepts embedded in the model, we spent three days reading the article aloud as a class. I asked students to keep a master list of all of the causes of hunger in Malawi as we read and discussed the article together. They were invited to raise their hands each time they read something that sounded like a cause of hunger in Malawi. When a hand went up, I asked the student to explain why he or she thought that particular item was a contributor to famine, and if the logic held, other students added that item to their lists. Students emerged from this experience not only with gargantuan lists of possible causes of famine but also with an understanding of how complex this issue is, both globally and in a country like Malawi.

Next I grouped students in fours and asked them to use the information on their lists to make a web showing all of the causes of famine in Malawi. I also encouraged them to try to identify links between the causes, and I told them that a messy web was not only acceptable but also preferable. My goal was to push their thinking so that they could surprise themselves with the large number of connections it was possible to make.

After the students completed their webs, I showed them the web I had developed at ISSI using the same article (Figure 7.1). The students were mesmerized by my web (and I am serious about this—the oooing and ahhing was really remarkable) and seemed to enjoy comparing it to their own, seeing where they had missed connections and discovering rather sophisticated ones that I had missed; I did some oooing and ahhing myself.

It was at this time, as well, that I gave a brief minilecture about systems thinking, explaining to the students the promise it offers for dealing with global problems. We talked about how it was not necessary to feel as though we must solve the entire problem of famine in Malawi, for example. We discussed how an all-or-nothing approach to solving global issues, in fact, might lead people—even those with good intentions—to turn their backs on helping. Most global problems are complex and therefore seem to be insurmountable. Rather than take an all-or-nothing approach, we talked about the benefits of entering the web of causation at a single point. Which point we choose depends on our interests. If we are interested in politics, we can deal with the issue of hunger and political corruption issue (see Table 7.1). If we are interested in economics, we can explore how the International Monetary Fund and the World Bank impact a country like Malawi. If we are interested in medicine, we can enter in at the point of disease control. If we are interested in agriculture or the environment, we can enter in at the point of Green Famine (Table 7.2), developing new agricultural techniques, or dealing with natural disasters.

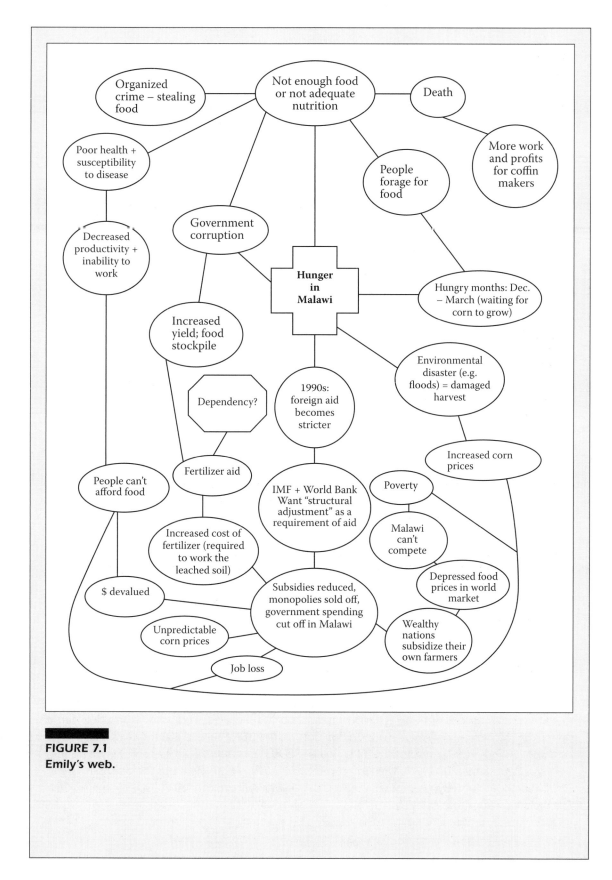

FIGURE 7.1
Emily's web.

TABLE 7.1

Corruption in Feeding The Hungry

According to Bearak (2003), in February and March 2001, flooding caused the corn plants in Malawi to fail to produce mature cornstalks. When the corn was harvested, the yield was about one third less than the previous year. In reaction to this, the Agriculture Ministry called for additional corn to be bought from Uganda, South Africa, and Tanzania. The Agriculture Ministry also asked their foreign aid donors to pay for this corn purchase. However, before giving the money for the purchase, the foreign donors asked about the whereabouts of Malawi's existing reserves of grain, which foreign aid donors had contributed to developing. They discovered, then, that the national reserves of grain were gone and that the profit made from its sale had also disappeared. At the time Bearak wrote the article, the details of where the grain had gone were still unclear, but Bearak suggests that the finance minister of Malawi was involved in corrupt bargains regarding the sale of the stored corn and that average Malawians went hungry because of it.

TABLE 7.2

Green Famine

A situation where the land is green and crops are growing, but in which people are starving. This may be because the rains have arrived too late for crops to be grown and harvested in time to prevent famine.

Source: http://www.worldwidewords.org/turnsofphrase/tp-gre2.htm.

The main point is that someone wishing to help can begin by addressing the problem someplace and can assume that a change in one area will impact the system in significant ways. As we talked, the students and I kept a list of our questions:

▌ What if the stored food in Malawi had not been sold on the black market?
▌ What if the farmers in Malawi were allowed subsidies and structural adjustment looked different?
▌ What if there was a government process that would empower local people to create their own ideas of how Malawi could be free from hunger?

Once the students were thinking about hunger and systems, they were given the opportunity to apply their understanding of these concepts. I asked them to choose one of four countries—North Korea, Afghanistan, Ethiopia, or Sudan—and to research the hunger issues faced by the people living in that country. I helped students kick off their research by giving each of them two news articles or news broadcast transcripts to read. The articles and transcripts came from either McNeil Lehrer News Hour on PBS or from the BBC (Ababa, 2003; *Aid agency warns on North Korea*, 2003; Anderson, 2004; Bearak, 2003; Bowser, 2003; *Crisis in Sudan*, 2004; Denny, 2005; Kirby, 2003, 2004; Loyn, 2002; Muir, 2002; *N. Korea crops hit by heavy rains*, 2004; *North Korea's empty shelves*, 2003; *Q&A: Sudan's Darfur conflict*, 2004; Suarez, 2001; *The North Korean famine*, 1997).

I asked students to read with the specific purpose of determining and taking notes on all of the causes of hunger in the country they had chosen. After they had completed this background

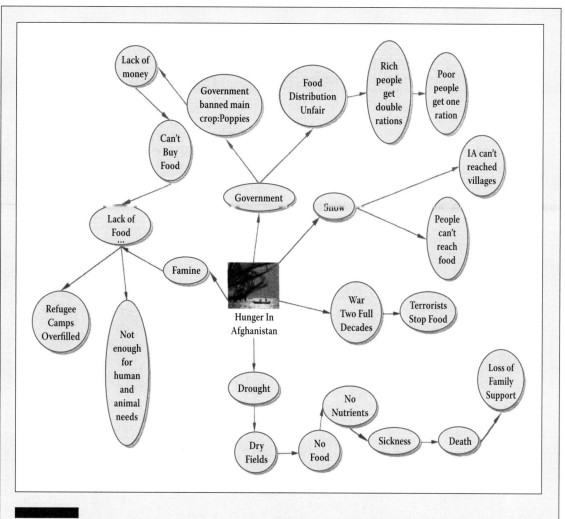

FIGURE 7.2
Hunger in Afghanistan.

reading, I invited students to use their notes to develop a hunger web, showing all of the interconnected causes of hunger in the country they had chosen to research. Figure 7.2 shows a web of the sociopolitical issues one student identified for hunger in Afghanistan. Even though this student predictably focused on issues of drought, war, and unequal food distribution, it is interesting that he also identified the problem snow creates for food distribution, the consequences of the government banning the opium poppy crop (the main source of income for many people), and overcrowding in refugee camps.

Along with the web, students were asked to develop a country profile, which was defined simply as a collection of statistics about the country that would help others understand that country and its context in the world. Country profiles included a vast array of information on everything from climate, terrain, natural resources, land use, population size, infant mortality rate, life expectancy, HIV/AIDS or other disease information, ethnic groups, religions, languages, literacy rate, government description (including age of suffrage), gross national product per capita, population below poverty line, labor force by occupation, agricultural products, industries, export and import partners, debt, economic aid, telephone systems, radio broadcast stations, highways, waterways, ports and harbors, airports, major cities, and the list goes on.

Students were asked to synthesize the information they could garner from maps, their hunger webs, and their country profile to write a two-page solutions paper explaining plausible local, national, and global approaches to solving the problem of hunger in the country that they chose. I challenged students to develop solutions that they viewed as truly workable. For example, if the people in a country had little access to mass media outlets, then a television or radio educational campaign was not plausible—that is, unless there was also a plan to provide televisions or radios to all of the people in the country. On the other hand, if it was clear that a tremendous amount of debt was hindering a country's ability to develop a farm aid program, then requesting that the United States and other countries forgive the country's national debt seemed in order. All in all, I wanted the students' solutions to be more realistic than imaginary. My directions were to develop real solutions they would feel confident about proposing to government officials and government agencies.

The insights students voiced in the solutions papers were complex and touched on some of the root causes of hunger in these four countries and around the globe (Table 7.3). Four major themes ran through the solutions papers: (1) greed and the unequal distribution of wealth, aid, and power; (2) lack of access due to a poor infrastructure (e.g., impassible roads, snow, lack of food storage facilities); (3) a failure to take collective community action (e.g., fund-raising, letter writing); and (4) an urgent need for global cooperation. The students felt good about their solutions papers, and so did I. Our project could not stop there.

In addition to presenting our study of hunger to other seventh graders in our school, we also presented our work to a fourth-grade classroom at a nearby school. To prepare for these events, my students discussed what they wanted to emphasize in their talks (all decided that focusing on hunger as a system was critical), rehearsed their talks in front of their peers, and made sure they were able to simplify language and ideas that might cause the fourth-grade students trouble. Needless to say, my students were shocked when the fourth-grade students asked questions that pushed their thinking. Not only did the younger children not have trouble following my students' presentations, but they also asked excellent questions. It quickly became obvious that there was widespread interest among both the older and younger students in seeing themselves as inquirers and world problem solvers.

Finally, we were lucky to have Steve Sharra, a guest speaker from Malawi, talk to our class. It would have been great if he had visited at the beginning of the project to start things off, but as it turned out, he was instrumental in helping my students articulate their understandings of hunger issues in Malawi. It raised the ante to have my class meet face to face with someone who was not only a Malawian author and poet but also someone who had worked on hunger issues in his own country. He was very impressed with the way my students presented their knowledge of the hunger problems in Malawi, and his reflections helped us deepen our understanding of the complexity of this issue. As a culminating experience, we related the problems of hunger in Malawi, North Korea, Afghanistan, Ethiopia, and Sudan to those closer to home. Although the hunger issues in Bloomington, Indiana, pale in relation to those in Malawi, they are still a major concern in the area. The local newspaper regularly runs stories about the need for food contributions to food pantries and shelters. Students were surprised to learn that in this town of 100,000, meals are served to 20,000 people a month (Denny, 2005). As we found with the issue of hunger globally, there are many interrelated causes at the local level as well. In the end, studying hunger in a global context led us back home.

TABLE 7.3

Examples of Solution Papers

Topic	Student Solution Paper
Barely Surviving: Problems of Geography and Climate in Afghanistan	Several things cause hunger in Afghanistan. The cause I want to focus on is one that I think Afghanistan has the most problems with. The problem I want to talk about is snow.
	Snow is a constant problem. It traps thousands of villagers with no food. IA (International Aid) can't get to some of these people. Consequently, the people are forced to walk for food or starve. Each year, American kids love snow and trot out to play in it. In Afghanistan, kids are terrified of snow.
	Locally, we can't do much about this problem. However, we should send villagers dry foods that they can keep throughout winter. We can send clothing and things we use to survive the winter, too. It never hurts to give kids entertainment so they can possibly ignore what hunger they have. Also, we shouldn't forget the animals. We can send feed or some such thing to help them.
	Nationally, we could send building supplies for winter storehouses. These people are so poor. They can't pay it all. We could send good winter wood, nails, and hammers.
	Globally, we can help a ton. We could convince the government to let us build winter villages. These could be villages that are like the ones the Afghans have, except they would be out of harms way. Afghans could get to them by walking or riding right before winter. We could keep stuff in the safe villages for them to survive. Then, once all danger is past, they could go back to their homes.
	All of those actions would help Afghanistan so much. They really do need help. All this (well most of it) can be easily done- if we have perseverance, that is.
The Need for Collective Community Action	Even though we aren't even near Afghanistan, we can still help their hunger problem. You might be saying, "What!"—but it's true. …All we would have to do is donate a dollar. In fact if every one in America and all of the other countries that can help can donate one dollar to Afghanistan, then the people in Afghanistan won't be hungry anymore. If we do this once every two months, they could almost be rich! How easy is that?[a]
Need for Global Cooperation	Lack of money is a huge issue for Ethiopia's hunger problem. I think that to try to fix this other countries could meet to decide on a way to have their countries donate money to the Ethiopians. This would be a donation, not a loan, so the Ethiopians would not owe the money back and sink farther into debt. This way, the Ethiopian government will be able to issue crops/ seeds to the people who need them both now and in the future.[b]

[a] *Note*: The rapid pace at which funds were raised for the Tsunami Relief effort in 2004, suggests that this student is indeed correct. Humans can collect a tremendous amount of money and resources when they work together and each contribute a little bit. The question then is, why were people so motivated to help in the face of a natural disaster, but are so unmotivated to assist countries dealing with famine issues that, sometimes, last for decades or more?

[b] This student showed an awareness of the "trap of debt" and the disastrous impact it has on some countries.

What Can We Learn from the Hunger Projects in Emily's Class?

"Think global, act local." Although this phrase is heard repeatedly in relation to social action projects, some global issues are of such magnitude that they need our attention immediately. Emily did just this when she created the Hunger Project curriculum with her seventh-grade class. Global hunger problems are huge. Every day, more than 16,000 children die from hunger-related causes—one child every five seconds (Bread for the World, 2006). The Food First/Institute for Food and Development Policy reports, "Enough food is available to provide at least 4.3 pounds of food per person a day worldwide: two and half pounds of grain, beans and nuts, about a pound of fruits and vegetables, and nearly another pound of meat, milk and eggs—enough to make most people fat! The problem is that many people are too poor to buy readily available food. Even most 'hungry countries' have enough food for all their people right now" (Poole-Kavana, 2006).

These statistics are staggering. Emily and other educators across the country who are committed to a social justice curriculum (Bigelow, 2006; Bomer & Bomer, 2001; Moore, 2004) feel that it is not enough for kids only to hear information like this. They believe it is our responsibility as teachers to help students delve into the messy sociopolitical and economic issues at the root of global catastrophes.

In reading Emily's vignette, we identify three theories that seem to have informed her classroom practice. We also make connections between Emily's work to that of other educators who are involved in teaching about world hunger issues.

Theory 1: In working to help students inquire into sociopolitical issues, it is often necessary to push ourselves out of our comfort zones.

Teachers who are adding sociopolitical content to their curricula often realize that they do not know enough about a particular event themselves to feel comfortable bringing the issue into their classrooms. Addressing sociopolitical issues in elementary and middle school classrooms is just plain difficult. In our work with teacher study groups, one request comes up repeatedly: "We need to find out more about _____." The blank is often a historical event, a sociopolitical issue, or a current world crisis. Because of this, we include two resources in this chapter that may be helpful when studying global hunger issues. One describes the work of Oxfam International, a nonprofit organization dedicated to finding lasting solutions to world poverty, suffering, and injustice (Table 7.4). The other is a fact sheet distributed by Food First/Institute for Food Development Policy (Table 7.5) titled *12 Myths about Hunger* (Poole-Kavana, 2006).

TABLE 7.4
Oxfam International

Oxfam International is a confederation of 12 organizations working together with over 3,000 partners in more than 100 countries to find lasting solutions to poverty, suffering and injustice. With many of the causes of poverty global in nature, the 12 affiliate members of Oxfam International believe they can achieve greater impact through their collective efforts. Oxfam International seeks increased worldwide public understanding that economic and social justice are crucial to sustainable development. We strive to be a global campaigning force promoting the awareness and motivation that comes with global citizenship while seeking to shift public opinion in order to make equity the same priority as economic growth.

We work with poor people
We seek to help people organize so that they might gain better access to the opportunities they need to improve their livelihoods and govern their own lives. We also work with people affected by humanitarian disasters, with preventive measures, preparedness, as well as emergency relief.

We influence powerful people
Experience of the real issues confronting poor people is linked to high-level research and lobbying aiming to change international policies and practices in ways which would ensure that poor people have the rights, opportunities and resources they need to improve and control their lives.

We join hands with all people
Popular campaigning, alliance building and media work designed to raise awareness among the public of the real solutions to global poverty, to enable and motivate people to play an active part in the movement for change, and to foster a sense of global citizenship.

Source: Oxfam International. Available from http://www.oxfam.org/. Copyright 2006. Reprinted with permission.

Because of Emily's training as a social studies teacher and her interest in global issues, she already knew many of the facts about world hunger issues. But the two-week intensive course she attended at the Center for Global Change gave her new tools and support to move forward with her students. The workshop enabled Emily to focus on hard issues with her students, without the hopelessness that often accompanies the teaching of big issues in the classroom. Emily moved beyond her own conception of how to teach sociopolitical issues and stepped into a new discipline: systems thinking. She was learning the new—something that is of vital importance to all of us as teachers. Our tendency to get stuck in our comfort zones—even if they are not all that comfortable—sometimes makes it difficult to see what moves might push our teaching forward.

But just attending the workshop was not enough. To begin using systems thinking with her students, Emily also had to find resources that are not mainstream in elementary and middle school classrooms.

Chapter Seven
Critical Social Practices

█████
TABLE 7.5
Twelve Myths about Hunger

Why so much hunger? What can we do about it?
To answer these questions we must unlearn much of what we have been taught. Only by freeing ourselves from the grip of widely held myths can we grasp the roots of hunger and see what we can do to end it.

Myth Number	Myth
1	Not enough food to go around
2	Nature is to blame for famine.
3	Too many people
4	The environment versus more food
5	The Green Revolution is the answer.
6	We need large farms.
7	The free market can end hunger.
8	Free trade is the answer.
9	Too hungry to fight for their rights
10	More U.S. aid will help the hungry.
11	We benefit from their poverty.
12	Curtail freedom to end hunger?

Notes: Based on the book *World Hunger: Twelve Myths* (Lappe, F.M., Collins, J., Rosset, P., & Esparza, L., 1998). For the reality behind each of these myths go to http://www.foodfirst.org/pubs/backgrdrs/1998/s98v5n3.html
Source: Poole-Kavana (2006).

She used a huge variety of articles and transcripts from the popular press and media as teaching materials. Taking the time to find these resources is a far cry from the ease with which we can open a textbook and turn to page 54. So, for many of us, addressing sociopolitical issues means not only pushing ourselves to learn new content but also realizing that we need to find new materials. All of this takes energy, but the rewards, as we see in Emily's case, make the effort—and at times the discomfort—worthwhile.

Theory 2: Students can engage in very sophisticated critical practices if their teacher is actively involved in the same practices and provides demonstrations that allow them to focus on sociopolitical systems and power relationships.

Since paying attention to sociopolitical systems and power relationships does not happen much in traditional classrooms, students need support as they venture into this new territory. A number of strategies can accomplish this. One fairly easy strategy is for students to compare their own understandings of an issue—in this case, global hunger—to what is presented in their textbooks. Often, textbooks do not provide even

Creating Critical Classrooms

cursory explanations of world hunger, quite a revelation for students to discover as part of their research.

Another strategy we find especially useful is one developed by Bigelow (2006). He wanted his students to understand in a personal way that hunger was not a natural problem, so he used the Irish Potato Famine as the backdrop for conducting a "trial role play to highlight the 'crime' of famine and to encourage students to reflect on responsibility for that crime" (p. 44). Bigelow notes that there was plenty of food being produced in Ireland during the famine years but that most of it was exported. After reading, viewing a video, and listening to songs, students were assigned to be members of different groups: British landlords, Irish tenant farmers, Anglican Church, British government, colonial capitalism. Each group was accused of murdering one and half million Irish peasants who died in the famine years of 1846 and 1847 (pp. 44–46). Bigelow wrote indictments for each group with specific charges, he played the prosecutor, and students had to prepare a defense for their group to make a case to the jury (another group). His goal in the role play was to have students begin questioning systems of meaning such as who is in power and how wealth is allocated.

An additional resource we like is Oxfam America's *Hunger Banquet* (http://www.hungerbanquet.org), an interactive online "game" about world hunger where students take on the roles of people from different parts of the world (Table 7.6). The use of drama is a powerful tool because it allows us to feel, in a deep way, the suffering and frustration of others. We believe that although not sufficient, empathy and understanding are important steps toward changing attitudes. Drama allows us to get outside of our commonplace ways of seeing, providing the potential to view the world from new vantage points. In this case, it facilitates new ways of looking at sociopolitical systems and power relationships.

Emily's work with her seventh graders provides yet another perspective and additional strategies for creating critical curricula in classrooms. Emily realized that she would need to become actively involved in the same practices as her students—and to provide demonstrations—for these middle schoolers to be able to focus successfully on sociopolitical systems and power relationships. So she started off the Hunger Project with a whole-class inquiry on hunger issues in Malawi, which preceded any small-group work. The whole-class focus on Malawi created a space where students learned from Emily's demonstration when she shared her own web. They learned from each other by sharing causes of hunger in Malawi as they read Bearak's (2003) article. In addition, Emily learned from the students as they shared the sophisticated connections they saw in Emily's web that she had missed. Emily realized that systems thinking is a very complex way to look at sociopolitical issues. By having students make webs and then look for connections among concepts on the web,

TABLE 7.6

Hunger Banquet

Banquet an Exercise in Real-World Inequalities

If you're afraid of venturing outside your comfort zone, stay away from the Shalom Community Center's third annual hunger banquet.

The banquet, scheduled for 6:30 p.m. Nov. 9 in the great hall of the First United Methodist Church, may make you fidget a bit.

The potential for uneasy feelings stems from the fact that those in attendance will eat status-based meals based on randomly distributed color-coded tickets - which will tell guests whether they are low, middle or high income.

The low-income group will move through a cafeteria line to receive what people typically eat for lunch at the Shalom Center - vegetable soup, bread and coffee.

Those eating the middle-income meal will sit at tables and enjoy a more expensive meal. The high-income guests will sit at tables draped with white linen, where they will be served a gourmet meal.

"At the previous two banquets, those in the upper income group said they felt uncomfortable with the quality and quantity of their meal in comparison to what those living in poverty received," Joel Rekas said. "Both years, those in the upper income group felt compelled to share some of their meal with those in the poverty group."

Rekas said the event is designed not only to raise money for the center's hunger relief efforts, but to highlight Monroe County's 19 percent poverty rate, which he said is the highest in Indiana.

"For one evening, people will get to step inside the shoes of those experiencing hunger," he said.

Rekas said the number of people in each group will reflect the percentages of those income groups in Monroe County, adding that the groups will sit together at tables in different parts of the room."

The evening is a very powerful experience," he said. "It's designed to demonstrate the effects of poverty and inequality on a personal and realistic level, and highlight the struggle many Monroe County residents have trying to feed themselves and their families."

Rekas said the event is particularly timely, given the struggle many food banks and pantries are having providing enough food for their clients."

This banquet gives people a time to reflect on the inequalities in Monroe County," he said. "It's my personal hope that everyone who comes leaves changed."

Middle Way House's Food Works will prepare the gourmet meal, area churches will provide the middle-income meal and the Shalom Community Center will fix the low-income meal.

The first two banquets raised about $1,700 per year. This year, with the event taking place in a more spacious venue, Rekas hopes 200 will attend - thus raising $4,000 in proceeds.

The funds will be used to support the Shalom Center, which serves an average of 5,000 meals a month to those in need.

Source: Dann Denny (October 25, 2006). Reprinted with permission from *Herald-Times*, Bloomington, IN.

Emily gave her middle schoolers concrete strategies for managing lots of different issues in a visually coherent way.

She also helped students complicate their notions of worldwide hunger problems by having them do an in-depth study of one country. Students had the opportunity to explore the similarities and difference of root causes of hunger in different nations. What is significant about this work is that Emily helped students look across national boundaries to identify common themes present in all four countries. So instead of didactically teaching students about hunger issues in developing counties, Emily gave the class a chance to conduct intensive research in small groups, to share findings with other groups, and to look for issues that crossed national boundaries. Emily was learning along with her students, not knowing which common themes or issues would arise from this activity.

Another strategy Emily used is worthy of note here. When the class was studying hunger issues in Malawi, she asked hard questions—questions she did not know the answers to such as, "What if the stored food had not been sold on the black market?" There is a range of sociopolitical issues wrapped up in this question:

- What is the black market, and how does it work?
- How prevalent is the black market in Malawi?
- Why and how is this market allowed to thrive?
- Who benefits and who is harmed by the black market?
- If the black market went away tomorrow, what effect would this have on the hunger problems in Malawi?

These questions are very different from the types of questions students are instructed to answer at the end of textbook chapters. In short, teachers can use a variety of strategies to help make global issues up close and personal—relevant to kids whose lives may not be directly affected by situations half way around the globe. Emily's work demonstrates how systems thinking can be a promising tool to help students engage complex sociopolitical systems and power relationships in meaningful ways.

Theory 3: Do not water down the curriculum.

As we support students to inquire into tough sociopolitical issues, complexity is something to expect, insist on, and encourage. Davis, Sumara, and Luce-Kapler (2000) make the distinction between complicated and complex systems. They describe complex systems in the following way: "Researchers have realized that these systems are not comprised of inert cogs or switches or microchips, but are themselves collectives of other, smaller dynamical systems. Economies, for example, emerge from, but are not reducible to, the activities of citizens" (p. 55).

We can see in Emily's work with students on the Hunger Project that she helped them focus on complexity. Complexity allows us to examine not one story about an issue but many stories and explanations. All kinds of stories can be told about world hunger, some more compelling than others. We see evidence of this in the myriad ways the popular media positions global hunger issues. Through the Hunger Project, students in Emily's class decided what kind of stories they wanted to tell. Their stories framed the presentations they made to kids at their own and other schools. They circulated new and powerful stories about global hunger in their community.

Invitation for Disruption 1:

Looking for the Sociopolitical

- During the next week, make a list at the end of each day indicating how many times you have dealt with complex sociopolitical issues in your teaching.
- During the following week, make a list of the ways you might include more sociopolitical issues in your teaching.
- Share your two lists with a colleague or at a study group meeting to get feedback from your peers.
- Make a third list of what you actually end up trying with students and discuss the results with a colleague or at a study group meeting.

Invitation for Disruption 2:

Rethinking Schools

- With a colleague, decide on a sociopolitical issue you'd like to work with in your classrooms.
- Go to *Rethinking Schools* (http://www.rethinkingschools.org/) and see what resources are available there.
- Try out an activity based on one of the articles.
- How did it go in your classroom? In your colleague's classroom?
- Think about other ways you might be able to use *Rethinking Schools*.

TABLE 7.7
How Critical Literacy Was Enacted in Emily's Classroom

Cultural Resources	Critical Practices Enacted	How the Teacher Took Up a Critical Stance
Emily's own interests led her to attend the Center for Global Change workshop.	Emily learned about systems thinking and how there are multiple causes and viewpoints when studying any complex issue.	Emily problematized her understanding of how to bring sociopolitical issues into the classroom.
Newspaper articles and TV news transcripts	Provided critical classroom resources that made complexity visible	Understood the multimodal nature of literacy and invited students to inquire into world hunger issues
Student-created webs became resources for organizing projects about hunger issues in North Korea, Afghanistan, Ethiopia, and Sudan.	Disrupted the commonplace by moving away from a textbook curriculum and helped students use literacy as a form of cultural citizenship	Helped students move beyond initial understandings and realized that since all knowledge is constructed, student-generated knowledge is just as legitimate as knowledge from more traditional sources
Presentations created for other students and 4th graders became a resource that provoked more questions about world hunger issues.	Students engaged in praxis to change the world and they shared their understandings with other students as a way to affect change.	Helped students understand that they had options in response and action regarding their new knowledge

Even the resources Emily used were complex. She used *New York Times* articles and a variety of transcripts from the BBC News and the News Hour with Jim Lehrer. Think of the complexity of these sources in relation to what would be presented in a textbook—if the topic was even covered. Complexity is messy and at times, unruly, but so is the world. A focus on complexity supports the process of understanding, and as Emily's vignette illustrates, it should be insisted on rather than shied away from.

How Was Critical Literacy Enacted in Emily's classroom?

Creating Critical Classrooms

Table 7.7 highlights the ways we see the critical literacy instructional model being realized in Emily's vignette.

TABLE 7.8
Exploring Rethinking Schools
Resources

	Synopsis
Rethinking Schools—the Journal	This quarterly educational journal provides timely analysis of policy debates and alerts teachers to innovative classroom practices.
Whose Wars?	Teaching about the Iraq war and the war on terrorism. This is the best collection available on how to teach about the war. It includes classroom-tested resources for social studies, language arts, and math classes. These powerful teaching materials incorporate poetry, imaginative writing, math activities, discussion, and critical reading strategies.
The New Teacher Book	This collection of writings and reflections—some by new teachers, others by veterans with decades of experience to share—offers practical guidance on how new teachers from kindergarten through high school can effectively navigate the school system, form rewarding professional relationships with colleagues, and connect in meaningful ways with students and families from all cultures and backgrounds.
Rethinking Globalization: Teaching for Justice in an Unjust World	This comprehensive new book from Rethinking Schools helps teachers raise critical issues with students in grades 4–12 about the increasing globalization of the world's economies and infrastructures and the many different impacts this trend has on our planet and those who live here.
Failing our Kids: Why the Testing Craze Won't Fix Our Schools	Includes more than 50 articles that provide a compelling critique of standardized tests and also outline alternative ways to assess how well our children are learning
Reading, Writing, and Rising Up: Teaching About Social Justice and the Power of the Written Word	This practical, inspirational book offers essays, lesson plans, and a remarkable collection of student writing, all rooted in an unwavering focus on language arts teaching for justice.
Rethinking Our Classrooms: Teaching for Equity and Justice	Creative teaching ideas, reproducible handouts, and lesson plans that promote values of community, justice, and equality
Rethinking Columbus (expanded 2d ed.)	Lesson plans, short stories, and interviews that reevaluate the legacy of Columbus in North America

Note: Available from http://www.rethinkingschools.org/.

In addition to the resources that Emily used, one of the best sources we know where teachers can get background information and classroom strategies on critical educational and social justice issues is the journal *Rethinking Schools* (Table 7.8). This publication was started in 1986 by local Milwaukee teachers to address problems such as basal readers, standardized testing, and textbook-dominated curriculum. For example, the Summer 2006 issue is titled *Feeding the Children, The Politics of Food and Schools*. In addition to Bigelow's article, "Hunger on Trial," this issue includes critical articles and classroom activities about childhood obesity, school cafeterias, federal school lunch programs, and more. Regularly reading *Rethinking Schools* is one way to find a wealth of

Chapter Seven
Critical Social Practices

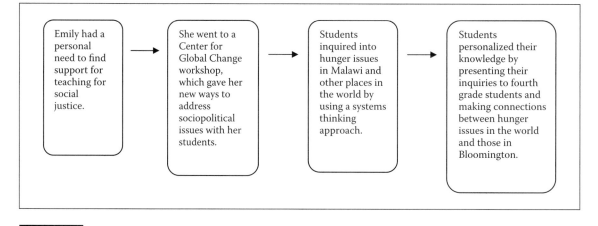

| Emily had a personal need to find support for teaching for social justice. | → | She went to a Center for Global Change workshop, which gave her new ways to address sociopolitical issues with her students. | → | Students inquired into hunger issues in Malawi and other places in the world by using a systems thinking approach. | → | Students personalized their knowledge by presenting their inquiries to fourth grade students and making connections between hunger issues in the world and those in Bloomington. |

FIGURE 7.3
How Emily moved curriculum between the personal and the social.

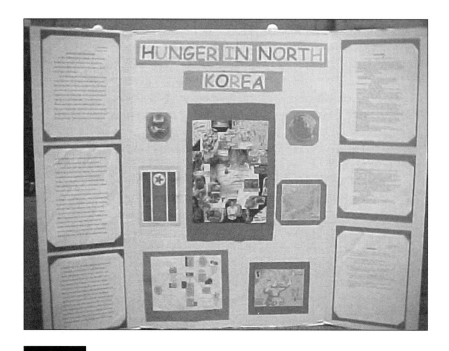

FIGURE 7.4
Hunger in North Korea.

resources that help us expand and complicate rather than water down the curriculum.

Figure 7.3 illustrates how Emily moved curriculum between the personal and the social.

Emily created a curriculum that allowed students to understand, in a deep way, how they were connected to issues on the other side of the world as well as right in their own backyards. In his thought piece,

Jerry Harste explores his own complicity and how he thought he was part of the solution of transforming our racist society until he spoke with a wise Mosotene chief in the highlands of Bolivia.

Lingering Questions

▪ How can I bring complex sociopolitical issues into the curriculum and not overwhelm students with a sense of hopelessness?

▪ Are some issues too tough for young students to deal with, or is it possible to present tough sociopolitical issues to students at any age if you plan carefully?

Thought Piece

Racism and Privilege—Having Our Hands in the Cookie Jar

Jerome C. Harste

Being "big and tall" (I like the British terminology better—they call Big & Tall stores "High & Mighty") has served me well. I notice as a teacher and even as a researcher that it is easier for big and tall people to command respect.

Age, too, can be an advantage. Looking a little older has made my professional development work with teachers easier. Though there is a premium on youth in our society, one can look too young and hence too green and inexperienced to command the respect of seasoned veterans in our field.

I am, of course, also male and white. These, too, are unearned privileges and, like size and age, serve me well. In most settings they give me a leg up. Classroom teachers are used to white male administrators and white male college professors despite the fact that more than 86% of all elementary school teachers are female.

Being male, white, and tall (someone once said I was stately, a comment I very much liked) is probably why I got my first teaching job over and above a female. There were not many males in the profession at the time, and I looked like I would be a good disciplinarian. I was offered and took a sixth-grade teaching job. Although I would like to believe otherwise, I do not think they hired me for my brains. Like all of my classmates, I had a teaching degree, but unlike them I was the first in my class to be hired.

I also suspect that I went on to get my master's and doctoral degrees because it was expected that a white male in elementary school would move up. In this sense I was destined to become a principal and, not surprisingly, earned a master's degree in educational administration and a doctorate in curriculum and instruction. I was one of the baby boomers, so it was supposed to be hard to get into graduate school. I applied to 10 different schools and found myself accepted by all 10. It never dawned on me until much later that an African American in the 1960s with the same qualifications might have had a very different tale to tell.

It took me a long time to realize that the very successes I was experiencing meant that I, consciously or unconsciously, had my hand in the metaphorical cookie jar of racism because of the privileges I received as a white male. As a progressive educator, I perceived myself as part of the solution. Realizing that I was also part of the problem was a difficult concept for me to get my head around.

On the surface, I was accepted to do master's and doctoral work because I had good test scores on the Millers Analogy Test and the Graduate Record Examination. Both of these, at the time, were considered the hard data on which such decisions were made. In retrospect, I realize that I scored so well in part because the people who wrote the tests were more than likely people like me with similar backgrounds and experiences. As a result, I was in a better position to pass the test than some of my peers from historically underrepresented groups who, unlike me, were at risk of not qualifying for entrance graduate schools. I have come to understand that blacks, Latinos, and other underrepresented groups are not asking for sympathy but rather for understanding that tests of this sort are not constructed based on their banks of experiences. If standardized tests were developed based on their background experience, the results might be quite different.

I remember being in the Peace Corps in Bolivia assigned to a Mosotene Indian village in the Alto Beni area of the Amazon. In one late-night conversation with the chief, he said, "You Americans are racists. You throw stones at black people." My immediate response was, "I never threw a stone at a black person in my life!" His retort stopped me cold: "Oh, yes, but you live in a society that allows people to throw stones at black people."

I remember staying awake that night thinking about his statement. I was guilty of racism by virtue of the fact that I lived in a society where such things happened, and I was doing nothing directly to intervene. At that time, racism was something distant from me; it was someone else's doing and, hence, someone else's problem. Taking racism on as my own problem forced me to think about the world very differently. Not only did I have my hand in the cookie jar, but also my basic beliefs about the United States and the society in which I was raised had to change. I had to acknowledge that yes, indeed, we are a racist society.

Although this is a difficult premise for many white folks to accept, starting from such a premise puts one in a very different place than denying that a system of white privilege exists and that such a system contributes to racism. Rather than putting me on the defensive, acknowledging the fact that we are a racist society readies me for action.

There are two parts to the hand-in-the-cookie-jar phenomenon. The first is the realization that you are involved: You are an integral part of not only of the problem of racism but of most other problems as well. This means you are part of the problems of homelessness, poverty, racism, ageism, sexism, the overuse of drugs, global warming, homophobia, gangs, bullying, the war in Iraq, illegal immigration, job loss, the increased use of Prozac among school-age children, the increase in numbers of children receiving remedial education, and even the children currently not well served by the No Child Left Behind legislation.

The second part of coming to grips with having your hand in the cookie jar is humility: the realization that you do not know everything—that others have real contributions to make. My Peace Corps experience taught me a lot. The Mosotenes were an Indian group the Bolivian government stumbled on during their agricultural reform movement. They were, even by Bolivian standards, an uneducated and illiterate population. Yet it was their chief who taught me to look at myself and my world differently. Despite my high school and college degrees, it was his sociological insight on our society that forced me to rethink a world I thought I knew. Humility means that you firmly believe that others have things to contribute, that the view from over there will contribute to a better view from here.

McIntosh (1989) talks about white privilege and all the things white folks take for granted. White folks can be fairly sure that they can find a house they can afford in a neighborhood of people who look like them. White folks can be fairly sure that their kids will go to a school where most of the teachers are the same color as their children. White folks can be fairly sure of finding band-aids that match their skin color. White folks can be fairly sure that their elected leaders will represent the values of their race and their politics. White folks can be fairly sure that the books their children are assigned to read in school will have characters with whom their children can identify.

These things are not natural for everyone. White privilege happens because the world is currently set up that way. The world is not an even playing field. And though white folks may never know what it is like to be a minority member in an other-dominated society, being positioned as such gives minorities something unique to contribute to the complexity of understanding our society. I do not mean to make light of, or offer easy solutions to, the difficult tasks that lie ahead. The bottom line for all of us to keep in mind is that there is no single privileged position.

I saw in the morning newspaper that there is now a new line of clothing called "Coexist" (Creps, 2006). The T-shirts in this line of clothing express *Coexist* as a word spelled out with symbols that include an Islamic crescent, the Star of David, and a Christian cross. Although acceptance of various religions may be a step in the right direction, understanding the hand-in-the-cookie-jar phenomenon is more than a call for tolerance. It is a call for introspection and for thoughtful new action. A better first step would be to examine the sty in one's own eye, asking, What are all the ways my current stance perpetuates the negative aspects (e.g., the inequities, the injustices) of what currently is? Tolerance does not move us ahead. It maintains the status quo. A second step is to explore collaboratively, What can we do to make this a better world? Our job as critical educators is to create a more just and equitable world. This calls for collaborative social action that is focused on changing the fundamental systems of meaning operating in society. Critical literacy begins in awareness, ends in social action, and, in between, supports us in envisioning a different world.

Chapter 8

Critical Social Practices
Taking Action to Promote Social Justice

Vignette

Putting Theory into Action

Dana Hubbard

Student teaching can be a stressful experience. The reality of the classroom and a heavily prescribed curriculum put pressure on student teachers to do what is required. My first student teaching assignment in a public school in one of the toughest urban neighborhoods in Indianapolis illustrates this point. Apathetic faces looked up only momentarily as I made my introduction; peer-to-peer chatter hardly skipped a beat. These fifth graders were clearly more interested in talking with each other than in hearing what I had to say. "How relevant," I wondered, "can my instruction be to these students' lives?" To most it was a foregone conclusion that what went on in the classroom was decidedly irrelevant and that "doin' school" entailed little more than doing time and fending off the thinly veiled litany of threats and judgments that accosted them daily:

You'd better do this or you won't pass.
You'd better do that or you won't be promoted to the next grade.
You'd better pay attention or you won't finish school.
You'd better finish school or you won't get a job.
You'd better change that attitude now…. What's wrong with you?

END

As a student teacher, I knew that my power to challenge this discourse was limited. I believed, however, that I did have some choices. Instead of appropriating the existing discourse, the task at hand was to transform these cynical comments into critical questions and then to enable the students to pose their questions to those who had power over their lives. It was time to put theory into action. I had read Freire (1970) and aspired to his notion that, as the teacher, I was not simply to deposit a preplanned lesson from my account into theirs and become a kind of teaching-clerk. Instead, Freire's work challenged me to transform the students' views and to make possible the literate expression of those views. Inquiry seemed like a promising methodology for accomplishing this. Contrary to the banking model of education, which negates any real possibility for questioning the order of things, inquiry encourages all kinds of questions, including tough ones about the nonneutral nature of education. As Freire suggests, education is either indoctrinating or liberating, and we choose which type we will teach.

My supervising teacher informed me that the district required fifth graders to study the legislative process and how laws get made. It would be my responsibility to teach this unit. Noting that the textbook explanation of this topic was both confusing and sleep inducing, I knew that I needed another way to arouse my students' interest. A field trip to the Indiana Statehouse had been scheduled as the traditional means to address this requirement. Although the school was located almost in view of the gleaming capitol dome, it might as well have been in medieval England for all the relevance the students perceived that it had to their lives.

Unfortunately, like the textbook, the field trip turned out to be both confusing and boring, especially for those who unconsciously recognized that their lives were already marginalized from any real participation in government. As my class prepared to leave the gilded statehouse, undifferentiated from a castle in most students' minds, the state senator for their district appeared and spoke to us. With no prompting, the senator focused his talk on how laws get made and how everyone—including fifth-grade students—can and should play a role in making the government more responsive to the needs of its citizens. He closed by inviting my class to submit proposals for new laws that would respond to problems they had observed in their community. This seemingly earnest appeal was met at first with incomprehension and then with incredulity by the class. The problem was how to make this direct invitation into the process of government real and pertinent to my students. On the short return bus trip, much discussion ensued about "what laws I would make if I were king." But after some conversations about democracy, the grandiose ideas came down to the quiet realization that maybe it really was possible for citizens to take action that could make their lives better. This was the spark of possibility that ignited the inquiry. My job now was to facilitate, to help the students go where they determined they should go.

Back in the classroom, I now had the students' attention as I walked them through the textbook explanation of how bills get made into laws with the help of the School House Rock video "I'm Just A Bill" (1973, Disney). The students noted that this verified what their representative had told them and started talking about different issues they saw as important to them and their families. One suggestion was to propose a law that would get rid of the "numbers house" (a house that served as a cover for gambling operations) located across the street from the school. A drive-by shooting had occurred there recently, and several students were terrified to walk by the place on their way to and from school. But others maintained that the place was already illegal and that they did not need a new law to get it closed down. Several said that their parents had complained to the mayor and that maybe that would help to get rid of it. Another suggestion focused on a proposing a law that would make it easier for people in their neighborhood to get jobs, but the students could not figure out how to get this idea into the form of a proposal. After further conversation, they eventually decided that more jobs would be available if new businesses like stores, restaurants, and movie theaters would open up in their neighborhood. What was stopping this from happening? This question did not stay out on the floor for long; they all knew the answer. The same thing that scared them was scaring other people as well: Their neighborhood was a dangerous place because of all the shootings that happened there.

Conversation now focused on the issue of cutting back on the number of shootings, and students concluded that they needed to come up with a way to get guns off the streets. I noted that every student in the class was paying close attention and contributing to the discussion of how to get this done. This was real life. Someone suggested making a law that would make guns illegal, but others claimed that this would not faze "bad people" who did not follow laws anyway. Someone else suggested making a law that would give people money to turn in their guns. The class agreed that this might work since people they knew were always in need of money. I asked the class to get into small groups and brainstorm ways to come up with money to pay for the guns that people would turn in. After much deliberation and negotiation, the class generated a list that I typed verbatim as a draft bill that they could send to the senator:

Senate Bill 1
Proposed by Mr. Hubbard's fifth-grade class

> This bill is to reduce the number of handguns in our state. The state will buy guns from owners for $100 each. The money to buy the guns will come from the following sources: (1) recycling the old guns; (2) a sales tax on tobacco and liquor; (3) a tax on new guns of an extra $10; and (4) a new state lottery game that will feature a message to make our state safer by getting rid of guns. People will turn their guns in to a police officer and get a voucher that they can cash in at a bank.

I asked the class to think about how they might convince the senator and others to give serious consideration to their proposal. After all, the senator might not know about what was going on in their particular neighborhood. How could they ensure that he understood what they were dealing with? Some students suggested inviting him to visit, but then they realized that shootings are not advertised in advance. How would they know what day to have him come? "What about your own stories?" I suggested. "You guys live here, and you know what it is like. Why can't you tell him yourselves?" At that point the class decided that writing letters to send with the proposal would be the best approach. They would start with their personal stories and then bring up their idea to make the neighborhood a safer place. The class was transformed by the idea that they were doing extremely important work. Their enthusiasm and sense of purpose are evident in the neat handwriting and careful attention to spelling in the three sample letters shown in Figure 8.1.

As promised, I bundled up all the personal letters with the class bill proposal and a cover letter that reminded the senator of what he had asked of us, in case he forgot. I placed everything in a large envelope and personally delivered it to the senator's office. The secretary was polite but wary as I explained my mission. I described how excited the kids were about taking the senator's invitation at face value. I said that they had worked so hard and that it would mean so much if they could receive a response from the senator. The secretary smiled blandly as she dropped the thick envelope into a wire basket and there, I believe, our bill died, unacknowledged.

In hindsight, this would be exactly the point where the real-world work of promoting the bill could have begun for the class. We could have written follow-up letters, made bill-related T-shirts, and tried

Dear Senator Howard,

We are making a bill to keep guns out of the neighborhood. We would appriecate if you would put this as a law.

People are dieing because of guns. President John F. Kennedy got killed (He got killed by a gun.) If you aban guns people will live longer lives. People rob stores with guns. I hope you aban guns so we can live longer lives.

Senate Bill 1

We got this program. That we buy guns back. We bye your gun for $100.00.

To get this money we will tax the guns, liqure & tobacco. We will sale lottery tickets. You would win $10,000 if you win. The tickets cost $2.00. The lottery tickets shape like a gun. The tax sale will be $10.00 extra.

Dear Senator Howard,

I think you should take guns from neighborhoods. And I also think you should put out of business gun stores. Because my brother got killed by a gun, and alot of other people got killed by guns or are being killed by guns.

Dear senator Howard. I think guns shuld Be Ban from the Hood. Becaus people are getting killd.

FIGURE 8.1
Kids' letters to the senator.

to get media exposure. All of these require real-world literacy skills and reflection on personal values. But time ran out, and I moved to another school for my second student teaching placement. My former students moved on to middle school and then to high school—or at least half of them did, according to the recent statistics I read in the local paper. I wonder if they still believe that their voices can count. I wonder if their voices ever will count.

Both the textbook and the video described the long process that a bill must go through before it has a chance of becoming a law. Both sources explained that a bill starts out as an idea that someone has for addressing an important issue, but the idea might be reshaped or expanded as it moves through different committees where other people add amendments or make changes in the language. Throughout this process, however, the underlying concept was made clear: Laws are the direct result of citizens' identifying needs and thinking generatively about how to make things better.

What Can We Learn from Dana's Experience?

Dana's vignette shows that all educators can make a difference—even student teachers, who often complain about their lack of empowerment. Working with someone else's curriculum, he still managed to focus on what he thought was important to his students. Even as a guest in someone else's classroom, he was able to develop his identity as an educator who followed Freire's (1970) ideas and consciously rejected the banking model of education, which equates teaching with some sort of depositing knowledge into students' heads. We have identified three theories that emerge from Dana's vignette.

Theory 1: Education is never neutral: It either liberates, domesticates, or alienates.

Dana became aware of this perspective by studying the writing of Paulo Freire, a Brazilian educator who dedicated his life to helping those in poverty learn how to use the power of literacy to challenge the status quo and improve their lives. Others have taken up Freire's themes and considered the connections between education and politics. Edelsky (1999, p. 121–123), for example, talks about the necessity of understanding that a teacher's approach to "classroom literacy can never be politically neutral. Literacy can be taught as a tool of critical inquiry or of passive transmission. It can be a vehicle for posing and solving important social problems or for accepting official explanations and solutions." Finn (1999, p. 172) uses Freire's theory as the basis for his claim that few working-class children will break through to greater economic success unless they receive an education that allows them to understand how to take action in their own self-interest: "Freire's vision was of class struggle. It was about empowering the powerless as a class so they can stand up for themselves. This is what made him

---

Invitation for Disruption 1:

Write a Letter to the Editor

Kids need to see examples of people they know taking social action. You can model the process for them while making a statement about something that is important to you.

- Think about a current educational issue that really bugs you. Too much standardized testing? Lack of resources? Laws that punish the victims?
- Write a letter to the editor of your local paper and send it in.
- Share your writing process (e.g., web, list, drafts) as well as the published version of the letter with your students. Invite them to write their own letters.

a transforming intellectual." Dana's approach can be characterized as helping his students see themselves as capable of taking action that will make their lives better. Finn refers to this kind of teaching as literacy with an attitude. Dana did not require his students to memorize and spit back the various steps in the legislative process. Instead, he encouraged them to consider how they could become active players in the system of power that ruled their lives.

Theory 2: Creating critical curriculum means delving into risky topics that surround children's lives.

Whole-language proponents have always urged teachers to begin any learning experience with what children currently know, perceive, and feel. "Curriculum has no other place to begin than with children's current concepts and language" (Short, Harste, & Burke, 1996, p. 83.) Critical literacy adds another dimension by attempting to frame these issues in a sociopolitical context. This opens up spaces to write about— and talk about—issues that might have been seen as inappropriate for school in the past. Dana's decision to invite his students to analyze their neighborhood in terms of why unemployment was so high led to conversations about guns on the streets, frequent shootings, and a general conclusion that the neighborhood surrounding this urban school was dangerous. A more faint-hearted educator might have backed away from this topic, opting instead to talk about the legislative process more generically. But Dana had already decided to follow Freire's (1998, p. 36) advice to begin with the students' personal experiences:

> Why not discuss with the students the concrete reality of their lives and that aggressive reality in which violence is permanent and where people are much more familiar with death that with life? Why not establish an "intimate" connection between knowledge considered basic to any school curriculum and knowledge that is the fruit of the lived experience of these students as individuals?

It did not matter to Freire (1998, p. 45) that some might consider these topics to be in bad taste; to him it was more important to ground instruction in the reality of students' lives so that they could begin to see possibilities for making positive changes:

> One of the most important tasks of critical educational practice is to make possible the conditions in which learners, in their interactions with one another and with their teachers, engage in the experience of assuming themselves as social, historical, thinking, communicating, transformative, creative persons.

Creating Critical Classrooms

This willingness to openly face the unsavory issues that people living in poverty face is echoed by West (1999, p. 294), who argues that the quest for truth requires us "to let suffering speak, let the victims be visible and let social misery be put on the agenda of those with power" and concludes that "pursuing the life of the mind is inextricably linked with the struggle of those who have been dehumanized on the margins of society."

Teachers sometimes claim that kids like the ones Dana encountered cannot be coaxed into writing because they have nothing to say, no experiences to write about. We suggest that this is not the case. These kids have lots of experiences. They may or may not be different from our experiences, and they might even be experiences we wish they did not have. No child should have to worry about getting shot while walking to and from school every day. Engaging with these experiences is difficult. But they are what these children bring to school, so they have to become the starting point for generating a meaningful curriculum.

Theory 3: It is not enough to treat critical literacy as a topic of conversation; we have to go out and do something as well.
"Critical whole language teachers do not want students to become apathetic, cynical, hopeless—to conclude that there is nothing they can do; that's just the way it is" (Edelsky, 1999, p. 29). Many of Dana's students already were apathetic, cynical, and, to varying degrees, hopeless when he walked into their classroom for the first time. But he did not allow them to stay that way. When they analyzed their neighborhood and decided that it was dangerous, he did not let them leave it at that. Instead, he pushed them to generate hypotheses for how to make life there better. He positioned them as people with agency—people who had the potential for making positive change. This line of thinking is articulated by Giroux and Giroux (2004, p. 84): "One imperative of a critical pedagogy is to offer students opportunities to become aware of their potential and responsibility as individuals and social agents to expand, struggle over, and deepen democratic values, institutions, and identities." The authors go on to argue that teachers can push their students toward action by helping them "unlearn the presupposition that knowledge is unrelated to action …. Knowledge, in this case, is about more than understanding; it is also about the possibilities of self-determination, individual autonomy, and social agency" (p. 84). In this case, Dana helped his students understand that there is more to knowing about how laws get made than the cute little song in the "I'm Just a Bill" video might suggest. Even though it helped them to understand the procedural aspects of the political process, Dana focused their attention on the need to do something to get this process working for them. He pushed them to design a bill that would respond to their neighborhood needs.

References to design come up frequently in discussions about the transformative power that comes from taking social action. According to

---

Invitation for Disruption 3:

Create Challenging Students

Kohn (2004, p. 192) urges teachers to create classrooms that are "conducive to challenge." In this environment, students learn to question what they are told. They become aware that teachers and textbooks do not have all the answers. Choose one of the following:

- Model your own fallibility by introducing a problem you might not be able to solve. Share your "backstage thinking" (Kohn, 2004, p. 186) as you work through it in front of your students. This might be a difficult math problem, a science experiment with an unknown outcome, or a first-draft attempt to respond to a writing prompt.
- Share an issue in the field that experts see very differently. Invite students to consider how it can be possible for experts to disagree.
- Present a real-world ethical situation where values like honesty and compassion seem to pull in different directions and where there is no easy answer. For example, when discussing child labor practices, it is tempting to conclude that all child labor should be terminated. Though this might be right on some level, it sidesteps the question of whether the children and their families will survive without that contribution.
- Discuss your efforts to create a classroom that is conducive to challenge with a colleague.

Kamler (2001, p. 54), "it is through the processes of designing that writers produce new representations of reality and at the same time remake themselves—that is, reconstruct and renegotiate their identities." Janks (2002) identifies design—along with domination, access, and diversity—as a framing concept for critical literacy education. Design is where human agency and transformation come into the process. It is a "productive power" that exemplifies "the ability to harness the multiplicity of semiotic systems across diverse cultural locations to challenge and change existing Discourses" (p. 2). Dana encouraged his students to remake themselves, if only for a brief moment in time. His curricular decisions set the conditions for learning experiences that responded to their issues. Instead of teaching at them, he worked with them on a project that they deemed important. Dana's design made it possible for kids who rarely paid attention to pay attention, for kids who rarely participated to participate, and for kids who saw their lives as hopeless to reconsider hope.

We have worked with student teachers who complained endlessly about the constraints they had to live with as a guest in someone else's classroom. We have heard diatribes regarding the limitations of mandated and standardized curricula that have no connection to children's lives. In Dana's case, however, we had a chance to see what is possible when a student teacher brings a strong theoretical stance to the experience. Instead of giving in to the negative ethos he encountered in this school, Dana countered it with a proactive response. He took action by moving forward with his intention to incorporate Freire's (1970) teachings into his own. We also believe that Dana's cooperating teacher played a positive role by giving him some space within the mandated curriculum to make the needed connections.

How Was Critical Literacy Enacted in Dana's Classroom?

Table 8.1 summarizes how Dana used the personal and cultural resources at hand to challenge the status quo and to move forward with a different kind of curriculum.

In addition, we can map out Dana's efforts to ground his teaching in the personal experiences of his students while helping them take social action that responded directly to those experiences (Figure 8.2).

What Dana's story makes clear is the idea that students are willing and ready to rise to the occasion when they perceive that the work they are being asked to do matters in the world outside of school. In other words, the messages we send them through our choice of curriculum and how we teach it make a big difference. In the thought piece that follows, Jerry Harste urges all of us to take a close look at the visual

TABLE 8.1

How Critical Literacy Was Enacted in Dana's Classroom

Personal and Cultural Resources	Critical Practices Enacted	How the Teacher Took a Critical Stance
Students' apathy with "doin' school"	Dana used their apathy to disrupt the curriculum.	Used tension as a resource
Field trip to the Statehouse	Focused on the sociopolitical (i.e., taking the students on site and turning the castle into a resource)	Was cognizant of his options; insisted on a different curriculum model
Class discussion of how they wanted to change their community	Engaged in inquiry to research social issues	Positioned students as active participants
Students' experiences with gun violence	Took action to promote social justice by creating a bill that students saw as important	Used tension from stories as a resource

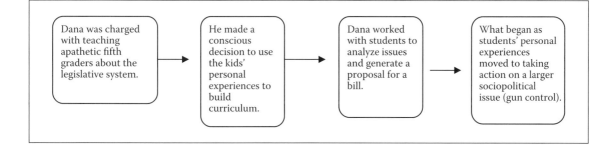

FIGURE 8.2
How Dana moved curriculum between the personal and the social.

messages we hang on our walls. He argues that school posters are more than decorative; they are also a form of communication.

Lingering Questions

▪ Think of a time when a student questioned your authority. How did you respond? What might have been a better way to respond?

▪ What are some mandates in your curriculum that you are less than enthusiastic about? How can these mandates be seen as perspectives that support or contradict other mandates?

Chapter Eight
Critical Social Practices

Thought Piece

School Posters

Jerome C. Harste

I think we need new school posters that reflect a new set of values and priorities. Even in a school as progressive as the Center for Inquiry in Indianapolis we have a poster that says, "Be Safe." This message bothers me. It implies that whoever is in charge assumes the children will not be safe—that they will do or are planning to do dangerous things. It suggests that the environment will not be safe unless the children receive constant reminders about it.

The unspoken message bothers me even more than the explicit message. Even though schools are supposedly for children, everyone knows that adults are really the ones in charge. Even if you disagree with me and think that "Be Safe" is a rather innocuous message as far as school messages go, the message implies a power relationship. The person who put the message up is the one in charge, and the person reading it is a subject. When analyzed in this way, it is clear that the hierarchical power relationship typical of schools is alive and well. Teachers or adults are on top. Kids are below.

FIGURE 8.3
"Have a Laugh" school poster.

I want schools and school posters to challenge and change these larger systems of meaning that we mostly take for granted. I want teachers and administrators to interrogate what they put up on the walls of their schools. I want school posters to send messages that disrupt these larger systems of meaning that everyone reads as normal or as just what schools have always done.

Think in terms of surface-structure and deep-structure meaning. There is often a difference between the two. Be safe, on the surface, seems like good advice, yet at the deep-structure level, it sends a message about schooling that all of us should be working to change. I want deep-structure messages that explore the possibilities of schooling and reflect the kinds of schools that could be.

Figure 8.3 shows a poster I made while conducting a workshop last summer. I had introduced Babbs (1998) as an artist whose style teachers might like to try to replicate. "Have a Laugh" is a very different message than one typically found on classroom walls. It suggests that schools ought to be fun places, even downright enjoyable. The implicit message sent is that adults in this building are expecting to hear giggling and laughter. It even implies that the adults in this school may actually like children. Now that is both a message and a reading that the walls of our schools should be sending.

Figures 8.4 and 8.5 provide a contrasting set of school posters. Figure 8.4 is a sketch of a poster I made while visiting a school. Figure 8.5 is one a teacher developed in a workshop I conducted at the same school and that now occupies the space that the poster in Figure 8.4 once held. In the "September: Back to Books" poster, the visual image is a boy holding a book above his head. The attempt is to portray books positively and as an ideal. The gesture is one someone might make at a sporting event. Books are like a trophy, and reading is something to be proud of. But despite all this, the poster associates books with work and with school. The

FIGURE 8.4
September: Back to Books" school poster.

FIGURE 8.5
"Sing, Dance, Live" school poster.

surface message is that it is now September, and since you have not been reading, it is now time to get back to the books. Even further, reading is hard work, so it is time to stop playing around as you did all summer and get back to the serious work of school. School has to do with books, not the real life stuff you have been doing for the past three months. Although the intent of this poster may be to encourage reading, it really positions reading rather negatively. Rather than associating reading with fun, it is associated with work. Plus, the poster is verbocentric. The only literacy that counts is print literacy, and even then, a particular kind of print literacy, the kind found in books.

In contrast to the poster in Figure 8.4, Figure 8.5 depicts a poster developed by a teacher in a summer workshop. He has taken the traditional 3 Rs of schooling—reading, writing, and arithmetic—and has superimposed on them "Sing, Dance, Live." Now doesn't that make schooling sound, if not more fun, at least more interesting and lively? He has not denied the traditional subjects, but he has managed to suggest that there is something different about life in this school and the difference is that students are encouraged to live richly through the arts. Like "Have a Laugh" this poster positions teachers, schools, and schooling more positively than "Be Safe" or "Back to Books."

Some posters simply lie, or if that is too strong for you, tell half-truths. Figure 8.6 is a rough sketch of one I found in a Canadian school, but it could have been found in almost any country in the world. All you would have to do is change the name of the country prior to the tag, "We All Belong!" The problem I have with this poster is that it perpetuates a platitude. We do not all belong. In the eyes of the dominant majority there are always some groups who are not good Americans, good Canadians, good Australians, or you name the country. Though in a democracy everyone should belong, in reality that is never the case. I think I could live with the "We All Belong" poster if the author were willing to make one simple change: to put a question mark where the exclamation point is now. This would signal to the reader that there is some

FIGURE 8.6
Pencil sketch of "Canada: We All Belong" school poster.

doubt about who belongs and who does not. It might be enough to start some much-needed conversations about what it means to be a Canadian or an American.

In a recent study of the posters found on the walls in two schools, Keller (2006) found that most fell into these categories:

- **Diversity:** For example, "Everyone smiles in the same language." This suggests somehow that sameness makes diversity acceptable. Compare this with a poster that acknowledges difference and demonstrates how difference might be used to create a richer world.

- **Competition:** For example, "Best students, Best staff, BEST SCHOOL." This poses schooling as a competition, much like a sports event, only with winners and losers—we versus them—and the end goal of academic excellence. Excellence, however, implies nonexcellence. Since only one or a few can attain excellence, most are, by default, left out. It is interesting that posters of this sort are as likely to be found in schools serving working-class children as in schools serving more affluent neighborhoods, even though any educator worth his or her salt knows that the playing field for participants from each of these settings is not equal.

- **Success, power, work ethic:** For example, "Today's Forecast: 100% Effort!" This poses hard work and success as the sum total of everyone's individual efforts. A poster with this message, like those proclaiming, "Knowledge Is Power," defines school as the unit that imparts knowledge and guarantees success in the global economy. The unspoken message, of course, is a reprimand: "Your lack of effort keeps others from being successful." Although you may say that there is some truth in both the explicit and hidden message, the problem, of course, is how schools define success. Most educational institutions have very narrow definitions of what constitutes success. These definitions almost assure that certain groups of students will never be as successful as children coming from homes where parents more closely reflect the dominant culture despite, and sometimes in spite of, whatever efforts they may individually make.

▮ **Cooperation, teamwork, community:** For example, "Education Is a Team Effort." This highlights the importance of cooperation and, in this case, because it was superimposed on a variety of different types of workers and professionals, the importance of business and education working together to create tomorrow's citizens. The word *team*, of course, frames the agenda as a sporting event, hence all the things that go with sports, such as competition, winning, pulling together, and catching the spirit. Though I believe strongly in the social nature of all learning, I would like to see school posters frame cooperation as a collective responsibility, even when they address issues of world peace. Playing the role of police officer for the world is, I believe, a foolhardy stance for the United States to take.

In closing, there is no set formula for developing the perfect school poster. The best we can do is challenge the status quo and invite some new conversations about schooling and what it means to be literate. But where better to start than with the walls of the classrooms that house our newest citizens and our future leaders? My advice is to take out your crayons, watercolors, or tempera paints and try your hand at creating a new school messag—one you truly value. Before you sit down to start painting, gather together a group of critical friends and interrogate the message in terms of what is explicitly going to be stated as well as what is implied. Once you get it to the point where you can live with the values it embodies, paint away, and once it is dry, post it. When it stops generating what you see as "much-needed new conversations in education" (that is how I'm recommending you assess its effectiveness), it is time once again to take out the paints, or better yet, invite your students to create a new poster following your lead. Figure 8.7 shows a poster Zachary, Grade 2, created in Tanya Korostil's second-grade classroom. His message to the world: "Have a Blast!" To which I say, "Amen."

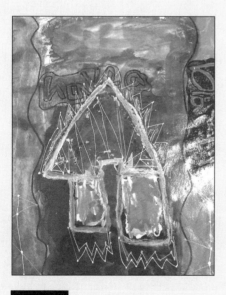

FIGURE 8.7
"Have a Blast!" school poster.

Taking a Critical Stance
Outgrowing Ourselves

Vignette

Learning to Teach by Teaching in the Margins*

Gerald Campano

As a fifth-grade teacher-researcher, I taught in an ethnically and linguistically diverse urban public school located on the south side in a neighborhood that was the most segregated from the city's population of non-Hispanic Whites. The school housed roughly 1,100 students. More than 90% were eligible for free lunch. With few exceptions, they were from families of the working poor. Their parents and caretakers often toiled in several low-wage, unstable jobs to make a living.

   This context led me to explore the question of what would happen if I invited children from immigrant and migrant backgrounds to read, write, and speak from their own experiences and the realities of their lives. One of my initial findings was that I had difficulty even posing my question. Because the school was officially designated as low performing, the teachers were under constant pressure to standardize curricula according to scientifically based research. Since I was new to the district, I struggled to weigh instructional mandates against my own desire to coconstruct a literacy curriculum with my students.

---

* Adapted from G. Campano. The second class: Providing space in the margins. *Language Arts*. Copyright 2005 by the National Council of Teachers of English. Reprinted with permission.

One day I had been laboring my way through a textbook. The students—not surprisingly—were watching the clock, anticipating recess. When the bell rang they thronged out the door. Only moments later I heard a knock and opened the door, and the students filed back in the classroom where they chose to spend the majority of their recess engaged in a range of activities. For example, they selected trade books to read, initiated their own writing projects, developed rhymes, created art inspired by Japanese anime, choreographed dance, wrote skits, and composed music. Perhaps most important, they shared familial and, by implication, cultural stories. In stark contrast to the formal school curriculum, they felt comfortable pursuing their own interests and desires and building on their own experiential knowledge.

This event prompted me to reflect on how the regular school curriculum may function to exclude or devalue the cultural resources of children, especially migrant children. It was a big struggle to develop an alternative pedagogy sensitive to the experiences and identities of my students against the currents of standardization and high-stakes testing.

This account is about my interactions with one child, Carmen. I frame Carmen's story as an interplay between two classes—a mandated class and a classroom—that occurred during the margins and in-between periods or cracks of the school day. The first class includes the time and energy spent on bureaucratically mandated tasks of which teachers are becoming all too familiar, including basal instruction, testing, test preparation, and codified teaching strategies that focus on the transmission of discreet skills.

The second classroom runs parallel to, and sometimes in the shadow of, the official first classroom. It is a space where the students and I coconstructed curricula based on students' experiences and their cultural and linguistic resources. This space developed by following the students' leads, their interests, desires, forms of cultural expression, and especially their stories. It occurred before school, after school, during recess, lunch, and occasionally on weekends and extended—at times—beyond the immediate classroom, into families' homes and community spaces. My account of Carmen suggests I may have failed her because the second classroom remained subordinate to the first.

Discovering Carmen's Roles

My goal for the year was to encourage Carmen to engage in complex literacy engagements that combined her more immediate life-world experiences with school-based knowledge and instruction. On several occasions in class Carmen began to write her family's migrant narrative, but the project was always deferred because of what then seemed more pressing demands such as implementing mandated curricula or giving tests. The school perceived Carmen as a reluctant learner in continual need of remedial instruction. She was marked as being in the lowest quintile band of students, according to testing. At the same time, she presented herself to me as a vital member of a larger community. Despite being perceived as deficient at school, she was very much an active contributor at home and in the neighborhood. She played an instrumental role in cooking, cleaning, and caring for her father, grandmother, and neighbors. She also had friends from a variety of backgrounds and often displayed empathy for their needs and vulnerabilities. I experienced two very different views of this girl: Carmen as a reluctant learner versus Carmen as capable and adept at negotiating the dynamics of her social milieu, creating solidarity with others.

It was at a basketball game that I first met her father, Marcos, and we shared pictures and stories, including my own Filipino grandfather's migrant narrative, while Carmen was playing. Marcos identified himself as Mestizo, of mixed Filipino and European decent. He told me he had spent the good part of his life performing migratory stoop labor in the vineyards throughout

California, Oregon, and Washington. He had to retire due to back problems, and spent the majority of his time making customized low riders with discarded car parts in his backyard. During the times I ate evening meals at their house, Carmen and I interviewed Marcos about his memories of working in the fields and his involvement with the Agricultural Workers Organizing Committee (AWOC) and the National Farm Workers Association (NFWA), founded by Cesar Chavez.

It dawned on me that Carmen's school experiences may not be too dissimilar to her father's migrant work experiences. Tests, evaluations, and programs were constantly foisted on her, and all too often, they too seemed to produce and to prolong her suffering. It was as if the school was reproducing conditions of insecurity and expected failure that were, in some ways, a mirror of the economic hardships many of the neighborhood families endured. It was also one of the first times I really understood the injustice of deficit-based instruction, which positions students as only receivers (and victims) of knowledge, not creators.

I was pleased when Carmen decided she was going to write her father's biography. Carmen and I listened to and discussed the transcripts of her father's interview. When she began writing about his life, she said it was the most she had ever written in school.

The story was never completed. I became absorbed with testing, evaluation, programs, and paperwork. I had five-paragraph essays to administer on mandated topics such as *snacks*. I never provided the adequate scaffolding for Carmen to lift her story out of obscurity—the deeper, more meaningful, and difficult work. Carmen's narrative could have also inspired a class inquiry into local history. We could have examined, for example, the histories of Mexican and Filipino laborers and how different ethnic groups cooperated to work toward a vision of social justice. The children's own familial stories could have become a curricular resource. But I had not fully developed a pedagogy that built on and developed the experiences and realities of the students' lives. And Carmen was subsequently subject to more intervention programs.

That summer Carmen received a letter, only weeks before sixth grade was to begin, that she would have to spend her final year of elementary in another school because the district had redrawn its boundaries. Despite all the talk in our district of the importance of creating a school community, she was removed from the community she had been a member of since kindergarten. Although this larger decision made sense to those on one level of the educational bureaucracy, it was experienced as arbitrary and cruel by Carmen, her father, and hundreds of other displaced children and their families, who were not involved in the decision-making process. Many wondered if the children were just numbers to be reshuffled. Would this happen in affluent districts?

One day, Carmen came to visit me after school, as she had been doing intermittently over several years. She told me, with sincere optimism, that she was not failing three of her classes. I was pleased to hear she had recently gone to a meeting of the local chapter of the Filipino American Historical Society on her own initiative, but I was disheartened that her interest in her roots was not being encouraged or developed within the context of her formal schooling. She gave me a video and some articles about Filipino American history from her father, "to keep," she said. He wanted to invite me to dinner again but was in too much pain. He was dying of cancer.

Carmen continued to nurture her father throughout the duration of his sickness and physical deterioration: "I was with him, like his personal nurse. I took care of him in our house, not the hospital. I was the only one with him while he was really hurt, until the very end. I heard his last words." Carmen missed a lot of school because she became her father's primary caretaker during the final months of his life. This served to compound her already low academic achievement and her own feelings of frustration. She had been retained, twice, and at 14 was embarrassed to still be in seventh grade at the neighborhood middle school. She began failing most of her classes and was developing an oppositional relationship with schooling. Although Carmen said she liked many of her teachers, she nevertheless felt infantilized because they still made her sound out letters and words, "just like I was doing in first grade."

Reflections on Carmen

Carmen was a remarkable young person, but the regular academic curriculum failed her. Out of school, she was a competent and invaluable contributor to friends and family. In school, she was positioned as reluctant learner who was often defiant and immature. She was not provided with the opportunities to incorporate her rich cultural identity and life experiences into her formal schooling.

In retrospect, I needed to listen first and understand the ways Carmen was already participating in the complex processes of building and nurturing relationships to survive. I also needed to be more imaginative about providing opportunities for Carmen to contribute to her own education by bringing her rich life experiences into the literacy curriculum. I never adequately provided the requisite structures of support that might have privileged her particular set of cultural resources.

I eventually discovered the powerful role that autobiography can play in enabling migrant and poor children to work through the challenges of their lives. I also discovered *teatro*, a form of political theater that has its roots in El Teatro Campesino of the migrant labor camps. El Teatro Campesino was a cultural tool created by migrant farm workers and performance artists including Luis Valdez to provide creative performances to farmworkers in California. The plays, presented on the back of flatbed trucks, depicted the farmworkers' struggles with a goal of raising workers' consciousness about the sociopolitical dimensions of their work. I began to see how teatro could become a vehicle through which the children could create individual and collective representations that critically examine their worlds, including their day-to-day lives in school.

Some of my most profound teaching moments occurred when classroom literacy engagements were based on the students' own cultural experiences and commitments. By finding a variety of ways to share their narratives, students could have a role in their own instruction and educational development. I also found that when this was done well, they invariably made substantial academic gains, even by conventional measures such as standardized test scores.

In a climate of standardization and high-stakes testing, a teacher's ability to fulfill the mandates of the school and, at the same time, accommodate the specific experiences and stories of students rests on his or her individual capacity to negotiate agendas that are often in direct conflict. Perhaps more than anything else, Carmen taught me to confront my own personal limitations as well as the pain of uncertainty and at times feelings of hopelessness in my life as an urban educator.

What Can We Learn from Gerald's Experiences with Carmen?

Gerald's struggle is a common one for teachers: How can we comply with district mandates while honoring the experiences and abilities of the children in our classrooms? His response to this dilemma was characterized by a continuing cycle of critical reflection, echoing Dewey's (1933) early work on reflective thinking. Dewey made a case for the importance of "turning a subject over in the mind and giving it serious and consecutive consideration" (p. 3). He believed that being in a state of doubt or uncertainty was an optimal place to be because then one could pay attention to the problematic and make it the subject of an ongoing cycle of reflection, deliberation, inquiry, and action.

At the center of our model of critical literacy instruction is critical stance—including consciously engaging, entertaining alternate ways of being, taking responsibility to inquire, and being reflexive. Gerald's vignette exemplifies these dimensions, and from his description, it is clear that this is no easy process. After a close reading of Gerald's narrative, we identified four theories that we believe informed his stance.

Theory 1: By consciously engaging with the issues and events that arise in our teaching, we can thoughtfully decide how to respond.

As the school year progressed, Gerald began to more fully understand that the formal, mandated curriculum in place at his school often functioned to exclude or to devalue the cultural resources many of his students brought to class each day. Carmen, like many of her peers, was labeled as a reluctant learner in need of remedial instruction. By making a conscious decision to get to know Carmen outside of the confines of the formal classroom, Gerald experienced her in a way that was closer to how she was known by her family and community: as a very competent young person. By consciously expanding his awareness of Carmen's many identities—especially those outside of school—Gerald began to understand the ways she was positioned and labeled by different groups. At this point, he had options about whether to respond to Carmen in the way she was viewed by the school or in some alternate way. Gerald consciously began to reframe Carmen's school identity to incorporate aspects of Carmen that were not valued at school. As Lakoff (2004) notes, reframing is no easy task; in fact, Lakoff believes that reframing is social change.

In describing how he may have failed Carmen, Gerald laments, "I had not fully developed a pedagogy that built on and developed the experiences and realities of the students' lives. I did not enable students to become agents in their own educational development." This may be true, but in one year Gerald came a long way toward developing a stance where he was consciously aware of the effects that dominant, one-sided perceptions can have on students' identities and their lives. He did this by working both within and against the system over time. Gerald did not all of a sudden adopt a critical stance. None of us ever does. But Gerald now has potential options, choices, and tools to use in reframing commonplace perceptions and interpretations of the students with whom he works.

Invitation for Disruption 1:

Disrupting Our Theories

- Jot down three statements that you strongly believe under each of the following headings:
  - What do I believe about language?
  - What do I believe about learning?
  - What do I believe about curriculum?
- During the next week as you are teaching, keep the list near. Note the times that you are enacting your beliefs with your students and the times when you are violating them.
- Take a careful look at the violations. Can any of these serve as an impetus for rethinking practice?
- If you could only keep one belief statement for each of your theories of language, learning, and curriculum, what would these statements be?
- This works really well if you and a colleague do this invitation together and discuss your beliefs.

Theory 2: By entertaining alternate ways of being, we may find that what we believe about teaching and learning is not working.

As a new teacher to the district, Gerald struggled to weigh instructional mandates against his own desire to coconstruct curriculum with his students. Instead of acquiescing to the prescribed curriculum or ignoring it, Gerald used the tension between the two as a resource. As a way of working with the tension, Gerald's first move was a familiar one—trying to make both the mandated and the coconstructed curriculum work. This view that an eclectic approach can work is common in our field. But if we pay attention to the effects that particular curricula and institutional mandates are having on particular students, we often uncover evidence that pushes us to begin abandoning an eclectic approach.

From the vignette, we can deduce the theories Gerald held about language, learning, and curriculum. He wanted students to "engage in complex literacy engagements that combined [their] more immediate life world experiences with school-based knowledge and instruction." Gerald believed that (1) language is learned through complex literacy engagements—that it does not need to be broken down into small bits and pieces; (2) students cannot learn school-based knowledge without connecting this learning to their life worlds outside of school; and (3) curriculum is a negotiation between what the school has deemed important and what is important in the lives of students.

At the same time, Gerald held a conflicting theory grounded in the reality of the school where he taught: that he needed to devote significant amounts of time to implementing the mandated curriculum. Because he had a conscious awareness of his own theories about language, learning, and curriculum, he began to see that the eclectic approach he was using in his classroom was not making sense. As the year progressed, Gerald began to understand how adhering to the demands of the mandated curriculum left his own theories and visions for curriculum unrealized. He found that the only time left for culturally responsive curriculum— curriculum that builds on students' experiences and their linguistic and cultural resources—was in the cracks, the second classroom, the time outside of the standard academic day.

In the years following this episode, Gerald continued to move toward a curriculum that valued students' identities outside of school and supported inquiries into social justice. But this movement was by no means linear. As educators we are always negotiating between our ideals and the realities of the contexts in which we work. Nonetheless, by enacting curricular structures such as writing autobiography and political teatro, Gerald moved closer to understanding the multimodal and multimediated nature of literacies and their relationship to power. Especially by using teatro, students were able to dramatically perform and to critique issues of injustice and inequity in their lives. Ladson-Billings (2002, p. 111) notes that by helping students become more aware of sociopolitical questions in society, teachers can assist students in becoming "bicultural and facile in the ability to move between school and home cultures." Gerald's goal was to create strong, literate beings who had the potential to move beyond being mere victims or consumers of curricula that devalued their experiences and abilities. By adopting a critical stance toward teaching—being willing to look at what parts of his teaching were not working—Gerald was able to move closer to creating learning spaces where the second classroom becomes the first classroom.

Theory 3: As teachers, we have a responsibility to inquiry.

The tension between implementing both a mandated curriculum and what Gerald believed was best for his students propelled a yearlong inquiry into his own teaching and family history as well as an inquiry into the lives of his students and their family histories. Gerald knew that inquiry is not just some cold, scientific set of procedures to follow, but rather it involves building relationships. When he first met Carmen's father, Marcos, at a basketball game, Gerald shared part of his own family history as well as found out more about Marcos and his background. As time progressed and Gerald got to know the family better, he and Carmen interviewed Marcos. They found out about his history of working in the fields and his involvement with the AWOC and the NFWA, founded by Cesar Chavez. This inquiry placed Carmen and Marcos on the front line of Gerald's learning and knowledge production, repositioning Marcos as a valuable resource rather than the school's one-dimensional perception of him as a parent of an underachieving student.

Although Carmen never finished her father's biography—a troubling coda for the school year from Gerald's perspective—we see Gerald making a courageous move to help students move toward cultural competency by supporting their ability "… to grow in understanding and respect for their culture of origin" (Ladson-Billings, 2002, p. 111). Through helping Carmen conduct an inquiry into the life of her father, Gerald was attempting to make school less alienating and more representative of students' home cultures. He also learned that there are multiple perspectives on how to do school, and they are not all equal.

In addition to inquiring into the lives of his students, Gerald problematized the commonplace notion that a scientifically based regimented curriculum is a good thing for students. This type of questioning is always risky business. Teachers who question methods of instruction, the prescribed curriculum, the role of students, or the goals of education may not only be challenging the norms of their particular school but society as well (Sparks-Langer & Colton, 1991; Zeichner & Liston, 1987). At best, this critical stance is a difficult road to travel; at worst it can jeopardize teachers' job security. As Gerald experimented with nonsanctioned viewpoints on curriculum, he moved beyond what Schön (1983) calls the illusion of expertise—he used inquiry as a tool to take down barriers that

---

Invitation for Disruption 3:

Reflection in Action on Ourselves

This invitation works like the previous one, but with a different focus.

- For a week keep a notebook with you at all times and set a timer to go off once an hour (e.g., at 10 minutes after the hour).
- When the timer goes off, stop and take a minute to notice what you are doing and how you are feeling. Jot down these observations without being judgmental.
- What do you notice when you review your notes for the week? Are you generally satisfied with what you have been doing with your students, or are changes in order? Are you enjoying teaching? What are your thoughts about the different feelings you experienced?

Chapter Nine
Taking a Critical Stance

inhibit looking at one's own role as a learner. He took on another aspect of a reflective stance, being truly in doubt about his practice, which enabled him to problematize and eventually begin to change his curriculum. To adopt a reflective stance, we all have to overcome the illusion that "we know" and take up the role of a learner. But Gerald did not stop here; he also examined and took responsibility for his role in maintaining an unjust curriculum—he moved from a reflective to a reflexive stance.

Theory 4: Being a critical educator requires mindfulness of our own complicity in maintaining the status quo or systems of injustice.

By adopting a reflexive stance, Gerald was bravely able to see his own complicity in what happened to Carmen and other students in his class. We have a window into the ups and downs of his teaching. He was pleased when Carmen decided she was going to write her father's biography, but the story was never completed as Gerald became absorbed with testing, evaluation, programs, and paperwork. Instead of just wallowing in guilt about what might have been, Gerald actively continued the ongoing process of transforming his teaching. He used Carmen, Marcos, and the other students in his class to outgrow himself and was able to envision alternate ways of being—ways that he was able to put into practice, in different degrees, in subsequent years. Dewey (1933) writes about the importance of having a willingness to accept responsibility for decisions and actions and not to accept things that do not make sense. Although it took more than one school year, Gerald actively sought ways to keep evolving as a teacher and to enact curricula that privileged the cultural resources students bring to school rather than ignoring them.

One especially interesting outcome of this work was that Gerald found when students were actively engaged in literacy practices based on their own cultural experiences and commitments, they actually made gains on standardized achievement tests. Thus, by putting students on the frontline of his learning, Gerald was able to deconstruct the academic achievement test–culturally responsive pedagogy binary. This commitment to conscious engagement, trying on alternate ways of being, responsibility to inquiry, and reflexivity served Gerald and his future students well.

How Was Critical Literacy Enacted in Gerald's Classroom?

Table 9.1 highlights the ways we see the critical literacy instructional model being realized in Gerald's classroom.

In addition, we can map how Gerald moved curriculum between the personal and the social (Figure 9.1).

Although the tension between his personal desires and the social norms of the school was painful, Gerald was able to use it as a resource

TABLE 9.1
How Critical Literacy Was Enacted in Gerald's Classroom

Cultural Resources	Critical Practices Enacted	How the Teacher Took Up a Critical Stance
Students' family and cultural stories	Disrupted the commonplace by letting students bring in their own stories and interests—even if it was just at recess, lunch, and before and after school	Consciously decided to find spaces in the school day for students' lives and interests to become part of the curriculum
Recess curriculum and mandated curriculum	Focused on the sociopolitical by reflecting on how the regular curriculum functioned to exclude certain cultural resources	Used tension as a resource to interrogate the effects of the mandated curriculum on students
Time spent with Carmen and Marcos outside of the school day	Disrupted commonplace view of both Carmen and Marcos	Was cognizant of the multiple and contradictory ways that Carmen and Marcos were positioned in school and in their community
Interviews with Marcos	Used counternarrative—Marcos's interviews—to understand that Carmen, like Marcos, was being positioned as a failure	Became aware of his own complicity in maintaining the status quo
What happened to Carmen	The next year, Gerald took action, evolving his curriculum to bring students' life experiences into the classroom.	Questioned his classroom practices and those of the school

to outgrow the way he created curriculum for students. In short, Gerald embodied professionalism by taking on the role of a teacher, a learner, and an intellectual. In the thought piece that accompanies this chapter, Jerry Harste discusses the importance of professionalism.

Lingering Questions

▌ What areas do you think need to be studied in your classroom? How could you go about doing this?

▌ What are the roadblocks that make conducting classroom research difficult? Are there ways you could overcome one of these roadblocks?

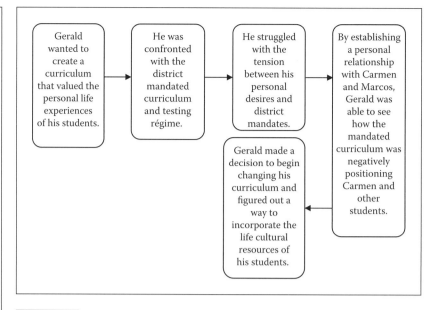

FIGURE 9.1
How Gerald moved curriculum between the personal and the social.

TABLE 9.2

Theories from *Creating Critical Classrooms*

Chapter Number, Topic, Title	Theories
2. Personal and Cultural Resources: "Using Life Experiences as an Entrée into Critical Literacy"	• Since all students are capable and bring a wide range of experiential, cultural, and linguistic resources to the classroom, our job as teachers is to figure out ways to regularly use these resources and to give them a place of prominence in what counts in our classrooms. • To be relevant to students' interests and knowledge, we build curriculum by creating connections between the classroom and life outside of school. • People must see themselves in literacy to become literate, and this involves starting with the personal and moving to the social.
3, Cultural Resources: "Using Popular Culture to Promote Critical Practice"	• Literacy keeps changing and is often linked to popular culture. • School can provide a site for interrogating cultural texts and repositioning oneself. • Children need to develop the language of critique to be truly literate in the 21st century.
4, Cultural Resources: "Using Children's Literature to Get Started with Critical Literacy"	• Teachers do not have to work alone. • Lingering in text is important. • Tension drives the learning process.
5, Critical Social Practices: "Disrupting the Commonplace Through Critical Language Study"	• No text is neutral. • Critical language study needs to be an integral part of the curriculum. • Curriculum should support the development of counternarratives.
6, Critical Social Practices: "Interrogating Multiple Viewpoints"	• Multiple perspectives complicate what we already know. • A focus on multiple perspectives involves the representation of people and ideas not prominent in school curricula. • It is important to weave diversity and seeing differently into the fabric of curriculum.
7, Critical Social Practices: "Focusing on the Sociopolitical"	• In working to help students inquire into sociopolitical issues, it is often necessary to push ourselves out of our comfort zones. • Students can engage in very sophisticated critical practices if their teacher is actively involved in the same practices and provides demonstrations of that allow them to focus on sociopolitical systems and power relationship. • Do not water down the curriculum.
8, Critical Social Practices: "Taking Social Action"	• Education is never neutral: It either liberates, domesticates, or alienates. • Creating critical curriculum means delving into risky topics that surround students' lives. • It is not enough to treat critical literacy as a topic of conversation; we have to go out and do something as well.
9, Taking a Critical Stance: "Outgrowing Ourselves"	• By consciously engaging with the issues and events that arise in our teaching, we can thoughtfully decide how to respond. • By entertaining alternate ways of being, we may find that what we believe about teaching and learning is not working. • As teachers we have a responsibility to inquiry. • Being a critical educator requires mindfulness of our own complicity in maintaining the status quo or systems of injustice.

"May You Live in Interesting Times"—The Politics of Eclecticism

Jerome C. Harste

This piece uses the old Chinese proverb, "May you live in interesting times," to talk about the politics of literacy. What makes these times so interesting for teachers of literacy is that despite phenomenal breakthroughs in our understanding of literacy, the federal government has now legislated the teaching of phonics but not, for example, preparing students to be critically literate. Strauss (2004) goes so far as to argue that when phonic advocates found out they could not easily win the phonics argument on intellectual grounds they turned to the federal government and pushed through phonics-first legislation. Phonics is in, not because that is the consensus of scholars in the field of reading education but because some group of scholars knew how to play politics. Lankshear and Knobel (2006) argue that truth is a forgotten concept in advertising, education, and politics; what matters is the narrative you spin.

It is little wonder, then, that educators often feel that because the teaching of literacy is a highly contested area the way to stay out of the debate is to advocate the teaching of a little bit of everything. Their thinking goes something like this:

> Given that there are experts who advocate teaching phonics first (i.e., meaning comes later), others who advocate breaking reading down into discrete skills—and teaching them very systematically and sequentially—and still others who advocate the use of holistic approaches (i.e., immersing children in books and in the functional use of reading and writing from Day 1), the sanest position to take is eclecticism, using the good parts of all of the approaches. Obviously each of these approaches has its good points—or else there would not be a debate—and I simply use what works given particular children and their needs.

Understanding Eclecticism

Just because eclectics argue for a little bit of everything, eclecticism is not a neutral position. To say everything works is to take just as much a theoretical position as to advocate for any one of a number of other positions: phonics, skills, whole language, critical literacy. Taking a position is not wrong. It is taking a position that does not challenge anyone, including yourself, that is the problem. Put even more straightforward, eclecticism is a position from which it is impossible to grow. If everything works then everything is either right or relative. When something does not work, it is not because what was done was wrong but rather because it was applied incorrectly or done at the wrong time. Eclecticism, in this sense, violates what we know about the learning process because it allows us to sidestep doubt rather than confront the theoretical beliefs that were at play when we acted.

There is still another thing that is wrong with eclecticism as a position. In language learning all things are not equal. Not all classrooms are equally effective; not all theories of reading are equal in terms of their explanatory power of the reading process; not all teaching methods are sound given what we know about the learning process; not all research merits direct application to instruction. Some answers are simply too simple to be true.

One of the things I learned as a researcher is that I had the most to learn in classrooms where teachers were attempting to apply the best of what was currently known about the teaching and learning of the English language arts. What I came to understand is that we grow at the frontier of our knowledge base. When we are using the best information we have available to us and things still do not pan out, we are pushed to reformulate our thinking and try again. And there is a practical side to all this. As a researcher I found it takes just as long to analyze the videotapes from a classroom in which nothing new is happening as it does in a classroom where teachers and children are pushing the envelope. Guess which setting is professionally more fulfilling.

Outgrowing Eclecticism

I see the alternative to eclecticism for teachers as professionalism. By professionalism I mean taking on the critical stance of a learner, part of which entails respecting what it is that others know and do within the fields of language and literacy yet being skeptical of it and keeping one's head. By keeping one's head I mean seeing teaching as a moral activity—including speaking up for those the larger society may want forgotten or ignored—and not letting our membership in the guild of teaching constrict and limit our language and thought. Said (2006, p. 2) makes the point more eloquently: "It's somehow important to balance and maintain a kind of coexistence between the necessities of the field and the discipline of the classroom, on the one hand, and of the special interest that one has in it, on the other, with one's own concerns as a human being, as a citizen in the larger society." For me, as for Said, the key is not to develop so much a sense of professional vocation as it a sense of intellectual vocation. "The intellectual, as opposed to the professional, is someone who is … an opponent of consensus and orthodoxy, particularly at a moment in our society when the authorities of consensus and orthodoxy are so powerful" (p. 3).

As an intellectual vocation, I see language teaching as involving an ongoing cycle of theorizing, evaluating, and instructing. I see the process of turning teaching into an intellectual vocation as a matter of using the gaps among theory, research, and practice as spaces within which to hone some sense of communal critical awareness, some sense of communal skepticism. I use the term *communal* to suggest that teaching as a profession always involves others. As teachers we are part of a professional community as well as part of the community, writ large. As professionals and as intellectuals we have the responsibility to grow and to contribute, simultaneously, to both these communities. Rather than collaborate with the centralizing powers of our profession or our society, it is important that we speak with our own sense of voice and our own sense of conviction, that we maintain some sense of independence, and that we not only keep the conversation going but also take positions that support reflection and growth on our part as well as on the part of others.

Theorizing. Theoretically, as English language arts teachers we need to have, minimally, some understanding of the reading and writing process, some understanding of both oral and written language development, and some understanding of the factors that affect both of these processes. Theoretically the question that drives teaching is, What is it that we currently know about literacy and literacy learning?

Articulating an answer to this question is a formidable task. But just like the conditions under which we take a driver's test, ignorance of the law—in this case, what is known—is no excuse. Similarly, it does not work to say, "No one told me," or "We didn't talk about that in the teacher education program I went through." As professionals each of us has to take personal responsibility for what we know and do not know. As professionals we have a responsibility to keep informed. That is why we join professional associations like the National Council of Teachers of English and the International Reading Association, why we take professional development seriously, why we attend conferences, why we go back to college to pick up additional courses and degrees, and why we read professional books and journals. There is, in fact, no guarantee that even doing all of these things will keep us up to date. The odds are just better, and engaging in all these activities encourages us as professionals to stay engaged. We take heart in knowing that on our tombstones they cannot write, "Didn't even try."

Evaluating. Evaluation, in this cycle of theorizing–evaluating–instructing, involves asking the question, In light of what we know about literacy and literacy learning (traditionally often thought of as reading and writing, language development, and the factors that affect these processes), how are these children doing? Evaluation in this model is not reduced to performance on standardized tests but rather to authentic instances of behavior from which sound decisions can be made. This does not mean that our decisions will not be biased. They will be. They will be made based on our reading of the best information we currently have available. But—and this is another big but—they will be done assuming that some part of what we are doing is in all likelihood wrong.

Importantly in this cycle, evaluation does not stand outside the process but is an integral part of the instructional process. From my perspective, any evaluation that does not result in the improvement of teaching and learning has to be seen as suspect.

Though *kidwatching* is a popular and powerful term for what we do (Goodman, 1978), evaluation, in the hands of a professional, involves more than watching children. It involves pushing our observations to the level of theoretical principles from which new hypotheses about instruction might be generated.

Instructing. The question instruction addresses in this theorizing–evaluating–instructing cycle is, In light of what we know about how these children are doing, how might we support their learning? Hypotheses about teaching do not come out of thin air but rather are grounded in decisions reached from evaluation, which in turn is both built from and anchored in what we know. When things under these conditions do not work, the results can be used to reformulate planks in our theory as well as suggest new areas in which to look for evidence of learning. In this sense the cycle is interactive as well as transactive, with each part affecting the other and the whole adding up to more than the sum of its parts. Evaluation and instruction, for example, need not be separate activities. Data on which sound professional decisions can be made can come from instruction as well as from more formal instances of evaluation.

Some Concluding Comments

The bumper sticker "Teachers Are Professionals" bothers me; especially since most of the time I see this bumper sticker on the back of teachers' cars. It strikes me as a defensive posture, although I understand that the real message being conveyed is "Let me do my job." At this level of intent, I like the bumper sticker, so long as doing our job is not doing as we are told, blindly following government mandates, directly applying the findings of research to practice, or becoming dilettantes, doing a little of this and a little of that without some bigger picture of what it means to be a professional.

From a sociopolitical perspective, in addition to worrying about how others are positioning us, we teachers need to worry about how we are positioning ourselves. Just as understanding literacy as a form of professional citizenship is important for teachers, so understanding literacy as a form of cultural citizenship is important for students. In both instances literacy and the times we live in are made more interesting by consciousness and resistance to the positions and identities that we are encouraged to assume blindly.

Within education generally, and literacy education specifically, eclecticism is fashionable—propelled and made ever more complex by the sociopolitical tenor of these times. On bad days I see eclecticism as a disease, curable by taking a position—any consistent theoretical position will do. On good days I see eclecticism as an invitation—an invitation to develop teaching as an intellectual vocation involving theorizing, evaluating, and instructing within a moral and critical public consciousness that challenges the sociopolitical forces currently at play.

Chapter Nine
Taking a Critical Stance

Invitations for Students

This section features a series of invitations for students that can be used in conjunction with the chapters in this book or as standalone curricular engagements. Each *invitation* is based on a particular social issue such as name-calling or consumerism and consists of a rationale, needed materials, and how to get started. We wrote the invitations for use as whole-class activities, but each one is followed by a *learning center extension* that was designed for students to do in small groups or on their own. As you will see, it takes little work to convert a whole class engagement into a learning center and vice versa. Each invitation consists of the elements described in Table 10.1.

TABLE 10.1
Elements of Invitations

Element	Description
Rationale	Sets the stage for getting started with students and gives background information about the content of the invitation
Materials	What you will need to implement the invitation in your classroom
Getting Started	The step-by-step description of how to implement this invitation as a whole-class engagement
Learning Center Extension	A different teaching strategy based on the same theme as the invitation, but designed to be used in a learning center; written in center-card format so that it can be reproduced and used directly by students
Learning Center Materials	What you will need to implement the center in your classroom
Taking Action	Suggestions for how you and your students might take action following the invitation; these are meant to serve as starting points from which you and your students can develop your own action plans

We invite readers to think of these invitations not as step-by-step recipes, but rather as springboards to developing your own critical classroom engagements. We envision these initiations as organic entities that will grow and change based on the needs of your class. We hope you and your students find the invitations as stimulating and enjoyable as we have found them when using them with both children and adults.

Digging Deeper into Texts through Drama

Digging Deeper into Texts through Drama, based on the subtext strategy developed by Jean Anne Clyde (2003), helps students take on the perspective of various characters in a story and think beyond the written text. Using process drama techniques, students are asked to act (typically using the text and pictures as clues) like one of the characters in a story and write out (on index cards) two things: (1) what they think that character might be thinking, and (2) what that character is actually saying.

Materials:

- Any picture book that you want to use for dramatization—in this case, Eve Bunting's *Your Move* (1998).
- Enough 3″ x 5″ index cards (different colors help), to put a stack at each table or with each group.

Getting Started:

1. Read a picture book aloud and ask students to select a character, step into role, and write out what that character is saying (on one side of an index card) in contrast to what that character might be thinking (on the other side of the index card). For example, using this strategy with Eve Bunting's *Your Move* (1998), there are four major roles:
   - James, the older brother (yellow cards)
   - Isaac, the little brother (green cards)
   - Mom (blue cards)
   - The leader of K-Bones, the neighborhood gang (pink cards)

2. A good way to begin is by referring students to the cover of the book where James is shown with his arms draped over Isaac's shoulders and Isaac has reached up to clasp James' arm. Essentially the scene is one of big brother protecting little brother. Given this picture as a reference point, students select a character and write out what it is they think that character is saying as well as thinking:

James is Saying: "Mom, don't worry. Go to work. You know I will take good care of Isaac."

James is Thinking: "Little brothers are a pain in the neck. I want to join the K-Bones. They have all the fun and they are my own age. I don't know why Mom hates them so."

Isaac is Saying: "Bye Mom. Me and James have big plans today. We won't get bored nor get in trouble."

Isaac is Thinking: "I hope James doesn't run off to be with the K-Bones all day and leave me on my own. The K-Bones scare me, and they don't like me either."

Although only two characters are shown here as an example, cards can be written for Mom and the leader of the K-Bones, even though they don't appear on the cover illustration.

3. Ask for two volunteers, one James and one Isaac, and have them stand in a tableau (frozen picture) based on the cover. First, direct the two characters to have a conversation based on their index card "saying" notes. The James character can read his "saying note," then the Isaac character, and finally have them ad lib a conversation for two turns beyond what they have written.
4. Next ask the same students to look at what they've written for their "thinking" notes. Ask the two characters to adopt body language and facial expressions that fit what they are thinking. They are usually very expressive and the class can comprehend without language being spoken.
5. Then ask if there is someone who has a different James and a different Isaac for the same cover picture. (This is a great way to demonstrate multiple interpretations of text.)
6. Continue working through the story by selecting key pictures as points to stop and invite students to write out what they think various characters are saying and thinking and act out the scene in tableau fashion.

7. When the story is complete, divide students into four groups by each of the four major characters in the story and have them look across the story as to what they and their classmates thought these characters were saying as well as thinking. Their task, at this point, is to identify the major premise (set of beliefs or values) that the character was operating from throughout the story. James, for example, sees belonging to the K-Bones as his road to developing an identity. The peer group is particularly important to him at this point in time in his life. Isaac, on the other hand, sees gangs as dangerous and James as a role model. Mother hates to leave her children alone but she knows she has to work in order for them to survive.

8. As a culminating activity have groups share what they see as the major systems of meaning (premises, belief systems, value systems) that were operating in the story, how these might differ from their own community, and what such differences signify.

Learning Center Extension: *Digging Deeper into Texts through Tableaux*

Hertzberg (2003) discusses how process drama is a great tool to help kids dig deeper into text meanings by having them read critically to understand characters' motivations and beliefs. She calls the tableau strategy (used in the invitation above) "still image." In this center, groups of students create a tableau based on a social issues book (see resources) and then present the tableau to the class during meeting time. Make sure to debrief with students after their presentations (e.g., How did you feel playing that role? Was it difficult? What did you learn about your character?)

> **Possible Social Issues Books**
>
> *Amelia's Road* (Altman, 1991)
> *Willy the Wimp* (Browne, 1995)
> *White Socks Only* (Coleman, 1996)
> *Radiance Descending* (Fox 1997)
> *My Man Blue* (Grimes, 1999)

Materials for Learning Center Extension
▌ A number of social issues books that you have read aloud and discussed with students prior to this invitation (see sidebar)
▌ 5x8 cards, markers, hole punch, string
▌ Table 10.1.1, Learning Center Directions

Taking Action

There are a number of ways to take action following this initiation. Here is one possibility: Groups can be invited to identify some problematic issues (like name calling or bullying) that they have observed in their classroom, lunchroom, on the playground, etc. and represent them in tableaux. If students identify multiple perspectives on the issues they are portraying, they can present more than one tableau. Follow this with a conversation about what the tableau(x) showed and why this issue is worth discussing.

Digging Deeper into Texts through Tableaux

1. Find three other people to work at this center with you. As a group, decide on a book that you all like and take turns reading it aloud.

2. While reading, pay special attention to what the characters are doing and thinking. Discuss what you all think are the most important issues in the book.

3. Each of you picks a character to play and together decide on a tableau (still picture, frozen picture) that shows your group's understanding of the story. Your tableau might not be an actual scene from the book.

4. To create a tableau, your group decides:

   - Who are we? (characters, roles)
   - Where are we? (setting, context)
   - What are we doing? (problem, tension)
   - Why are we doing it? (focus, theme, issue)
   - How will we show this? (body language, movement, mood) (Hertzberg, 2003)

5. You will probably try out a number of tableaux before you find the one that captures your ideas the best.

6. Make "name cards" for your characters to hang around their necks.

7. Perform your tableau in front of the class during meeting time. You may want to hold the tableau perfectly still for a minute and then have each character say one line that sums up who he or she is and what he or she is feeling.

Double Standards—
Bringing Consumerism
Home

Advertisers have become extremely adept at gearing ads toward particular target audiences. You and your students can find some amazing examples of this by comparing ads from the same company in publications geared for two different audiences. With the ever-increasing bombardment of ads into our homes, on our computer screens, and even in our classrooms, it behooves us to begin interrogating how sophisticated advertisers have become in exploiting the desires and needs of different demographic groups.

> **Parent Magazine Suggestions**
>
> ▪ Family Circle
> ▪ Kraft Kitchens
> ▪ People Magazine
> ▪ Ebony
> ▪ Today's Parent
> ▪ US Magazine

Materials
▪ Parent and teen magazines

Getting Started
1. Write a letter home asking parents or guardians to send in as many back issues of parent magazines as they might be able to part with (see sidebar). At the same time, ask students to bring in copies of any teen magazines (see sidebar) that they might own or have available. Since bookstores destroy magazines at the end of each month, it might be possible to convince a manager to donate a few old copies to the school.
2. Once you have a fairly good-sized collection of magazines, pair students up to look for ads from the same company across both teen and parent magazines.

> **Teen Magazine Suggestions**
>
> ▪ MAD Magazine
> ▪ Spin Music
> ▪ Transworld Skateboarding
> ▪ Teen Vogue
> ▪ Smack Down Wrestling
> ▪ Sports Illustrated Kids
> ▪ Gamepro
> ▪ Teen

3. The results of this activity can be pretty startling. In one classroom, students found that McDonald's advertised its "premium green salad lunches" to parents in *People Magazine* but had ads saying things like, "Have you had your hands on a great set of buns today" on the Internet and in their ads in teen magazines. Similarly, a Skechers shoe ad showed a girl vampire biting the neck of a boy in the teen magazine *Smack Down*, whereas the Skechers ad for parents in *People Magazine* showed American Idol winner Carrie Underwood sitting on the floor surrounded by cute puppies and, of course, Skechers shoes.

4. Once students have collected, analyzed, and discussed contrasting sets of advertisements, open up a whole-class conversation as to what this means and why it is important to understand how advertising works.

Learning Center Extension: *It's All in the Numbers*

On a now-defunct website, the City of Casey published sample demographics in its "Home-Based Business Manual" (http://www.homebusiness manual.com.au/hbm/prom otion/advertising.asp). Table 10.2.1 is useful in helping students understand why advertisers create different ads or commercials for different target audiences.

Materials for Learning Center Extension

- Sample demographics chart (Table 10.2.1)
- Whole-class demographics chart copied onto chart paper (Table 10.2.2)
- Teen and parent magazines used in the previous invitation
- Table 10.2.3 Learning Center Directions

TABLE 10.2.1
Sample Demographics Chart

Demographic Group	Characteristics
People in their 20s	Like novelty and uniqueness and product appealing to peer pressures
People in their 30s	Are looking for product to give them recognition and stability
	Are more family orientated and do not have much money
People in their 40s	Are looking for products that will satisfy a desire to be self-indulgent as they have more money to spend
People in their 50s	Are looking for products that give them recognition, indicate power, and show their competence
People in their 60s	Are looking for products that are practical, reliable, and have quality
	Are usually looking for bargains

Note: For a whole-class demographics chart, copy this onto chart paper, and put up at the center, leaving lots of space for students to add their own characteristics.

TABLE 10.2.2
Whole-Class Demographics Chart

Demographic Group	Characteristics
People in their 20s	Like novelty and uniqueness and product appealing to peer pressures
People in their 30s	Are looking for product to give them recognition and stability Are more family orientated and do not have much money
People in their 40s	Are looking for products that will satisfy a desire to be self-indulgent as they have more money to spend
People in their 50s	Are looking for products that give them recognition, indicate power, and show their competence
People in their 60s	Are looking for products that are practical, reliable, and have quality Are usually looking for bargains

TABLE 10.2.3
Learning Center Directions

It's All in the Numbers

1. With a friend, take a good look at the sample demographics chart at this center. Think about and discuss the following questions:

   - Do you agree or disagree with the way different age groups are positioned in the chart?
   - Why do you think the sample demographics chart did not include toddlers, children, or teens?
   - Think of as many reasons as you can that the people who made the sample demographics chart stopped with people in their 60s.

2. Find a couple of adults who fall into one or more of the age categories represented on the sample demographics chart and interview them. Find out what these adults look for in products or services. After the interviews, you can do the following:

   - Add characteristics to the whole-class demographics chart based on your research
   - Create your own demographics chart
   - Create your own activity on this topic

3. **Extension:** You might want to use the sample demographics chart, the whole-class demographics chart, or the demographics chart you created and take another look at the ads in the parent and teen magazines. Did the ads follow the correct demographic characteristics listed on the chart or not? How were they similar or different?

4. **Reflection:** From the work you have done at this center, how do you think advertisers make decisions, plan ads, or buy space in certain publications?

Taking Action

There are many ways you and your students might take action following this invitation. One idea is to have interested students could make posters illustrating double-standard advertising to put up around the school.

Fairy Tales with an Edge

Since most fairy tales have an all too predictable structure and message, this invitation is designed to give students an opportunity to challenge the status quo. The class will be writing emancipatory fairy tales—tales that go against the grain of what might be considered "normal" in this genre. The dictionary defines "emancipatory" as being free from bondage, oppression, or restraint.

Emancipatory Fairy Tales

▌ *Little Red Riding Hood: A Newfangled Prairie Tale* (Ernst, 1995)
▌ *Into the Forest* (Browne, 2004)
▌ *The Paper Bag Princess* (Munch, 1983)
▌ *Princess Smartypants* (Cole, 1997)

Materials:

▌ Traditional version of a fairy tale
▌ Newer (emancipatory) edition of the same fairy tale (see sidebar)
▌ *The King and His Three Daughters*
▌ *Triple Entry Journal* (see Table 10.3.1)

Getting Started:

1. Read aloud a traditional and then a newer/emancipatory version of the same fairy tale to the class.
2. In small groups, have students analyze what changes the author of the emancipatory tale made to the original story and describe the effects of those changes. It might help if students draw a triple entry journal to record their analysis (see Table 10.3.1).
3. Students report back their analyses to the class and summarize their findings.
4. Next, students will rewrite a fairy tale with a partner to make it emancipatory.
5. Read aloud *The King and His Three Daughters* and give each pair of students a copy.

6. Ask students to rewrite this story (or make up one of their own) so that it is "emancipatory." This could be accomplished by making gender, personality, setting, or plot changes.
7. Have a few students read their emancipatory tales aloud.
8. Have a discussion of how easy or hard it was to change the story to make it emancipatory.
9. Students can also discuss whether they think emancipatory tales ruin the fun of fairy tales or if they serve a useful purpose.

The King and His Three Daughters

There was once a king who had three lovely daughters. One day the three daughters went walking in the woods. They were enjoying themselves so much that they forgot the time and stayed too long. A dragon came and kidnapped the three daughters. As they were dragged off, they cried for help. Three heroes heard the cries and set off to rescue the daughters. The heroes then returned the daughters safely to the palace. When the king heard of the rescue he rewarded the heroes.

TABLE 10.3.1
Triple Entry Journal

Fairy Tale: Date: Group Members:		
Event in the original fairy tale	Changes the author made in the new version	How this change affected the meaning of the story

Learning Center Extension: *Picture Books with an Edge*

Bronwyn Davies (2003) has done some fascinating research reading feminist stories to young children. From her research, it isn't clear whether these tales—take *Oliver Button is a Sissy* (De Paola, 1979) for example—actually convey a feminist message (characters taking on non-traditional gender roles) or simply reify traditional gender roles (Davies, 2003, p. 50). This center activity is a chance for your students to interpret some emancipatory picture books and for the whole class to conduct research on these interpretations.

Materials for Learning Center Extension

- Emancipatory picture books (see sidebar)
- Table 10.3.2, Learning Center Directions
- Analyzing Picture Book Characters (see Table 10.3.3)
- Collection box for student work

Taking Action:

One way to take action after this invitation is to have students engage in research to understand how their family and friends view the ways particular characters are depicted in Fairy Tales.

- Students can survey adults (teachers, parents, and friends) about how women are depicted in fairy tales. The survey might include the following question: Tell me three words that describe each of these characters: Cinderella, Red Riding Hood, and Grandma (in Little Red Riding Hood).
- When students have interviewed three people each, compile the results as a class, looking for trends.
- What did the students learn from the survey?

> **Emancipatory Picture Book Suggestions**
>
> - *Oliver Button is a Sissy* (De Paola, 1979)
> - *Max* (Isadora, 1984)
> - *Amazing Grace* (Hoffman, 1991)
> - *Piggybook* (Browne, 1990)

TABLE 10.3.2
Learning Center Directions

Picture Books with an Edge

1. Read one of the books at this center by yourself.

    Fill out the *Analyzing Picture Book Characters* sheet, being as honest as you can.

    When you are finished, put the sheet in the collection box.

2. Your teacher will ask a group of students to tally up the responses on a big chart so everyone can see the variety of responses.

    After the chart is up at this center, return here with two friends.

    Study the chart closely and write up a group statement that tells the following:

    What items on the chart surprised your group?

    What are the reasons your group was surprised?

    Put your statement up on a board at the center and share your statements at a class meeting.

TABLE 10.3.3

Analyzing Picture Book Characters

Name:	
Book:	
Date:	

The most prominent male character:	Five adjectives that describe this character:
The most prominent female character:	Five adjectives that describe this character:
Which character did you like best in this book?	What are your reasons for this choice?
Which character did you like least in this book?	What are your reasons for this choice?

If you could change on thing about this book, what would you change and why would you change it?

Happy Holidays for Whom?

Holidays are a time when companies know that many of us will be buying presents for our friends and family. It is very revealing to interrogate how holiday ads are constructed and how they try to position both the consumers and gift recipients.

Materials
▪ Advertisements from magazines, newspapers, and junk-mail fliers that feature a particular holiday when people are likely to buy presents for others
▪ Multiple copies of the "Holiday Ad Inquiry" handout (Table 10.4.1)

Getting Started
1. You and your students bring in advertisements from magazines, newspapers, and junk-mail fliers that feature a specific holiday like Christmas, Easter, Valentine's Day, or Father's Day. Collect enough ads for groups of four to have at least eight ads each.
2. Invite students to look through these advertisements and to note who is featured and what is being sold; allow at least 15 minutes.
3. In addition, students can answer the following questions about ads that particularly interest them:
   • Who is the intended consumer (i.e., buyer)?
   • How does this ad position the buyer are well as the recipient of the gift?
   • What do you think the advertiser believes to have created this ad in this particular way?
   • Are any stereotypes are being perpetuated? If so, which ones?

The "Holiday Ad Inquiry" handout will help students keep track of their research.

4. A variation on this center is to use gift bags—the kind given for birthdays—in lieu of advertisements, as it is interesting to explore how girls are positioned by Miss Piggy or Barbie bags and how boys are positioned when their gift is given in a superhero or Kermit bag. Each group needs one or two bags.

TABLE 10.4.1
Holiday Ad Inquiry

Holiday:

Store that produced the ad:

Description of items for sale and the way they are placed on the page	Who is the intended consumer (buyer)?	How does this ad position the buyer and the recipient of the gift?	What does the advertiser believe to have created this ad?	What, if any, stereotypes are being perpetuated?

Learning Center Extension: *Messages in Halloween Costumes*

Halloween costume ads are far from being innocent, as they display an array of costumes to purchase—many geared specifically to boys or girls. This center allows students to explore what is in and out for Halloween as well as to understand the messages that costumes can convey.

Materials for Learning Center Extension

▌ Halloween costume ads collected by you and your students
▌ A piece of butcher paper used as a graffiti board
▌ Table 10.4.2, Learning Center Directions

Taking Action

There are many ways your students may want to take action following this invitation. One example is to have students interview members of the recipient audience for holiday ads (i.e., fathers for Father's Day) to see what it is that they might really want for a present. Students then compare these data with those generated from the advertisements they examined. There is almost always a wide discrepancy. As an example, in one class most of the students' mothers said they wanted a hug for Mother's Day, yet the bulk of the advertisements focused on beauty products and cosmetics of one kind or another. On a different note, students might research how holidays like Mother's Day, Father's Day, and Valentine's Day actually got started—making special note of things that surprised them. They can decide what information they learned from their research is important enough to share with others and how best to present their findings.

Creating Critical
Classrooms

TABLE 10.4.2
Learning Center Directions

Messages in Halloween Costumes

1. With a partner, spend about 15 minutes examining and discussing the Halloween costume ads at this center. What did you notice about the ads? Jot your observations down on the graffiti board.

2. Talk about three of the following questions that you and your partner have not yet discussed.

   - How are girls, or females, positioned in the costume ads?
   - How about boys, or men?
   - According to the ad, what can girls be for Halloween? How about boys?
   - How are different age groups positioned in the ads?
   - What differences or similarities do you notice about costumes for toddlers, children, teens, and adults?
   - What do you notice about the ethnicities of the models?
   - Are any ethnic groups left out of the ads?
   - If so, who is left out, and why do you think this happened?

3. **Reflection:** What is in and out this Halloween? If you were asked to report to the local business community about what you discovered about Halloween ads, what would you say?

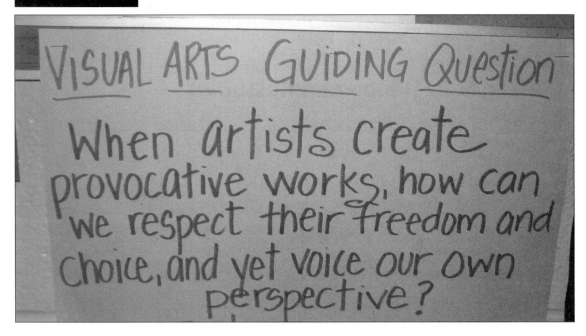

■Poster by Daphne Draa, Art Teacher, Center for Inquiry

Honing Your Visual Literacy

Although Kress and van Leeuwen (1996) would be the first to admit that we have much to learn about how cultures read and make sense of visual images, their initial framework can be used as a starting point for honing our own and our students' knowledge of visual literacy.

Materials

- One copy per student of the handout "Areas of a Canvas" (Table 10.5.1)
- Two copies per student of the handout "Analyzing a Canvas" (Table 10.5.2)
- Two pieces of student- or teacher-generated art (Figures 10.5.1 and 10.5.2). As an alternative, any two pieces of art can be used, including poster art or photography.

Getting Started

1. Have students read through the handout titled "Areas of a Canvas" (Table 10.5.1). Answer any questions they might have.
2. Distribute the handout. "Analyzing a Canvas" (Table 10.5.2). Then, using a piece of student-generated art, either (a) invite students to try their hand at analyzing a piece of art; or (b) walk students through the different areas of a canvas and how they might be read. For example, in the piece of student art titled "School Protest" (Figure 10.5.1) the top left and right quadrants in the upper half of the picture feature protesters who are, one supposes, leading the way for others to follow. Although the placards are not all that readable, if one looks closely, the topmost placard reads "Save Our Schools." These upper quadrants of a canvas represent the *ideal*. In the context of this

picture where all of the figures seem to be following the lead of the figures depicted in the upper quadrants, protesting is positioned as something good. The bottom quadrants of a canvas represent the *real*. The feet of the protesters anchor them to the ground. They are grounded in the real. The group of protesters forms one dominant *vector* that runs from the bottom left quadrant (*here and now, real*) to the top right quadrant (*new, ideal*). The *gaze* of the characters is off the page (we see only the backs of their heads), yet we assume they are either looking at the backs of their fellow protesters or upward toward the top right quadrant (some *new, ideal* state of being). The center or *focus* of the picture seems to be on the protest itself. The *colors*, though not shown, are muted with lots of off-greens and darker colors all of the same tonality, making the scene seem serious.

3. To help students gain further confidence in their ability to analyze and read visual works, invite them to work with a partner and use Table 10.5.1 and Table 10.5.2 to read a second student-generated piece of art. (This could be a piece of student art from your own classroom or the "Art Wars" poster [Figure 10.5.2] that a student in one of our classes created.)

4. Have students share the data they recorded on their graphic organizer as well as their interpretation of what this data means.

5. As a culminating experience ask students to take a minute to use the framework described on the handout "Areas of a canvas" to talk about how the authors of either of the pieces of art they have analyzed might have visually designed their work to make their messages even clearer to their intended audiences.

TABLE 10.5.1
Areas of a Canvas

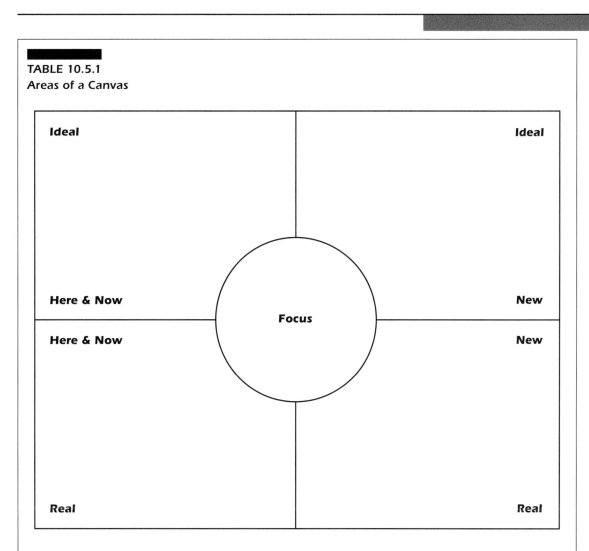

Top & Bottom. The top of a picture is "the ideal;" the bottom, "the real."

Left & Right. The left side of the picture is "the here and now;" or given; the right side, "the new."

Center. Note where your eye falls when you first look at a picture. The center of the picture provides a focus.

Vectors. Vectors are lines or alignments in a picture that carry your eye up, down, or sideways in a picture. Typically they go from "the real" to "the ideal" or from "the here and now" to "the new." They may go, however, go diagonally crossing quadrants in interesting ways.

Colors. Colors are often used to set the mood. The use of bright colors suggest something positive or hopeful while the use of dark colors suggest dreariness and doom. Pastel colors are calming and often are used to suggest innocence.

Gaze. In pictures or photographs containing characters, the gaze is often important as the direction of the gaze creates a vector that moves the eye from one point in the picture to another. A gaze upward and off the page may suggest the future (an idealized perfect state) and be read a hopeful. A gaze downward anchors the picture in "the real" or here and now.

Exaggeration. Pay particular attention to exaggeration; items, like hands, that are drawn out of proportion to the rest of the figure or arms that are too skinny for the body depicted. Extra large hands may suggest the importance of hard labor and work, for example. Skinny arms may suggest idleness or helplessness.

TABLE 10.5.2

Analyzing a Canvas

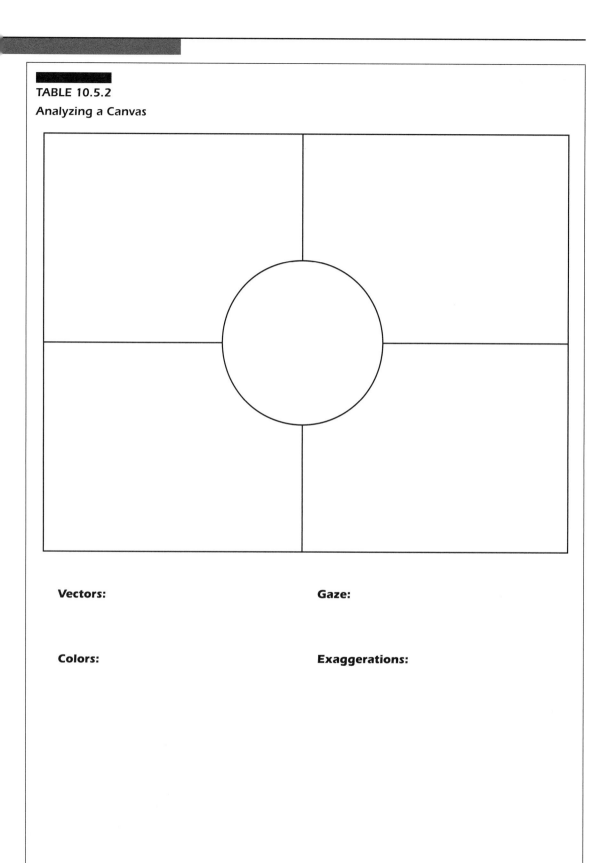

Vectors: **Gaze:**

Colors: **Exaggerations:**

FIGURE 10.5.1
School Protest. Artwork by Mitzi Lewison.

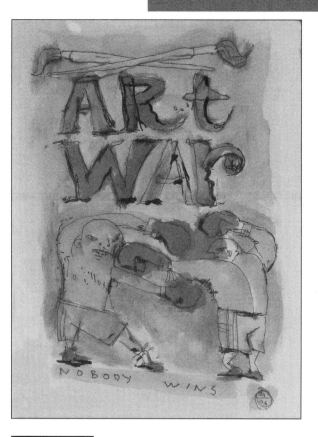

FIGURE 10.5.2
Art Wars. Artwork by Scott McDonald.

Learning Center Extension: *Understanding Graphic Design*

Graphic designers, such as those hired by big ad agencies, know how to produce graphic images that sell products and attract consumers. No item in an effective advertisement is random; all have intent. This center invites students to apply what they know about visual literacy to analyze advertisements.

Materials for Learning Center Extension

- A collection of full-page advertisement from various magazines or any collection of visual images purposefully put together to represent a product or institution
- A single copy of the handout "Areas of a Canvas"
- Multiple copies of the handout "Analyzing a Canvas"
- Manila folder labeled "Analyzed Designs"

Taking Action

Identify some local, national, or global cause you feel strongly about— for example, putting an end to bullying, implementing universal health care, or ending world hunger. Using what you know about visual literacy, design a poster and display it publicly. One week later take the poster down, but stay and survey people who come by. Find out if they walked past this area last week, if they saw a poster, and what they remember about it. Use this information to design a more effective poster.

TABLE 10.5.3
Learning Center Directions

Understanding Graphic Design

1. Together with a partner, try your hand at analyzing one of the advertisements at this center. Using the handout "Areas of a canvas" as a reference, record what information is located in particular quadrants of the advertisement. Record this information on your worksheet "Analyzing a Canvas."

2. After analyzing and interpreting the data you collected, use the back of your worksheet to write out the conclusion you and your partner reached as to what the advertisement is saying and how you see the design working. (Leave your worksheet in the manila folder for others to enjoy).

3. **Reflection:** Check the manila folder titled "Analyzed Designs" to see if other students came to the same conclusions you did. Talk about differences and what you make of them.

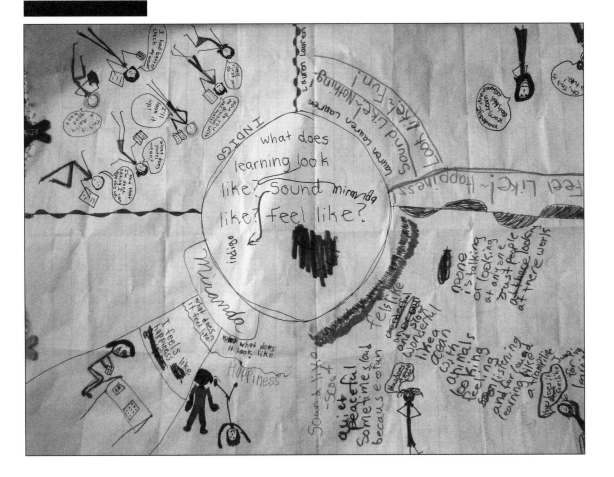

Keeping the Conversation Going

It is important to keep visible records of significant classroom conversations. Vasquez (2006) uses the walls in her classroom to create a **learning wall** (Figures 10.6.1 and 10.6.2) to post artifacts of the critical conversations that students have throughout the school year. A learning wall makes curriculum visible to everyone including children, fellow teachers, administrators, and parents. Heffernan (2004, p. 32) calls this record of classroom conversations **a history trail** and notes that in addition to being a record of conversations, "the physical representation of key conversations in classroom life later becomes a resource for student writers." Because one of the goals of a critical classroom is to support the development of reflexivity, this invitation operates as an audit trail that students and teachers can use in reflecting back on curriculum, synthesizing engagements for purposes of seeing a larger whole, and interrogating growth that has and has not taken place in becoming critically literate.

> **Possible Artifacts for Learning Wall**
>
> ∎ A photocopy of one of the pages of a children's book that was read and discussed along with a quote that captures the conversation
> ∎ A piece of writing that a child had produced
> ∎ A picture of an activity in which the class had engaged
> ∎ Newspaper articles that led to extended conversations
> ∎ Letters sent and received as part of, for example, various social action projects

Materials
∎ A large wall covered with colored butcher paper
∎ Access to a color copy machine
∎ Colored paper, yarn, and other assorted materials

Getting Started
1. After a classroom conversation about an important topic, students decide how to best represent this event on the learning wall (see sidebar).

FIGURE 10.6.1
Learning wall, Alaskan Workshop.

2. It is a good idea to hold regular class meetings so students can decide what should be added to the learning wall for the week.
3. Vasquez (2006) labels certain ideas "hot topics" and uses yarn to show how various curricular engagements relate to each other as well as how this topic is revisited over and over again throughout the year (Figure 10.6.2).
4. When visitors come into to the classroom, students can walk and talk them through the curriculum by using the learning wall as a reference.
5. The wall itself becomes a resource for generating new topics of study and inquiry.
6. The wall also supports students' reflecting on and seeing the connections between and among the various elements of the curriculum.

FIGURE 10.6.2
Learning wall, Vasquez Classroom.

Learning Center Extension: *Walking Journals*

Walking journals are another way to keep important conversations going in your classroom. Each journal takes up a critical issue that has been the topic of discussions with your students. One of the benefits in using walking journals as a regular feature in your classroom is that these journals can be created to reflect topics of immediate classroom interest. It works best if there are several journals circulating at once.

Materials for Learning Center Extension

■ Walking journals are created by stapling 8½ × 11 sheets of paper together or by buying commercially available journals.

■ Paste in a provocative article from the newspaper (or another text or quote that fits with your curriculum) in the front of the journal. Or, instead of starting with a published text, students with strong opinions on a subject can make the first entry in the walking journal.

■ Give each journal a title (affixed to the outside cover), and tape the directions for using walking journals in the opening end pages of the journal itself (Table 10.6.1).

■ Table 10.6.1, Learning Center Directions

TABLE 10.6.1
Learning Center Directions

Directions for Walking Journals

This is a walking journal. Someone has already put something at the front of this journal. Now it is your turn.

1. Respond to the original entry as well as any of the entries that others have made. Make sure you remember to date and sign your entry.

2. It is possible that one of the entries might make you think of something else. It is okay to write about that, give an example of some point that someone else has made, or even go off in a new direction.

3. **Reflection:** What new ideas did you come away with after reading and responding?

Keep these journals walking! It is one way that we can be sure the issues that are important to us are being discussed.

FIGURE 10.6.3

Taking Action

Kids can start important conversations in their homes or in the community about the issues in walking journals:

▮ Take home a walking journal and give it to your parents, another adult you know, or a friend so they can respond to the issue.
▮ After the person has responded in writing, read his or her response and start a conversation, exploring how your ideas are similar or different.
▮ Make sure you remember to bring the journal back the next day.

■Artwork by Indigo Ensign, Center for Inquiry

Kids at the Mall

Local issues get a lot of attention in local newspapers and on local television news shows, but they rarely become curricular topics in schools. Instead of building curriculum from the questions and concerns of children, it is more often delivered as content in a vacuum. Students learn about a particular topic because it is included in the next chapter of the textbook. This invitation shows how local issues can serve as a starting point for inquiry-based curriculum with a critical perspective. In this case, kids are invited to pursue questions of equity relating to new rules that have been adopted at various malls, but any local issue will work.

Materials
❙ Assorted news articles focusing on mall rules. You can find articles by going to Google and putting in *malls* and *rules* as the search terms. Some sample articles and websites are included in Table 10.7.1.

Getting Started
1. Divide students into groups of three to five, depending on how many articles you have available.
2. Distribute a different article to each group, and ask students to read their article aloud together and be prepared to share it with the class in 10 minutes.
3. Each group presents what they see as the major points of their article.
4. Involve the whole class in a discussion about any patterns or anomalies they noticed among the various group reports.
5. Distribute copies of the "New rules at the mall" data sheet (Table 10.7.2) to students, and ask them to read it and talk

in their groups about the various perspectives they can see. They might think about questions like the following:

- How do these views support or contradict each other?
- How are the adults hearing or not hearing the teens' issues?
- How can you tell who has power?
- How can you tell who does not?

6. Invite students to dramatize and expand the various perspectives represented. For example, what else might a mall executive, teenager, or parent say?

7. As a culminating activity have groups share what they see as the major systems of meaning (e.g., premises, belief systems, value systems) that appear to be operating in these news stories. The students can reflect on issues such as the following:

- Why do different people have such different opinions on mall rules?
- What does this suggest about some adults' views of teenagers?

TABLE 10.7.1

Internet Articles about Rules at Malls

Article and Source Information

Mall won't allow teens without parents (n.d.). KVOA News 4, Tucson, AZ. Retrieved September 24, 2006, from http://www.kvoa.com/Glo bal/
story.asp?S=3236395&nav= menu216_3_6

Mall bans teens without parents (2005, April 20). CBS5.com, San Francisco, Oakland, San Jose, CA. Retrieved September 24, 2006, from http://cbs5.com/ watercoo ler/watercooler_story_110072833.html

Mall to kids: Gotta shop with Mom and Pop (n.d.). Nick's News Weekly Stories. Retrieved September 24, 2006, from http://www.nick.com/all_nick/tv_sup ersites/nick_news/stories_weekly.jhtml?pollId=
320010265&wstory=2

Carlile, J. (2005). *Targeting badly behaved Britons.* MSNBC Alert. Retrieved September 24, 2006, from http://www.msnbc.msn.com/id/7897532/

Canning, A. (2004). *Cincinnati Mills enforces code of conduct.* WCPO.com. Retrieved September 24, 2006, from http://www.wcpo.com/news/2004/local/08/24/mills.html

Russell, J. (2005). *At regional malls, a teen test.* Boston.com News. Retrieved September 24, 2006, from http://www.boston.com/ne ws/local/articles/2005/09/11/
at_regional_malls_a_teen_test/

Mall deals with young patrons differently (2005, 04/29). Rockingham News. Retrieved September 24, 2006, from http://www.seacoastonline.com/ 2005news/rock/04292005/news/39885.htm

TABLE 10.7.2

New Rules at the Mall

In April 2005, managers of the Pheasant Lane Mall in Nashua, New Hampshire issued an edict that barred unaccompanied shoppers under the age of 16. Articles in the New Hampshire Sunday News (April 24) quoted a mall executive and a parent who were interviewed for stories about the new ruling:

Speaker or Source	Quote
Simon Group executive	"It's not that we don't want the teens to come in. We want the parents to come in with them, because we are here to conduct commerce. That is our purpose for being here. It's being disorderly and disruptive. It's using foul language. It's yelling from the top level to the bottom. It's throwing things. People have felt intimidated. It does not make for a pleasant shopping environment."
Parent	"Where are they gonna go now, the street corner? They've got really no place else to go if they want to hang out with friends. You can only go bowling or to the movies so many times. I don't think this if fair. There are really good kids. They may be loud sometimes, but they just want a place to hang out."

Teenagers who were interviewed echoed the sentiment of needing a space to hang out with friends. One talked about the limited access kids have to places where money is no object and they can just be:

15-year-old teen	"We hang out at the bowling alley sometimes—if no one's paying attention. But eventually they ask us to leave because we don't spend a lot of money."

Another hypothesized that some adults didn't approve of the way she and her friends dress:

17-year-old girl	"For some reason they think we're gonna be bad people because of how we look. I mean, if I go into Abercrombie and Fitch, they will ask me to leave. It doesn't matter—people can be wearing anything at the mall and still be hassled over it. And there's the whole thing of racial profiling. You can't start talking about gangs without hassling Hispanic and black kids more than everyone else. I'm not saying that they are all in gangs, but I'm saying that's how some people think. That's how ridiculous the whole thing is."
Editorial, *Union Leader*, April 24, 2005	Tossing the teens out of the mall into … what? "Had more children behaved themselves, executives at Pheasant Lane Mall in Nashua would not have felt the need to require minors under the age of 16 to be accompanied by a parent. Malls are businesses, not public play areas …. It would appear that there is a high demand in Nashua for a safe, teen-oriented hangout. The first people to create one that teens will pay to frequent probably could make a comfortable living filling that void in the marketplace."

Learning Center Extension: *Mall Survey*

This center provides an opportunity for students to extend their inquiry into rules at malls (or the local issue you are studying) through the use of surveys. They are invited to survey kids about their self-reported mall behaviors and survey adults from various demographic groups about their opinions about "kids at the mall."

Materials for Learning Center Extension

- "New rules at the mall" (Table 10.7.2)
- Table 10.7.3, Learning Center Directions
- Multiple copies of the "Mall survey for kids" (Table 10.7.4) or students can make their own
- Multiple copies of the "Mall survey for adults" (Table 10.7.5) or students can make their own

TABLE 10.7.3
Learning Center Directions

Kids at the Mall

1. With a friend, reread "New Rules at the Mall."

2. Think of questions you could ask other kids to find out if some of the adult complaints about kids at the mall have any truth?

3. Construct a survey instrument. The "Mall survey for kids" is an example. If you are having trouble thinking of questions, here are a few suggestions:

   - How often do you go to the mall?
   - Does anyone go with you? If yes, who?
   - Estimate what percentage of time at the mall you are buying things and what percentage are you hanging out.

Come up with at least five questions.

4. Practice giving the survey by a role play with your friend. One of you takes the role of the interviewer (who take notes on the responses to your questions), and the other is the interviewee (the person answering the questions). Switch roles.

5. Find five kids from other classrooms or your neighborhood to take the survey. Make sure you keep track of the name of each person you interview and take notes on each response.

6. When you have completed five interviews, look across the responses and write a sentence that summarizes your findings for each question.

7. Present your summaries to the class. Discuss how your research relates to the situation at the Nashua Mall.

8. **Extension:** As an out-of-school activity create one or two interview questions for adults to find out their opinions about kids at the mall. It might be something like, "Should kids be allowed to go the mall without an adult?" Interview five adults and take notes. You can use the "Mall Survey for Adults" as an example of a way to keep track of who you interview and each person's responses. To stretch your survey even further, try to find at least one person to interview in each demographic category listed on the "Mall Survey for Adults." How do your findings support or challenge what you discovered from interviewing other kids? How do they relate to the data sheet about the mall in Nashua, New Hampshire?

9. **Reflection:** From the data you have collected, how do you think malls should treat kids? What would it take to make this happen?

TABLE 10.7.4
Mall Survey for Kids

	Question #1:	Question #2:	Question #3:	Question #4:	Question #5:
Kids Interviewed (First name and age)	Answers				
1.					
2.					
3.					
4.					
5.					

TABLE 10.7.5
Mall Survey for Adults

Question:	
Demographic Group	**Opinions**
Parents of teens	
Parents of young children	
People who do not have kids	
People who own or work in stores in mall	
Mall owners or executives	

Taking Action

Students might decide to get involved with mall issues in their own community if they discuss the following questions:

- What social action might be taken to get the mall rules changed? Who needs to take this action?
- What social action might be taken to end the bad behavior of some kids at the mall? Who needs to take this action?

Lingering in Text

This invitation supports students in revisiting previously read texts and in developing a set of critical questions for interrogating texts. "Chart-a-Conversation" (adapted from Smith, 1996) allows students to experience, firsthand, the power of lingering conversations around particular texts. Because of the way chart a conversation has been designed, students end up with a visible record of the ideas they generated as well as how conversations with others enhanced their comprehension and understanding of the text. Sumara (2002) argues that part of taking on a critical stance is savoring the text by taking the time to thoughtfully linger in text.

Materials

▌ A very simple children's book such as *Where the Wild Things Are* (Sendak, 1963). Although any text might be selected, using *Where the Wild Thing Are* demonstrates how generative this strategy is even when using books that use very few words.

▌ "Chart-a-Conversation" handout (Table 10.8.1)

Getting Started

1. Introduce this invitation to students by reading aloud *Where the Wild Things Are* or any other simple picture book.

2. After the oral reading of the book you selected, ask students to get into groups of three to complete one "Chart-a-Conversation" graphic organizer per group, with one student acting as scribe. Ask students to discuss the book in groups, writing responses to things they liked about the book in the "Like" column, things they disliked in the "Dislike" column; patterns they notice in the "Patterns" column (e.g., the wordless pages in the middle of

the book, the fact the book started and ended with food, repetitious phrasing); and problems they have with the book in the "Problems" column (e.g., some people dislike the fact that food is used as punishment; some fundamental Christian groups have tried to get this book banned as they see the story as encouraging children not to listen to their parents; some are bothered by the fact that it was a little boy acting up rather than a little girl, thus perpetuating a common stereotype).

3. Once student groups have at least one response—and hopefully more—in each column, come together as a class so groups can share responses. Before sharing, ask each group to select a new scribe and ask him or her to use a writing instrument that is different from the writing instrument that the first scribe used. So, if the first scribe used a pencil, the second could use a pen, for example. A good way to share is to have each group report just one response and to keep rotating through the groups until all of the ideas in a column have been talked about. The new scribe's responsibility is to record all the responses that other groups say they "Like" that their group did not write on their graphic organizer. Then move to the other columns of "Dislike," "Patterns," and "Problems."

4. When everyone has shared and the class has worked its way through the columns, ask students to go back to talking about the book in their small groups, only this time to talk about at least one of the new ideas that they got from listening to what other groups had on their papers. These will be easily identified as they have been written with a different writing instrument. As groups are discussing, sit in for a few minutes on each conversation to hear what students have elected to talk about during this second discussion period.

5. As an after-the-fact activity ask students to write an individual reflective piece in their journals about what they learned about reading comprehension, extended conversations around books, or lingering in text. They can share their journal entries in their small groups or at a class meeting.

TABLE 10.8.1

Chart-a-Conversation

Book:		Date:	
Group Members:			
Like	Dislike	Patterns	Problems

Learning Center Extension: *Writing in the Margins*

As adults, we often read books more than one time and write notes in the margins. It is always a revelation to find out how brilliant or clueless we were when we last read the book. This center activity gives students a chance to do some margin writing of their own.

Learning Center Materials

▮ Three (or more) short stories or essays that you have photo-copied and bound. It is good to pick materials that your students are familiar with, possibly texts you have read aloud or ones that relate to a current theme cycle.

▮ Different colored pens

▮ Table 10.8.2, Learning Center Directions

Taking Action

When a controversy arises in your community, print out articles about the controversy from the local newspaper. Students can respond by lingering in text or writing in the margins. Students who feel strongly about the issue one way or another can work together and decide how to make their voices and perspectives heard, either by other students at school or by members of the community.

TABLE 10.8.2
Learning Center Directions

Writing in the Margins

1. Choose one of the three stories, or essays, and a colored pen to write comments.

2. If you are the first person at the center to read a story, you will be the first person to write comments and responses to the text in the margins. You can write your initials next to each of your comments.

3. If someone has already read the story you decided to read, you do the same activity as in #2 with a different colored pen, but you have the choice of the following:

   - Responding to the text
   - Responding to someone else's margin response
   - Responding to both

4. You will probably want to check back at the center occasionally to see if anyone has responded to your comments.

5. **_Reflection:_** As you read through what your classmates wrote in the margins, which ideas surprised you the most? Which helped you understand the story or essay in a new way? Let the writer know.

Motivated Signs

Everything in a picture book—be it a phrase, a particular word choice, a picture, or the use of color—is assumed to be motivated, or done purposefully. At this invitation, students are invited to read *Into the Forest* (Browne, 2004) and analyze the words, pictures, and symbols that Browne uses. *Into the Forest* is Anthony Browne's version of "Little Red Riding Hood." This story begins with a young boy hearing thunder and lightning during the night. When he awakens the next morning, his father is missing. Whether what he actually hears is thunder and lightning or his parents squabbling is up for debate. Nonetheless, whichever interpretation is chosen, a reader is likely to read these signs as ominous, and, in this fashion, Browne sets the reader up by conjuring up images of absent parents and unhappy childhoods. Grandmother is, of course, sick, so the boy is sent to take goodies to her house. On the way he meets several characters from children's books, and it is left to the reader to determine the underlying meaning of each interaction.

Materials

- Multiple copies of *Into the Forest*—enough so groups of four each have a book
- "Motivated signs" handout (Table 10.9.1)

Getting Started

1. Discuss with the class how authors and illustrators use words, pictures, color, and symbols for specific purposes. Explain that words, pictures, and symbols are all called *signs*. Signs in books are similar to road signs, but instead of giving us directions they tell us what the author was trying to get across to readers.

2. In groups of four, have each group examine the cover of the book, *Into the Forest*. Ask the students the following questions, which should lead to a lively class discussion about the signs Browne chose for the book cover:
   - What do you notice about words, pictures, and symbols on the cover?
   - What are some reasons that Anthony Browne might have chosen these signs for the book cover?
3. Ask the class to read the book slowly in their small groups, paying attention to signs. At any time they can stop reading and talk about the signs.
4. After students have finished reading, they decide on the five most important signs in the book and fill out one "Motivated signs" graphic organizer per group.
5. After the students have completed the "Motivated signs" graphic organizer, have a grand conversation (Peterson & Eeds, 1999) about the different perspectives and reasons for choosing a particular sign as the most important. You might want to conduct this as a debate.

TABLE 10.9.1
Motivated Signs

| Name of Book: | | |
| Team Members: | | |

Write or draw what your team sees as the five most important *signs* in the book (one in each box below).	Why did you think this sign was important?	How do you think the author wanted you to read this *sign*?

When you are finished, circle the sign your group thinks is the most important in the book.

Learning Center Extension: *The Signs of Anthony Browne*

This center gives students a chance to further investigate the intriguing way Browne uses signs in his books. Browne is especially interesting to study because his illustrations are influenced by the surrealist movement (specifically Magritte), Salvador Dali, comic books, painters who used strong lighting effects, and fellow author–illustrator Chris Van Allsburg (Booktrust, 2006, http://www.booktrusted.co.uk/education/browne/browne.html).

Materials for Learning Center Extension

- A variety of books by Browne—at least four different titles (see sidebar)
- A large poster with the title "The Signs of Anthony Browne"
- Markers
- Table 10.9.2, Learning Center Directions

Taking Action

Many of Browne's books have important social themes and also very imaginative illustrations with lots of small signs—some almost hidden—that add layers of meaning to his books. Students can create some socially conscious signs for the classroom or school.

Creating Critical Classrooms

TABLE 10.9.2
Learning Center Directions

The Signs of Anthony Browne

Anthony Browne is an author-illustrator who has a unique way of using words, pictures, color, and symbols for specific purposes.

These words, pictures, and symbols are all called *signs*.

Signs in books are similar to road signs, but instead of giving us directions, they tell us what the author was trying to get across to readers.

1. Read two of Browne's books with a partner, paying special attention to the signs he uses.

2. After you finish each book, individually write or draw what you see as the three most important signs in the book. **Don't show your partner your signs.**

3. After you have finished the two books and jotted down important signs, share your work with your partner.

   - On what important signs did you and your partner agree?
   - Which were different?
   - Find out why your partner chose different signs than you did.
   - Did you notice any signs that Browne used in more than one book?

4. On the poster at this center called "The Signs of Anthony Browne," draw or write any insights you have about Browne and his signs.

5. **Reflection:** With your partner, look around the classroom and see if you can agree on the three most important signs in the room. Why did you choose these three? Share your choices at the next class meeting.

Multiple Perspectives

An old saying reminds us that there are two sides to every story. But how many times have we read something in a book or in the newspaper and assumed that whatever it was saying must be true? This invitation invites participants to consider the motives that might be driving any text.

Materials

■ Books with different perspectives on a particular topic. Make sure that you do not represent only your personal perspective or what might be seen as politically correct. For example, war and weapons are frequent topics in the news and many people have strong opinions about them. Although children are hearing much about war and weapons, they might not realize that there are many different views regarding these topics. To make the idea of multiple perspectives more transparent, we recommend using both fiction and non-fiction (see Table 10.10.1).

■ Large sheets of butcher paper—one for each group of four to five students)

Getting Started

1. Divide students into work groups, and give each group some markers and a sheet of butcher paper to serve as a graffiti board.
2. Read aloud the first book you have chosen. In this example, we use *Feathers and Fools* (Fox, 1989), a story about two groups of animals that collect weapons for protection from each other but that all end up dead when the weapons finally get used.
3. Ask students to jot down their thoughts about what the author of this book thinks about war and weapons.

TABLE 10.10.1
Multiple-Perspectives Text Set: Books about War

Book Title	Author
Alpha, Bravo, Charlie: The Military Alphabet	Demarest (2005)[a]
Battle	Holmes (1995)[a]
Feathers and Fools	Fox (1989)
Gleam and Glow	Bunting (2001)
Hiroshima No Pika	Maruki (1980)
Hiroshima: The Story of the First Atomic Bomb	Lawton (2004)[a]
Sadako and the Thousand Paper Cranes	Coerr (1977)
The Butter Battle Book	Seuss (1984)
The Cello of Mr. O	Cutler (1999)

[a] Denotes a nonfiction book.

4. After students have had about five minutes to write, they can share their responses with the whole class.

5. Read aloud a few short sections from the second book. In this example, we use *Battle* (Holmes, 1995), a nonfiction book that shows various weapons people have used through history to protect themselves or to wage war on others. Ask students to write about how the author of this book views war and weapons.

6. As a whole class, have students do the following:
   - Share responses that compare or contrast the perspectives of the two books
   - Discuss how it is possible for people to have such diverse opinions on the same issue
   - Think of issues in their community that people see differently

Learning Center Extension: *Multiple Perspectives in the News*
It is relatively easy to use Internet search engines to discover how different reporters talk about the same event. Choose any event where some type of controversy has ensued.

Materials for Learning Center Extension
- Table 10.10.2, Learning Center Directions
- Here, we use two sports stories that describe the same event from different perspectives. The event was a basketball game between the Indianapolis Pacers and the Chicago Bulls that ended in a brawl (Tables 10.10.3 and 10.10.4).

TABLE 10.10.2
Learning Center Directions

Multiple Perspectives in the News

With a friend, read the two articles at the center and consider the following questions:

1. What is the main issue in these two articles and what are the different viewpoints?

2. What instances of language can you find that might show which side a particular author supported?

3. Is either piece neutral (straight actual reporting)? How can you tell?

4. On what points do the authors seem to be in agreement?

5. On what points do they disagree?

6. **Reflection:** Is it possible to be neutral when telling others about an event? Or is what we see always influenced by what we bring to the situation?

TABLE 10.10.3
Story from Detroit Pistons' perspective

Malice at Palace
By Michael Rosenberg

Go away, Ron Artest. Go far, far away.

Last week, you were an amusing circus act.

For much of Friday night, you were the best player in the building.

And then you were something beyond Idiot and several miles past Nuts.

And now you need to disappear—not for a week, not for a month, and not for any amount of time that can be defined in conventional basketball terms. We're not measuring this in games missed. It goes beyond that.

An intense regular-season game morphed into one of the ugliest nights in sports history Friday, and it's all because of Artest, the Pacers forward. Without him, there is no riot at the Pistons-Pacers game. Period.

Let's replay what happened: Artest committed a hard foul on Ben Wallace, which happens. Wallace retaliated with a shove to Artest's face, which was over the top, but it happens.

Artest went to lie down on the scorer's table like a sunbather and briefly grabbed a headset from the Pacers' broadcast team—which doesn't happen, but wasn't a huge deal. As other players scuffled, a fan threw a water bottle at Artest's head.

That was stupid and irresponsible—BUT IT HAPPENS. It shouldn't, but it does. And the expected level of decorum for players and coaches is higher than it is for fans.

Then Artest jumped up and ran into the stands with fists flying. He got there so fast, he almost knocked me over before I knew he was there.

Stupid me, I was watching the court.

Then Pacers Jermaine O'Neal, Eddie Gill and Stephen Jackson jumped into the stands. Pistons broadcaster Rick Mahorn, trying to play peacemaker, followed. It was hard to tell who was trying to break up fights and who was trying to start one. Fans screamed, "I punched Artest!" Or, if they were on the receiving end, "He hit me! He hit me!"

The next thing you knew, Artest coldcocked somebody, and O'Neal was said to have done the same, and chairs flew at the Pacers.

And a lot of it was inexcusable. But none of it would have happened if Artest had done what athletes are trained to do forever: Ignore the fans.

You never, ever, EVER run into the stands. And if you dispute that, please tell me one time, just when, when a situation got better when a player bolted into the crowd.

As Palace president Tom Wilson said, "we're paid a lot of money" to maintain poise in that situation.

"I don't know that there was a security failure," Wilson said.

Wrong. Somebody let Artest into the building.

That can't happen for a long time, and it won't. Expect the longest suspension in NBA history. And expect police charges, although none was filed Friday.

What Artest did has nothing to do with sports, nothing to do with the Pacers–Pistons rivalry and very little to do with the water bottle. He has teetered on the wall between sanity and insanity for a while, and Friday he fell on the wrong side. No, not fell. Jumped.

This is obviously a man in need of some serious help. Last week, when he asked coach Rick Carlisle for some time off to promote his CD, he was an amusing sideshow. There goes Ron-Ron again. Ha-ha.

And Friday, he played brilliantly. He was the reason the Pacers won, 97–82. Then he was the reason the game ended with 45.9 seconds left.

Over the loudspeakers, fans were asked to leave the Palace. Then, and only then, did the clock wind down from 45.9. It was way, way, way too late.

Finally, long after the game was officially over, the Pacers' team bus departed the parking lot.

It moved past the Pistons' cars, all of which were running, so that the Detroit players could make a quick exit. (None spoke to the media.)

Rain fell on the Palace parking lot. And as the bus wedged between a dozen or more police cars and a few ambulances, this much was clear: Ron Artest was in the wrong vehicle.

Source: Rosenberg (2004). Reprinted with permission.

TABLE 10.10.4

Story from Indianapolis Pacers' perspective

Players' Union Blames Refs, Security in Appeal

By Tracy Dodds

The NBA Players Association filed the expected appeal Tuesday, specifically asking that arbitrator Roger Kaplan review the suspensions made by NBA commissioner David Stern after the brawl in the final minute of the Indiana Pacers' game at Detroit on Friday.

Although the season-long suspension of Pacers forward Ron Artest is getting the most attention, the union is asking for a review of the rulings against all nine players penalized—five Pacers and four Pistons.

Billy Hunter, executive director of the players' association, told *The Star* that the union has asked for an expedited appeal. He expects a response within 10 days.

As commissioner, Stern has sole discretion under collective bargaining rules over penalties for on-court behavior, and all appeals are made to him. Hunter contends Kaplan should be called in because part of the incident occurred in the stands.

"It depends on how strict you interpret the on-court clause," Hunter told *Bloomberg News*. "If you use a strict interpretation, then he's (Stern) out of the ballgame."

Later Tuesday, ESPN reported it had footage of Pacers rookie center David Harrison striking a fan as the team left the court following Friday's game. Harrison was not penalized because it was determined he went into the stands as a peacemaker.

The NBA considers the case closed, according to Brian McIntyre, senior vice president of basketball communications, and provided a statement:

"ESPN provided the NBA with all footage from the broadcast and it was reviewed by the league office prior to commissioner Stern's determination of penalties. The decision was made not to suspend David Harrison because of the circumstances in the vomitorium at the time the incident occurred as the players were attempting to leave the floor."

As for why the union thinks the Pacers' suspensions should be reviewed, Hunter said the penalties are not in line with penalties of the past; that Artest's history should not have been a factor; and the players' actions should be considered in light of the "total chaos."

"Our contention is that what happened was a general breakdown," Hunter said. "We don't condone what happened. Our players should not be going into the stands. By the same token, the fans should not be coming out of the stands to confront the players. The area of the court should be a no-man's land for the fans, just as the stands are a no-man's land for the players.

"As it unraveled, if the referees had done their job, all of this might not have happened.

"We contend that the referees were in checkout mode. Although they were physically on the court, with 45 seconds to go it seemed their minds were elsewhere."

Hunter contends that after Ben Wallace reacted to Artest's foul, the referees should have grabbed both players and "sit them down."

"When you watch the film, you see that Artest, to de-escalate the situation, lays down on the table," Hunter said. "When Reggie (Miller) left the bench, it was to try to keep people separated. Artest was trying to disengage…. Then you see a missile come down and hit Artest.

"At that point, you see no security. No security. But for the players and other team officials and even media people (former Piston Rick Mahorn), no one was trying to get control. Still, there was no security. There was no security, still, when the chair is thrown.

"We think it was a total breakdown for Palace security."

Palace Sports & Entertainment, Inc., was named as a defendant in one of two lawsuits filed Tuesday by individuals who claim to have been injured in the brawl. Hunter said he considered federal court an option if the union is not satisfied with the response to its appeal.

Although Kaplan's term as arbitrator expired in September, Hunter said the collective bargaining agreement provides that, because a new arbitrator has not been named, Kaplan should be the person to hear the appeal.

Hunter cited the punishment of 26 games imposed by the commissioner in 1977 when Rudy Tomjanovich was seriously injured by a punch thrown by Kermit Washington as a comparison to show the severity of the "remainder of the season" suspension to Artest.

"In this case, Stern is saying that but for the fact that Artest has prior (problems) he would not have suspended him for the entire season," Hunter said.

"If you really look at what he did, (the suspension) is not justified….

"What Stern is arguing is progressive discipline and we don't have progressive discipline. And if that is his thinking, that clearly doesn't apply to Stephen Jackson and Jermaine O'Neal. This is their first incident. Does that mean that in order to justify 30 games (suspension for Jackson) and 25 games (suspension for O'Neal) that he has to ratchet Artest up to 73?"

Rev. Jesse Jackson also expressed concern about Stern's admission that he could not "factor out" Artest's history.

"Due process should not be suspended," Jackson said Tuesday in an interview with *The Star*. "When they speak of Artest's record, those infractions didn't have anything to do with Friday night…. If he and Wallace had gotten into a real thunder brook on the floor, that's one thing.

"This is a separate issue. There is a broader context."

Source: Dodds (2004). Reprinted with permission.

Taking Action

Here are a few ways that students might take action following this invitation.

■ Every war brings out multiple perspectives on, for example, whether it should be fought in the first place or how it should be fought. Students choose a current or past war to investigate in terms of those who supported it and those who did not. What reasons did each side give for their view?

■ Symbols are often used during wartime to keep the people at home feeling like they are involved in the effort even though they are not in the armed services. For example, "Uncle Sam Wants YOU" posters were common during World War II, and yellow ribbon "Support Our Troops" stickers were common during both Iraq wars. Students can survey a specified number of people who lived during the time they are researching to get their views regarding the symbols used at that time.

Multiview Books

Multiview books are structured so that characters speak for them-selves. Each page or section features the voice of a different character. Although they may all be experiencing the same events, their reactions make it clear that they are not coming to the same conclusions. These books can help children understand why people react differently to difficult social issues.

Materials
- A multiview book (see Sidebar)
- Multiview Book Analysis handout (Table 10.11.1)

Getting Started
1. Read a multiview book aloud to your class. If you choose a chapter book, you will need to allow extra time or read it over several days. Shorter multiview books work well being read dramatically with different students getting into character and taking on different voices.
2. Analyze the features and discuss how the text was constructed. How many characters are in the book? How many times did each one appear?
3. Divide the class into groups of four and ask each group to complete a multiview book organizer. For example, if you are using *Voices in the Park* (Browne, 1998), you might use the issue *meeting new people* and begin with Charlie's mother. Her perspective was that she was suspicious of Smudge and her father and did not want her son to play with someone who looked rough to her. Other issues that might be raised with this book include *having fun* and *taking care of pets*.

Multiview Books Text Set

Voices in the Park
  Browne (1998)
Seedfolks
  Fleishman (1997)
Bat 6
  Wolff (2000)
From Slave Ship to Freedom Road
  Lester (1998)
Making Up Megaboy
  Walter (1998)
Under Our Skin: Kids Talk About Race
  Birdseye & Birdseye (1997)

4. Bring the groups back together to share their interpretations of characters' perspectives.

5. Discuss what might be difficult for an author who is writing a multiview social issues book. What strategies might an author use when writing a book like this?

TABLE 10.11.1

Multiview Book Organizer

Issue:	
Character	Perspective on the Issue

Learning Center Extension: *Write Your Own Multiview Book*

This center provides an opportunity for students to work with others to compose a multiview book similar to the one they analyzed in the first activity.

Materials for Learning Center Extension

▌ A collection of multiview books (see sidebar)

▌ Table 10.11.2, Learning Center Directions

TABLE 10.11.2
Learning Center Directions

Write Your Own Multiview Book

At this center you will be working with a small group to write your own multiview book.

1. With your group, choose an issue that your characters will confront.

2. Decide how many characters you will create and who will represent the voice of each one.

3. Decide how many times each of your characters will appear and in what order.

4. Once you know who your character is, jot down what she or he likes, dislikes, and thinks about.

5. Use the "Multiview Book Analysis" handout to plan your characters and their actions. Make sure you plan for different perspectives. Do not make them all the same.

6. Write your pieces

7. Put the book together and share it with the class.

8. **Reflection:** What did your group learn by making a multiview book?

Taking Action

Share your new multiview books with another class and discuss why it is important to look at issues from multiple perspectives.

Name Calling

Name calling and bullying are problems in schools as well as in the larger society. Although the number of students bringing guns to school continues to grow, one common thread in these cases seems to be that guns are seen by many of the kids who bring them as needed protection against other kids who pick on them. One university researcher has estimated that bullying accounts for around 60,000 students missing school every day (Kauffman, 2006). Even if we do not call people names ourselves, by not speaking up we are in effect part of the problem in that our silence condones the activity. This strategy invites students to inquire into name-calling practices and to consider how to take action to challenge them.

Picture Books About Name Calling

Sister Anne's Hands,
  Lorbiecki (2000)
Oliver Button Is a Sissy,
  De Paola (1979)
The Sissy Duckling,
  Fierstein (2002)
Crow Boy,
  Yashima (1955)
Molly's Pilgrim,
  Cohen (1983)
Angel Child, Dragon Child,
  Suerat (1990)
Simon's Hook,
  Burnett (2000)

Materials

▮ One or more picture books that focus on or include an instance of name calling (Sidebar)

▮ Victim/Perpetrator/Bystander/Ally handout (Christensen, 2003) (Table 10.12.1)

Getting Started

1. Give each child a copy of the Victim/Perpetrator/Bystander/Ally handout, and explain the various roles.

   • The victim is the target of the name-calling behavior and the one being marginalized.

   • The perpetrator is the one doing the name calling or other discriminating behavior.

   • A bystander is someone who watches the event but does not take any action to stop the name calling or to help the victim.

   • An ally is someone who actively intervenes to support the victim or to challenge the name calling.

2. Divide students into groups of three or four. Explain that they will be filling in the organizer as you read aloud.

3. Introduce the story you have chosen and read to the place in the text that is right after the point where the first instance of name calling occurs. Stop reading and ask each group to talk about how the organizer might be used to represent what is happening in the story. Invite children to fill in the name of any characters in the story who might be playing any of the roles listed on the organizer and how they take on that role. For example, *Sister Anne's Hands* (Lorbiecki, 2000) tells the story of an African American nun who found a paper airplane in her classroom with the verse, "Roses are red. Violets are blue. Don't let Sister Ann get any black on you." This would be a good place to stop reading and talk about whom they see as playing the different roles.

4. Finish reading the story and ask children to discuss in their groups whether they want to change their charts or make new entries. Discuss how it is possible for a character to play multiple roles and be mentioned in more than one column. For example, the narrator of the story, Anna, started out as a bystander but later became an ally when she consciously began to use many colors in the hands she drew. Similarly, in this or other stories, there might be different ways of defining bystanders. Some might argue that people who do nothing to help a victim are really perpetrators.

5. Have groups share why they categorized the characters in the book as they did. Accept different interpretations and the reasoning behind each. Ask students to draw a line under the data recorded for the book just read on their Victim/Perpetrator/Bystander/Ally handout and try the same procedure with another book.

TABLE 10.12.1

Victim, Perpetrator, Bystander, Ally Organizer

Victim	Perpetrator	Bystander	Ally

Source: Linda Christensen, 2003.

Learning Center Extension: *Become School Anthropologists*

Equip students with clipboards so they will be able to write down any and all instances of name calling they hear on the playground or in the cafeteria for a specified period of time. In this center, students classify these recorded taunts into categories and analyze what the name caller was trying to accomplish with each type of taunt. Make sure students are aware that this is not a tattle-tale activity targeting particular kids but is one to help them understand the broad issues of name calling and bullying at school. This center is designed so students can see that name calling has a particular effect, even when the person doing the name calling may not even be able to define the terms being used (e.g., "You're so gay!").

Materials for Learning Center Extension

- Clipboards and paper for students
- Victim/Perpetrator/Bystander/Ally handout
- Table 10.12.2, Learning Center Directions

Taking Action

- Invite students to explore how prevalent name calling is in our society. Generate a list of sites that might be monitored, including such things as political speeches, popular TV shows, and conversations at home. Assign different groups of students to monitor different sites and to agree on a format for keeping track of findings (e.g., what names are being used, what is trying to be accomplished, who benefits, what was the effect).
- Start a problems journal in your classroom. Risë Reinier decided to start a problems journal in her sixth-grade classroom to respond to widespread complaints about name calling and bullying. To help children make better decisions under pressure, she invited them to write down their version of what they saw as a problem. At town meeting—typically the last hour of the day on Wednesdays and Fridays—these problems were read and discussed. Risë did not offer solutions or alternatives but rather let the students make recommendations. She did, however, take notes on what alternatives classmates came up with. Once a problem was discussed at town meeting the parties involved needed to select one of the solutions generated by their classmates and try it. Often a single discussion took care of the situation, but if it did not, problems could be written about again in the problems journal and could go through another round of discussion and recommendations.

TABLE 10.12.2
Learning Center Directions

Become School Anthropologists

1. Work with your teacher to identify a time for your group to observe other students on the playground, in the cafeteria, or even in the classroom. Decide how long your observation time will be.

2. As you watch other children, take field notes on exactly what you see happening, and note the behavior of all kids who are present, even if they are not directly involved.

3. As you take notes, do not write down specific names, but identify your informants (i.e., people you are watching) scientifically by calling them descriptive terms such as big boy #1, small girl #2, and loud adult #1.

4. When you get back to class, use the Victim, Perpetrator/ Bystander/Ally handout to organize and analyze what you recorded. For example, if you saw someone being called a name, note who it was and what she or he was being called in the "victim" slot. Then fill in the descriptions of others who were playing any of the other roles.

5. Keep your Victim/Perpetrator/Bystander/Ally handout in a safe place. In a week, you will discuss your analysis with others who have also done this invitation.

6. **Reflection:** According to an old nursery rhyme, "Sticks and stones can break my bones, but names can never hurt me." Think about what this nursery rhyme is trying to get us to believe and who might want us to believe that. Who benefits if we do buy into it and who loses?

Picture It

The old adage that a picture is worth a thousand words is probably true in that words need to be processed in a linear way whereas pictures can be grasped more holistically (Eco, 1970). Although a picture might show relationships at a glance, these same connections might be less obvious in a text. In this invitation students are given statistical data and are asked to use their knowledge of visual literacy to create posters that highlight, rather than bury, what they see as one (or more) of the major stories these data tell.

Materials

- Copies of the "Animal Euthanasia" handout (Table 10.13.1) or some other statistical data
- Handout, "Areas of a Canvas" (Table 10.13.2)
- Blank 8½ × 11 sheets of typing paper
- Art materials such as construction paper, crayons, colored pens, glue, and scissors

Getting Started

1. Organize students in groups of three and explain that they will be working with reading statistics, which is a special kind of reading. Also explain that the statistics they will be reading today are about the euthanization of animals in shelters. Some students will not know that euthanize means "to kill an incurably ill or injured person or animal to relieve suffering" (*Encarta World English Dictionary*, Microsoft Corporation, 1999). This is important information to know while reading the statistics.

2. Ask groups to interpret the "Animal Euthanasia" handout. You might ask questions like the following (accept all reasonable responses):
   - What do these data say?
   - What conclusions can someone reading this handout reach? For example, most animals that end up at an animal shelter are euthanized. Cats are more likely to be euthanized than dogs.
   - Why do you think the statistics writers used the word *euthanized*?
3. Once groups of students agree on what this handout is saying, have them write their statement in the center of a clean 8½ × 11 sheet of paper. Their job now is to make a web of reasons for why the statement in the middle of their sheet of paper might be true. For example, if more pets wore identity tags, more would be returned to their owners. Cat owners are particularly bad at having their pet wear identity information. Pet owners need to get their pets neutered to stop euthanasia.
4. After students have had an opportunity to share and discuss their webs, invite them, using the art materials provided, to take their favorite interpretation and to design a poster that gets people thinking critically about the issues talked about in the "Animal Euthanasia" handout.
5. Review the principles found in the "Areas of a Canvas" handout before they lay out and design their poster.

TABLE 10.13.1

Animal Euthanasia

A recent study estimated that there are 65,000,000 dog owners in the United States and 77,600,000 cat owners. Unfortunately 15,000,000 dogs and cats end up at animal shelters each year.

- Roughly 64% of the total number of animals that entered shelters is euthanized (56% of all dogs; 71% of all cats).

- 72% of owned dogs and 84% of owned cats have been spayed or neutered.

- Only 15% of dogs and 2% of cats that enter animal shelters are reunited with their owners.

- On the average, only 18 to 21% of the animals at an animal shelter get adopted.

Sources: American Humane Society (www.americanhumane.org); The Humane Society of the United States (www.hsus.org)

TABLE 10.13.2
Areas of a Canvas

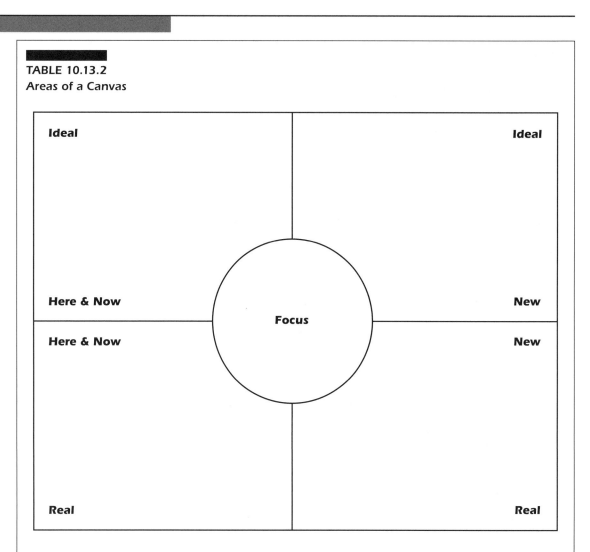

Top & Bottom. The top of a picture is "the ideal;" the bottom, "the real."

Left & Right. The left side of the picture is "the here and now;" or given; the right side, "the new."

Center. Note where your eye falls when you first look at a picture. The center of the picture provides a focus.

Vectors. Vectors are lines or alignments in a picture that carry your eye up, down, or sideways in a picture. Typically they go from "the real" to "the ideal" or from "the here and now" to "the new." They may go, however, go diagonally crossing quadrants in interesting ways.

Colors. Colors are often used to set the mood. The use of bright colors suggest something positive or hopeful while the use of dark colors suggest dreariness and doom. Pastel colors are calming and often are used to suggest innocence.

Gaze. In pictures or photographs containing characters, the gaze is often important as the direction of the gaze creates a vector that moves the eye from one point in the picture to another. A gaze upward and off the page may suggest the future (an idealized perfect state) and be read a hopeful. A gaze downward anchors the picture in "the real" or here and now.

Exaggeration. Pay particular attention to exaggeration; items, like hands, that are drawn out of proportion to the rest of the figure or arms that are too skinny for the body depicted. Extra large hands may suggest the importance of hard labor and work, for example. Skinny arms may suggest idleness or helplessness.

Learning Center Extension: *A Picture Is Worth 1000 Words*

Although many people see writing as hard and making a picture as easy, graphic designers know this is not necessarily so. To create a powerful graphic from a written text, graphic designers have to unpack and fully understand the materials they are turning into graphic form. This center invites students to use what they learned about the grammar of visual design from Invitation 5, "Honing Your Visual Literacy," in this chapter, to unpack a fact sheet and express what they see as its major message in visual form.

Materials for Learning Center Extension

- "Areas of a Canvas" (Table 10.13.2)
- Table 10.13.3, Learning Center Directions
- Fact Sheets 1 and 2 (See Sidebars)
- "Analyzing a Canvas" (Table 10.13.4)
- Art materials such as construction paper, crayons, colored pens, glue, and scissors

TABLE 10.13.3
Learning Center Directions

A Picture Is Worth 1,000 Words!

1. As the head of your own graphic design agency you have been hired to create posters that highlight why everyone should get out and read a banned book during "Banned Book Week."

2. Using the art materials provided and referring to the "Basic Areas of a Canvas" handout, design a poster that gets people thinking critically about the underlying issues you see buried in these data.

3. Hint: Start by "reading" the fact sheets and webbing out reasons why banning particular books on the list— (or any book on the list, for that matter—) might be, (in some people's opinion,) a very bad idea and what other alternatives might be worth fighting for.

4. Remember your company's motto: "A Picture is Worth 1,000 Words."!

5. **Reflection:** How easy or difficult was it to share your ideas about banned books in poster form? Why do you think this is?

Fact Sheet 1: Democracy Depends on Everyone's Having Free Access to Information

The most frequently cited quote that argues this point is that of Justice William O. Douglas of the United States U.S. Supreme Court (*Adler v. Board of Education*, 1951):

Where suspicion fills the air and holds scholars in line for fear of their jobs, there can be no exercise of free intellect .... A problem can no longer be pursued with impunity to its edges. Fear stalks the classroom. The teacher is no longer a stimulant to adventurous thinking; she becomes instead a pipeline for safe and sound information. A deadening dogma takes the place of free inquiry. Instruction tends to become sterile; pursuit of knowledge is discouraged; discussion often leaves off where it should begin.

Fact Sheet 2: Most Challenged Books of 21st Century (2000–2005)

In anticipation of the 25th anniversary of Banned Books Week (September 23–30, 2006), the American Library Association (ALA) compiled the top 10 most challenged books from 2000–2005, with the *Harry Potter* series of books leading the pack. The list is as follows:

1. *Harry Potter* series by J.K. Rowling
2. *The Chocolate War* by Robert Cormier
3. *Alice* series by Phyllis Reynolds Naylor
4. *Of Mice and Men* by John Steinbeck
5. *I Know Why the Caged Bird Sings* by Maya Angelou
6. *Fallen Angels* by Walter Dean Myers
7. *It's Perfectly Normal* by Robie Harris
8. *Scary Stories* series by Alvin Schwartz
9. *Captain Underpants* series by Dav Pilkey
10. *Forever* by Judy Blume

Between 1990 and 2000, there were 6,364 challenges reported to or recorded by the Office for Intellectual Freedom (see *The 100 Most Frequently Challenged Books*[a])

- 1,607 were challenges to "sexually explicit" material (up 161 since 1999)
- 1,427 were challenges to material considered to use "offensive language" (up 165 since 1999)
- 1,256 were challenges to material considered "unsuited to age group" (up 89 since 1999)
- 842 were challenges to material with an "occult theme or promoting the occult or Satanism" (up 69 since 1999)
- 737 were challenges to material considered to be "violent" (up 107 since 1999)
- 515 were challenges to material with a homosexual theme or "promoting homosexuality" (up 18 since 1999)
- 419 were challenges to material "promoting a religious viewpoint" (up 22 since 1999)

Other reasons for challenges included "nudity" (317 challenges, up 20 since 1999), "racism" (267 challenges, up 22 since 1999), "sex education" (224 challenges, up 7 since 1999), and "anti-family" (202 challenges, up 9 since 1999).

Please note that the number of challenges and the number of reasons for those challenges do not match, because works are often challenged on more than one ground.

Seventy-one percent of the challenges were to material in schools or school libraries.[b] Another 24% were to material in public libraries (down 2% since 1999). Sixty percent of the challenges were brought by parents, 15% by patrons, and 9% by administrators, both down 1% one percent since 1999).

[a] The Office for Intellectual Freedom does not claim comprehensiveness in recording challenges.
[b] Sometimes works are challenged in a school and school library. Table Invitation 13.5

TABLE 10.13.4

Analyzing a Canvas

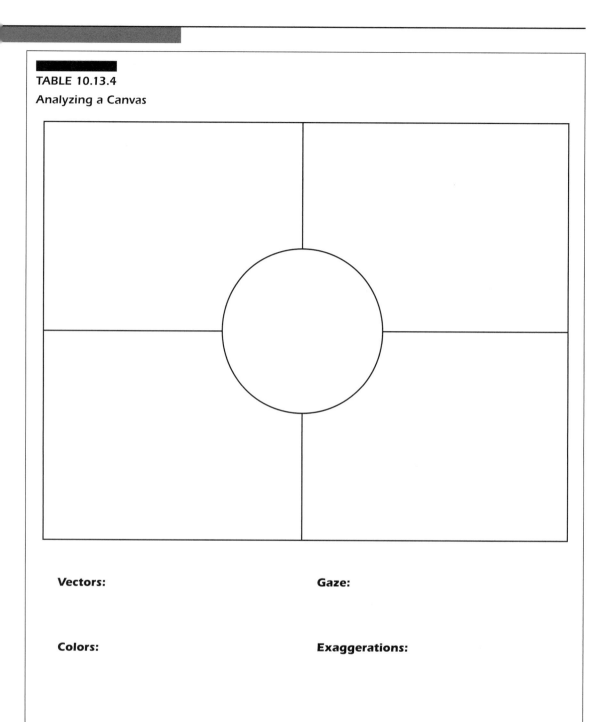

Vectors: **Gaze:**

Colors: **Exaggerations:**

Taking Action

Think about which groups really need to know and understand the information you have highlighted in the posters you developed. Once you have decided on the groups you need to reach, take the posters you created and see if any of local agencies will let you post them (e.g., doctor's offices, banks, post offices).

Kids may also want to:

▌ Create a poster for a burning issue of their own
▌ Interrogate and act on other statistical data that come from your community and raise important critical issues

Poignant Passages

Occasionally, when reading, one comes across a passage that merits extended discussion. Fry (2005), for example, when reading *Cinderella* (Brown, 1971) ran across a passage in which the king's son decided to throw a party. The next sentence read, "He [the King's son] invited anyone who was anyone, including our two young misses, for they cut quite a figure in the land." At this point, Fry stopped, wrote the sentence on the board, and invited the students to jot down who it was they would invite to a party they were giving if their criteria was "anyone who was anyone." The writing that the children did opened up a powerful conversation through which they explored what values and assumptions were operating in their own lives. Fry followed up this discussion by inviting students to take a moment to speculate again, with paper and pen in hand, on what they thought "the two young misses" actually did that got the king's son to see them as "cutting quite a figure in the land."

Materials

- A book with a passage that is striking because it reflects particular values and assumptions that you see as meriting interrogation. Though there is no particular formula for which passages to choose, phrases and sentences that initially surprise and cause a rereading are a good place to begin.
- For the purposes of illustration, we use *The Carpet Boy's Gift* (Shea, 2003)—a book about Nadeem, a boy who was sold to a carpet maker so his parents and younger brother would have enough money to live.

Getting Started

1. Read *The Carpet Boy's Gift* aloud to your class. It will undoubtedly generate discussion about issues of fairness and child labor. When there is a lull in the conversation, write this quote from the title page of the book on the board and read it aloud:

> I appeal to you that you stop people from using children as bonded laborers because the children need to use a pen rather than the instruments of child labor.
>
> **—Iqbal Masih, 12 years old**

2. Ask students to write their thoughts about the phrase "the children need to use a pen." Do they agree or disagree with the phrase and why?
3. After students have had about five minutes for a quickwrite, they can discuss their responses in small groups or as a whole class.
4. Next, read aloud the short section at the end of *The Carpet Boy's Gift* about the life of Masih, which describes his incredible courage and eventual death as a result of standing up to fight child labor practices in Pakistan. Reread the quote from Masih and ask students to write their response to the quote as a whole.
5. Have students share their responses.

Learning Center Extension: *Catchy Newspaper Phrases*

Although literature is usually a good source for this invitation, newspapers can also provide a wealth of text worth a second visit. This is a good way for students to have written conversations about what is in the news.

Materials for Learning Center Extension

▌ A stack of recent front sections from your local newspaper
▌ Table 10.14.1, Learning Center Directions
▌ Copies of the "Newspaper Phrases Response Sheet" (Table 10.14.2)
▌ A folder labeled "Newspaper Phrases" for completed response sheets

TABLE 10.14.1
Learning Center Directions

Catchy Newspaper Phrases

1. With a partner, browse through the front pages of the newspapers at this center and find an article that has a phrase that catches your attention. It might:

   - Surprise you
   - Anger you
   - Cause you to reread
   - Make you laugh
   - Make you ask questions

2. Use the "Newspaper Phrases Response Sheet" to do the following:

   - Write down the headline and date of the article that has the phrase that caught your attention.
   - Write down the phrase itself.
   - Write your and your partner's response to the newspaper phrases.

3. After you have finished with your response sheet, put it in the "Newspaper Phrases" folder.

4. Read through some of the response sheets that other students have completed, and write in your responses to their newspaper phrases in one of the boxes at the bottom of the sheet.

5. **Reflection:** What phrase in the this folder did you and your partner think was most powerful? What made it so powerful?

TABLE 10.14.2

Newspaper Phrases Response Sheet

Names: _____   _____

Headline and date of article:	Phrase or sentence that caught your attention:	What you and your partner have to say about this phrase:

Other Responses

What _____ and _____ have to say about this phrase	What _____ and _____ have to say about this phrase
What _____ and _____ have to say about this phrase	What _____ and _____ have to say about this phrase

Taking Action

After reading *The Carpet Boy's Gift*, student will often want to learn more or take some action regarding child labor practices. The book has a wealth of resources and information at the back where students can do the following:

- Learn more about Iqbal and other child advocates
- Learn about the United Nations and "The Rights of the Child"
- Learn about other books that explore child labor issues
- Learn about where the products we buy come from and how to tell if the company has responsible labor practices

Chapter Ten
Invitations for Students

Reading from Different Stances

When we read something, we usually have an initial response or reaction, which may change if we have to defend our response, if we talk to someone with a different interpretation, or if we engage in conversation. To be critically literate we need to know about alternate ways of responding as well as know how our response positions us in the world. Too often in the past, we have prepared readers without this kind of agency. Oh, they could respond to a text and even pass a comprehension test, but they never thought through or took responsibility for the position that response reflected. This curricular invitation supports readers in developing the habits of mind to seek out multiple—and even conflicting versions—of every story they hear and to take agency in fashioning those responses to reflect how they want to position themselves as well as how they wish others to see them in the world.

Materials

- Handout: *Different Interpretive Stances* (adapted from Bleich, 1993) (Table 10.15.1)
- Text to read aloud. For purposes of explanation, we use *Fox* (Wild, 2006) a picture book which could be used even with older readers.
- Handout: *What's Your Stance?* (Tale 10.15.2)
- *Examples of Different Interpretive Stances* (Table 10.15.3)

Getting Started

1. Give each student a copy of the *Different Interpretive Stances* handout. You probably will want to discuss the stances and let students ask any questions that they may have.

2. Divide the class up into six groups, and assign each group the responsibility of responding to the text you are about to read from one of the six stances on the sheet.

3. Read a text aloud. For example, we use *Fox* (Wild, 2006), a story about Dog and Magpie and their troubled friendship.

4. Students then meet in their "stance" groups, and each group comes up with their own definition of the stance they have been assigned. Also they can list the types of people who might normally respond this way (see the *What's Your Stance* handout, which may be helpful).

5. When students have finished their stance definition and lists of people who are likely to respond from this stance, ask them to generate several examples of what a reader making that type of response would say. For examples from *Fox*, see *Examples of Different Interpretive Stances* (Table 10.15.3).

6. When groups are finished, ask each one to explain the stance assigned to them in their own words, tell about the kinds of people they think might usually respond from this stance, and the examples they came up with from the book that was read aloud.

7. Ask students to take five minutes to reflect on what they learned about being a reader from engaging in this invitation. Given our experience, students typically see the invitation as teaching them that there is a range of ways readers can respond to a text. While this is an important conclusion, it is equally important to talk about the functionality of particular responses under various conditions. Make the point that as a literate being we not only have a choice in how to respond to a text but we have a responsibility to elect a response type that reflects how it is we wish to be positioned in the world and what kind of identity we wish to take on.

TABLE 10.15.1
Different Interpretive Stances

Stance	Example
Metaphorical	Responds by making analogies, or connections, to prior events and life experiences
Philosophical	Looks for universal truths or messages that go beyond the text
Aesthetic	Responds to the emotional experience of reading; tracks highs and lows during the roller coaster experience of reading
Analytical	Responds to how the text works and why the author wrote it in a particular way; takes a close look at texts and considers why certain words (e.g., characters, settings) were chosen and how they create the effects they do
Intertextual	Makes sense of the text in terms of, for example, other texts, movies, or books.
Critical	Looks for societal stereotypes and patterns or how the text makes us look differently at everyday events; points out the stereotypes that the text perpetuates; helps us see the big issues that lie just beyond the text

Source: Bleich (1993).

TABLE 10.15.2

What's Your Stance?

Book:	
People in Our Group:	

Stance:	Formal Definition:
	Our Own Definition:

The kinds of people we think might read from this stance:

1.
2.
3.

How we responded to the book by reading from this stance:

TABLE 10.15.3
Examples of Different Interpretive Stances

Stance	Examples of Student Responses
Metaphorical	We made lots of personal connections to this story, even though it was about animals. For many of us this story reminds us of all those people who are jealous of what you have and do everything possible to make sure that you are as unhappy as they are.
Philosophical	This book reminds us of when people say, "The grass is always greener on the other side of the fence." We think this because the characters are greedy. Magpie is not happy with what she has so Fox easily tricks her.
Aesthetic	We had all kinds of feelings when we read the book. First, we were happy for Magpie and Dog. Then, we felt fear, like Magpie, when Fox showed up. Then we were hopeful and finally we felt bad. We were kind of glad that Fox did not eat Magpie.
Analytical	We were interested in trying to figure out how the author wrote this book. Instead of print, like we usually see in books, the author uses child-like handwriting. We wonder if she wants us to believe the person telling the story is a kid. We also liked the way some of the pictures are upside down and that the text goes in all different directions. You have to keep turning the text as you read it. We are changing the way we hold the book while the characters are telling the story from their own perspectives.
Intertextual	This reminded us of some other folk tales with animals. It also is about a fox, but we thought how he was a little like a wolf in some of the fairy tales. Juan said the fox reminded him of coyote, in the coyote tales from New Mexico.
Critical	This book is about greed. It was about animals, but it could also be about greedy people. We wished it would have had some solutions to greed, but it did not. We talked about how the book could have ended differently.

Learning Center Extension: *Becoming Agents of Texts*

This center gives students additional opportunities to see what it feels like to respond to texts from different stances. They can try on alternate ways of reading.

Materials for Learning Center Extension

- Handout: *Different Interpretive Stances* (Table 10.15.1)
- Writing paper or journals
- Table 10.15.4, Learning Center Directions

Social Action

With a group of friends, read a book or see a movie that's controversial (make sure you get parent or guardian permission).

- Analyze the book or movie using the handout Different Interpretive Stances (Table 10.15.1)
- Students can decide how they want to make their analysis public

Learning Center Directions

Becoming Agents of Texts

1. Find a friend that likes the same book or story as you do and work together at this center. Get the book from the classroom library and bring it with you.

2. Use the "Different interpretive stances" sheet as a guide. Pick three stances that you both want to try out.

3. Read the book, a few pages at a time with your friend.

4. Stop and decide how someone reading the book from the first stance you picked would respond to what you read.

   - What would he or she think or say about what you just read?
   - What questions would he or she have?
   - How did it feel reading and responding from this stance?
   - Is this a stance you would like to try when you are reading another story?

5. Jot down notes about these questions on a piece of paper or in a journal. See if you and your friend have the same or different responses to the questions.

6. Read a few more pages and do talk about the questions in #4 again, but this time for the second stance you picked to try on. Then the same for the third stance.

7. **Reflection:** What did you learn by trying on different stances with your friend? Share your thoughts at the next class meeting.

Political Cartoons

R. J. Matson of the *St. Louis Post Dispatch* is a political cartoonist. One of his most recent cartoons shows a man in an SUV getting directions from a gas station attendant. The attendant is saying to the driver, "You want to drive $5.00 down that road, make a left turn at the light, then bear right, and you will be there in another $2.25." (This and other political cartoons are available at http://www.cagle.com/teacher/2.asp). To understand as well as to create effective political cartoons, the artist must be sensitive to what is going on in the world as well as to what dominant values need to be questioned. What made this particular cartoon so effective when it was published was that it addressed one of the hottest issues in the political and economic world at the time. With the price of gas at the pump increasing daily, the public had begun an outcry that was slowly being heard in Washington, especially since, in 2006, oil companies posted the largest earnings in history. Matson's cartoon played to the audience's anger and frustration by suggesting that even commonplace ways of giving directions were no longer appropriate for drivers with price concerns on their minds. This invitation challenges students to read political cartoons in terms of identifying what values the cartoonist is speaking for or against. It also encourages students to try their hand at creating their own political cartoons.

Materials

- Copies of "The World Is Just" (Figure 10.16.1) or another cartoon you prefer
- "Analyzing a Cartoon" handout (Table 10.16.1)
- Copies of at least two other cartoons collected from websites or news outlets

Getting Started

1. Put students in groups of three or four and introduce "The World Is Just" or another political cartoon you have decided to use with the whole class. Invite students to talk in their groups about what they see happening in the picture without considering the caption:
   - How realistic is the picture?
   - Could this scene really happen?

   Explain that cartoons often exaggerate aspects of life that might have some basis in truth. In this case, students might argue that larger fish eat smaller fish, but the chances of the scene's happening exactly this way are small.

2. Ask students to look at the captions and consider what the three fish are saying. Invite them to talk in their groups about how the message of each fish positions it in terms of power and agency (i.e., the ability to take control of a situation and do things for oneself).

3. Ask students to talk in their groups about the overall message of the cartoon. What point is the cartoonist trying to make? What does this suggest he or she believes about the world?

4. Pass out copies of the "Analyzing a Cartoon" handout and let students work together to fill in the first row for the cartoon they have analyzed together. Table 10.16.2 shows a possible response on the handout for this cartoon, and Figure 10.16.2 shows what one student wrote about the cartoon.

5. Have groups report out on their work. Ask them to judge whether the message of the cartoon is one they want to accept or reject and to explain their decision.

6. Provide a selection of other cartoons and ask each group to go through the same process for two others.

FIGURE 10.16.1
"The world is just" cartoon

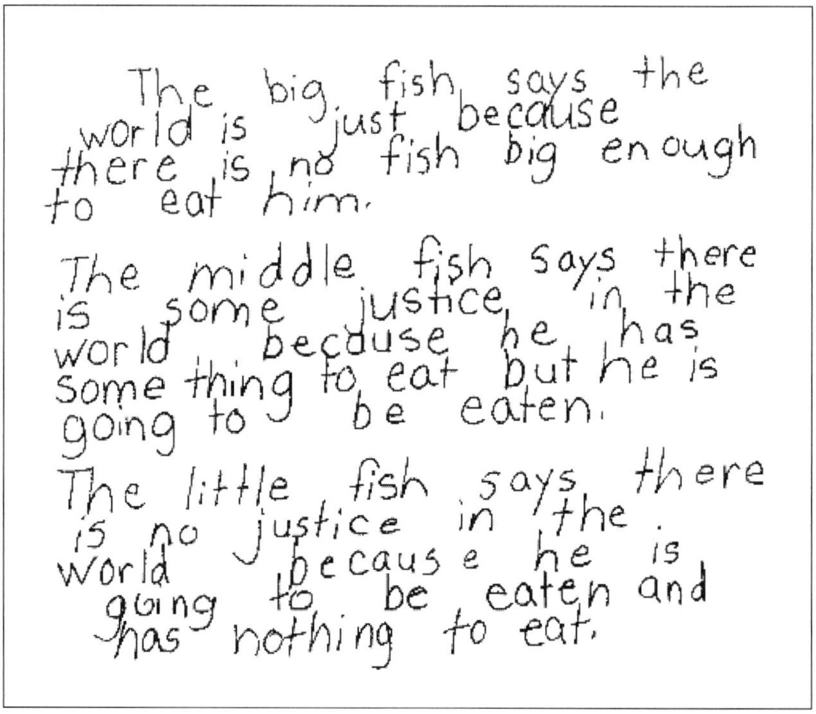

> The big fish says the world is just because there is no fish big enough to eat him.
>
> The middle fish says there is some justice in the world because he has something to eat but he is going to be eaten.
>
> The little fish says there is no justice in the world because he is going to be eaten and has nothing to eat.

FIGURE 10.16.2
Student writing sample for fish cartoon

TABLE 10.16.1

Analyzing a Cartoon

Cartoon & Source	Picture Shows	Caption Suggests	Message

Source: Linda Christensen, 2003.

TABLE 10.16.2

Sample Response to "The World Is Just" Cartoon

Cartoon and Source	Picture Shows	Caption Suggests	Message
"The World Is Just" Rethinking Schools.	Small fish being eaten by medium fish; medium fish being eaten by large fish.	Small fish sees no justice in the world; medium fish sees some justice; large fish says there is justice.	Your belief about whether there is justice in the world depends on how much power you do or do not have.

Learning Center Extension: *Try Your Own Hand at Cartooning*

This center invites students to analyze political cartoons in terms of how the artist exaggerates certain aspects of a picture to make a specific point. It also invites them to think of an issue they see as important and to address that issue through a cartoon they create.

Materials for Learning Center Extensions

- Collection of cartoons or access to selected cartoon websites
- Blank paper, pencils, markers
- Table 10.16.3, Learning Center Directions

TABLE 10.16.3
Learning Center Directions

Try Your Own Hand at Cartooning

At this center you will be exploring some of the elements of cartooning and trying your hand at creating a cartoon for a message you believe is important enough to share with the world.

1. With a partner, look though the collected cartoons and find one that you want to study further.

2. Examine this cartoon in terms of what is exaggerated. Can you identify any stereotypes?

3. What does the cartoon suggest about power? (Who has it? Who doesn't?)

4. Think of a message about a public issue that you care about and want to express in your cartoon. Jot the it down. Make sure that your message doesn't marginalize anyone in your class or school community.

5. Brainstorm with your partner about how you can use exaggeration to make your point.

6. Decide what your cartoon will show in terms of the picture and caption.

7. Sketch your cartoon and get feedback from your partner.

8. Make any changes to improve your cartoon and leave it at the center for others to enjoy.

9. **Reflection:** Some people say that art can convey a message better than words. How does the cartoon you studied (or your original cartoon) support or contradict this statement?

Taking Action

Have a class discussion about school issues that bug people. Maybe it is the food in the cafeteria, bullying that happens at recess, or peer pressure to dress a certain way. Students may want to design cartoons that address these specific issues and display them in hallways or other areas outside the classroom.

Researching Advertising Techniques

As consumers, we are bombarded on a daily basis by messages that try to get us to believe specific things about ourselves, our families, and various products on the market. This invitation is designed to help kids become savvy consumers who are able to deconstruct ads in terms of identifying the techniques that companies use to get their messages across to their target audiences.

Materials
- A stack of magazines and newspapers (which you or your students have collected)
- "Advertising techniques" poster (Table 10.17.1)

Getting Started
1. Starting with a stack of magazines and newspapers, invite students to use the "Advertising Techniques" poster as a tool for finding and analyzing prototypical, or classic, examples of each of these advertising techniques.
2. Once students have collected and shared what they see as prototypical examples of each category, you can begin to make the issue more complex by having students identify ads that use a combination of techniques, emphasizing not only the techniques used but also their effects.
3. As a culminating activity, ask students to share or find ads that fall outside the categories of techniques listed on the poster. As a class, name and create new categories of advertisements to add to the poster.

4. Use this final list of advertising techniques and the examples to create a class-made poster to use as a reference for the "Researching Advertising on Television" center.

TABLE 10.17.1
Advertising Techniques

Plain Folks	You should believe what people who are just like you are saying about the product.
Expert.	You should believe what the expert is telling you about the product.
Statistics	You should believe what the charts and graphs are showing.
Bandwagon	Everyone is buying this product so you should buy it too.
It's a Deal	You should buy this product to save money.
Lifestyle Improvement	Your life will be better if you buy this product.
Repetition of Image or Slogan	You should buy this product because they show the product or say the slogan over and over.

Learning Center Extension: *Researching Television Commercials*
As a way to expand this invitation, have students investigate the advertising techniques used in television commercials. Students can look for similarities and differences between print and TV advertising techniques.

Materials for Learning Center Extension
- "Advertising Techniques" poster created by the class
- Table 10.17.2, Learning Center Directions
- Multiple copies of the "Researching Advertising on Television" handout (Table 10.17.3)

TABLE 10.17.2
Learning Center Directions

Researching TV Commercials

1. At home, pick a 30-minute television show of your choice to watch.

2. Using the "Researching Advertising on Television" Graphic Organizer, record the name of the show and time it was shown, and write a brief description of the first six commercials that air (just describe the commercials rather than give your opinions about them).

3. Once you have collected this information at home, work with a partner (or in a small group) and share the data you have collected.

4. Pick three (or more) of these questions to answer with your partner or group:

   - Who was the target audience of a particular commercial?
   - Are there assumptions or stereotypes being made by the producers? If so, what are they?
   - What kind of person would believe this commercial or buy the product?
   - How is this target audience positioned by the commercial?
   - What identity is the advertiser trying to give to the target audience?

5. **Reflection:** What was most surprising about your research findings? Report your findings and your thoughts about the television advertising industry to the whole class during class meeting time.

TABLE 10.17.3

Researching Advertising on Television

Show Name:	Product Name	Description of Commercial
	1.	
Time:	2.	
	3.	
	4.	
	5.	
	6.	

Taking Action

There are a number of ways that students may decide to take action based on the research they have conducted. One possibility is to invite students to design a truthful ad for a product they really like and to send it to the company that manufactures the product.

Touchstone Texts

A touchstone text is book, article or some other piece of writing that has been selected to be read and reread aloud several times over the course of a unit of study (Sumara, 1995). As a result of participating in this curricular invitation students come to understand the value of revisiting books, songs, and other materials in that texts take on meaning as a function of familiarity and understanding of a topic. They also can be used for multiple purposes.

Materials

- A picture book for a read-aloud that addresses major issues surrounding a topic being studied. (Because you will be reading your commonplace text to the class on several occasions, it is important that you select a book you read well and that has enough depth to merit extended conversation.)
- Art paper, marker, and other materials.
- An overhead transparency of a page in the text you will use for a writing mini-lesson.

Getting Started

1. For the purposes of illustration, we use for this invitation *Freedom Summer* (Wiles, 2001) in connection with a focused study on American history and the civil rights movement. *Freedom Summer* is the story of two friends, one white and the other African American, who live in Mississippi during the summer of 1964. Taking place in the aftermath of the passage of the Civil Rights Act, the book recounts how many towns decided that rather than opening public pools to African Americans, they would simply fill them in with dirt. Although there is no particular

order in which the following activities need to be completed—nor are the ideas offered here a finite set—the overall aim is to have students visit and revisit a text by responding to it in some appropriate fashion after each reading.

- **Sketch To Stretch** (Harste, Short, & Burke, 1988): Using *Freedom Summer* as the commonplace text, have students work in groups of three or four. Give groups colored markers and large sheets of paper and ask them to discuss the text and to create a sketch symbolizing what the story meant to the group.
- **Save the last word for the artist:** Ask groups of students to hold up their sketch while classmates hypothesize what it is they thought the artists had tried to say. Once all of the students (not in the group that produced the sketch) have stated their hypotheses, the artists share what they were thinking as they created the sketch. Sharing continues until all groups have a turn. Sketches are then posted in the classroom so they can be referred back to in subsequent class discussions.
- **Wonderful Questions Booklets:** During a subsequent reading of Freedom Summer, ask students to jot down what questions the book raised that they might try to find answers to using the Internet. Begin this reading by having each student make a wonderful questions booklet for use in recording questions. (See Figure 10.18.1 for directions on how to make a one-page stapleless book that in this instance served as a wonderful questions booklet.) Have students share and post the findings from their Internet research.
- **Debate:** As a result of the questions students raised in their wonderful questions booklets, groups of students may want to debate the legality of the behavior displayed by the townspeople in the story. In many classrooms this has started an inquiry into Jim Crow laws.

2. A completely different way to use a touchstone text is for examples of writer's craft strategies. Heffernan (2004, pp. 54–56) uses touchstone texts (in this case we would use *Freedom Summer*) for writing mini-lessons to help students discover how the author uses (1) power words; (2) time shifts; (3) snapshots (showing, not telling); and (4) paragraphing. For example, one passage from *Freedom Summer* reads, "John Henry swims better than anybody I know. He crawls like a catfish, blows bubbles like a swamp monster, but he doesn't swim in the town pool with me. He's not allowed." This passage is a great example of

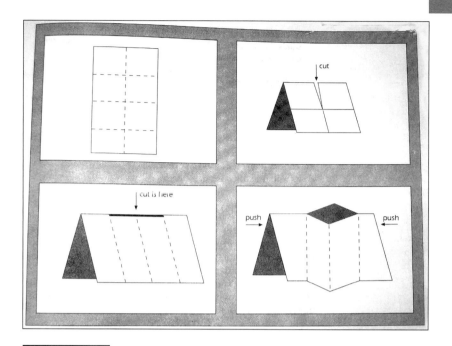

FIGURE 10.18.1
One-page stapleless book

how snapshots (e.g., "crawls like a catfish," "blows bubbles like a swamp monster") are so much more powerful than simply saying, "John Henry was a good swimmer." It is also a great demonstration of how simple words can at times be very powerful (e.g., "He's not allowed"). After introducing examples of powerful writing invite students to try their hand at creating and sharing their own powerful images in things they are writing. When conducting this strategy we have found it helpful to put the page of text you are using for a mini-lesson on a transparency.

3. As you can see from the aforementioned activities, there are endless ways to use touchstone texts. Do not be afraid to use a powerful book over and over and over.

Learning Center Extension: *What Does It Mean To Be Patriotic?*
Songs can often be thought of as commonplace texts in that they are
played over and over again, coast to coast, on popular radio stations
throughout the nation. For purposes of illustration, we use John
Mellencamp's song "To Washington" and Toby Keith's "Courtesy of the
Red, White, & Blue." Any two songs with contrasting themes will work
for this invitation.

Materials for Learning Center Extension
- Two popular songs with contrasting themes.
- Table 10.18.1, Learning Center Directions

TABLE 10.18.1
Learning Center Directions

What Does It Mean to Be Patriotic?

At this center we use music help you think deeply about what it means to be an American. You will listen to two songs, both of which are controversial.

1. With a friend, listen to "To Washington" by John Mellencamp. This song contains the lines, "So a new man is in the White House/With a familiar name/Said he had some fresh ideas/But it's worse now since he came."

2. Next, listen to "Courtesy of the Red, White, & Blue" by Toby Keith. This song contains the lines, "My daddy served in the army/Where he lost his right eye/But he flew a flag out in our yard/Until the day that he died."

3. You might want to listen to these songs several times so you are familiar with the lyrics. Then have a conversation around these questions:

   - What do you see as the message of each of these songwriters?
   - What do you think each of these artists saying about America?
   - Do you think both of these songs are patriotic? Why or why not?

4. **Reflection:** Write a five-minute "quickwrite" on how you would define patriotism. During the class meeting your teacher will lead a discussion based on your quickwrites.

Social Action

If you have used *Freedom Summer* in this invitation, you might want students to explore current discriminatory attitudes. Race theorists argue that instead of thinking that segregation is something that happened in past, we need to acknowledge that we are and always have been a racist society. Students might plan a public debate on the issue: Are we a racist society? To prepare they can (1) gather evidence for and against this argument; and (2) present the debate to other classes or parents.

Unpacking Appealing Ads

The people who create ads want us to believe that we need certain products or services so that we will buy them. To see how advertisers accomplish this, it helps if we examine our own wants, needs, and desires.

Materials

- Videotape of commercials from a major-event TV show
- Multiple copies of the "Why ads and commercials are appealing" handout (Table 10.19.1)

Getting Started

1. To study how advertising affects each of us personally, tape a group of commercials during a NASCAR race, the Olympics, the final game of the World Series, the Rose Bowl, or during a very popular TV show—as these are times when businesses spend a lot of money on advertisements.

2. As a class, examine the following questions. Students can use the "Why Ads and Commercials Are Appealing" handout to help keep track of their ideas in this inquiry.
   - What appeals to you about these commercials?
   - Why are these things appealing to you?
   - What does this advertiser know about you?
   - What kind of identity does the advertiser expect you to take on?

3. When the class has finished viewing and discussing these commercials, ask students to rank in order which of the commercials most appeal to them (use handout notes to help rank) and to then begin probing why and what this says about the students (and us) as consumers.

4. It is also important to point out and discuss trends such as the following:

- Why did these companies buy advertising time during this particular program?
- What similarities are there, if any, among the commercials?
- Are any groups being made fun of on the commercials you are examining? If so, what groups?
    - Why it is that some commercials are more likely to make fun of certain groups than others?
    - If you substituted a different group (e.g., women for farmers, African American men for Caucasian men) how would the commercial be received?

TABLE 10.19.1

Why Ads and Commercials Are Appealing

Product:

Ad/Commercial Description:

What appeals to you about this ad?	Why are these things appealing to you?	What does the advertiser know about you?	What kind of identity does the advertiser want you to take on?

Learning Center Extension: *Appealing Magazine Ads*

An alternative way to do this invitation is to ask students to bring in examples of print advertisements that they find clever, appealing, or compelling.

Materials for Learning Center Extension

▌ Print advertisements brought in by you and your students

▌ Multiple copies of the "Why Ads and Commercials Are Appealing" Graphic Organizer

▌ Table 10.19.2, Learning Center Directions

TABLE 10.19.2
Learning Center Directions

Appealing Magazine Ads

1. With a friend, examine the magazine ads you brought into class. Look especially carefully at the ones you found particularly appealing.

2. Use the "Why Ads and Commercials Are Appealing" sheets to answer the following questions for three different ads:

   - What appeals to you about these ads?
   - Why are these things appealing to you?
   - What does the advertiser know about you?
   - What kind of identity does the advertiser want you to take on?

3. **Extension**: Interview people that are a different age than you (older or younger) or of a different gender to find out if they find the ads you chose appealing. If yes, what were their reasons? If no, why did they think differently from you?

4. **Reflection**: What do you know about print advertising now that you didn't know before you started this center?

Taking Action

Here is a suggestion to start you and your students thinking about the kinds of action you might want to take following this invitation: If there are any commercials that your students find particularly offensive in the way they try to position consumers, they could write letters to the parent company of the product or write a blog entry on the topic.

Unpacking Fairy Tales

Some texts are perceived as innocent. Fairy tales, for example, are often seen as something all parents should read to their children. This invitation is designed to support children in becoming more consciously aware of the underlying messages in fairy tales. The more significant learning, however, might be their growth in understanding that all texts contain both implicit and explicit messages that need to be interrogated and not simply taken for granted.

Materials
- A traditional fairy tale like "Little Red Riding Hood," "Cinderella," "The Three Little Pigs," or "Goldilocks and the Three Bears"
- Large sheets of butcher paper (one for each group of four to five students)
- Markers

Getting Started
1. Divide students into work groups and give a sheet of butcher paper and markers to each group. Explain that the butcher paper will serve as a graffiti board. Have everyone in the group write their name somewhere around the edge of the butcher paper.
2. Introduce the traditional fairy tale you have chosen to read aloud. Read to the place in the text that is right after the point where the main character is first described. Stop reading and ask each group to collaboratively sketch the main character in the middle of their graffiti board.
3. As you read the tale aloud, pause periodically and invite students to jot down words and images that represent the messages they perceive as being sent by the text. It is important for the students

FIGURE 10.20.1
Little red graffiti board.

to understand that they need to draw images as well as to write words. For example, if you are reading "Little Red Riding Hood," students may write things like, "Young girls and old ladies need to be taken care of and rescued by men when they get into trouble," or they may draw a wolf in a circle with a "no" symbol across its front. There is no right set of messages to be discovered. Figure 10.20.1 shows the ideas generated by one group of teachers.

4. For each message they identify, ask students to think about how that message positions different people—or groups of people—in terms of power and agency (i.e., the ability to take control of a situation and do things for oneself).

5. Go around from group to group, round-robin style, and have each group share one of their reactions to the book. Keep going around until the groups have shared all their reactions. Discuss some of the major similarities and differences in interpretations, and have students speculate why differences in reactions occur.

Creating Critical
Classrooms

Learning Center Extension: *When Fairy Tales Go Public*

This center asks you and your students to look for instances in the popular media where themes from fairy tales are used. Of particular interest are how themes are elaborated as well as distorted.

Materials for Learning Center Extension

- Songs, children's literature, cartoon clips from TV, movies that portray themes from a particular fairy tale.
- Table 10.20.1, Learning Center Directions
- Table 10.20.2, Analyzing Fairy Tale Artifacts handout
- In this case we use "Little Red Riding Hood" as an example.
  - Song: "Lil' Red Riding Hood" (Sam the Sham and the Pharaohs, 1966). Available at http://www.itunes.com.
  - Cartoon: "Red Riding Hood" (Figure 10.20.2). Other fairy tale cartoons available at http://cartoonbank.com/.
  - Movie: *Hoodwinked* (Weinstein Company, 2006). Rated PG for violence. Trailer available at http://www.apple.com /trailers/weinstein/hoodwinked/trailer/.
  - Poem: "Little Red Riding Hood and the Wolf," in *Revolting Rhymes* (Dahl, 1995). Contains violence.

TABLE 10.20.1
Learning Center Directions

When Fairy Tales Go Public

At this center you will be exploring the many ways that *Little Red Riding Hood* has been used in public places.

1. With a partner, pick one of the artifacts at this center (e.g., a song, book, video, cartoon).

2. Spend some time looking at or reading the artifact.

3. Use the "Analyzing Fairy Tale Artifacts" handout to analyze two of the artifacts at the center.

4. Keep your completed "Analyzing Fairy Tale Artifacts" handout in a safe place. In a week, you will discuss your analysis with the rest of the class.

TABLE 10.20.2
Analyzing Fairy Tale Artifacts

Date:		
Names:		
Artifact	Why did the author make this artifact (song, book, movie, cartoon) in this way? What's the point?	Why do you think this artifact is appropriate or not appropriate for children?

FIGURE 10.20.2
Red Riding Hood Cartoon.
(CartoonStock.com. With permission.)

Taking Action

Violence is often seen as acceptable if it occurs in fairy tales but not acceptable in other types of media. Have students decide what they think about the violence in the original "Little Red Riding Hood" and the violence in Roald Dahl's "Little Red Riding Hood and the Wolf." After your class has a chance to discuss the different types of violence, have a debate about whether the original "Little Red Riding Hood" or Dahl's "Little Red Riding Hood and the Wolf" should be banned or used in classrooms. Students may want to dramatize the debate and present it to other classes at the school.

What Differences Make a Difference?

Like ethnographic research, teaching has to be up close and personal. This invitation acknowledges the real differences among us (i.e., that we are *not* just the same) and that we can use these differences as a resource. Because so much of American society is grounded in European traditions, values, and beliefs, it is not uncommon for students of European ethnic origins to think of themselves as having no culture. Rather than deny our differences—and the privileges or marginalization that goes along with these differences—we need to learn how to use difference as a vehicle for outgrowing our current selves as both individuals and as a society.

Materials
- Cultural artifacts or facsimiles brought in by students
- Markers, colored paper, and other poster supplies
- Several large pieces of butcher paper used as multiple graffiti boards, each labeled "Our Heritage"

Getting Started
1. This invitation starts by creating an "Our Heritage Museum." Ask students to bring in three artifacts (one of which is a book or some type of printed material) that represent their various ethnicities or family backgrounds. Other items could include crafts, music, photos, or any of a number of other mementos or artifacts. Be prepared to help students who are not living with parents or relatives, do not have family knowledge, or do not

have artifacts to bring to class. Unless everyone can participate comfortably, this invitation can be harmful rather than helpful.

2. Each student gets a small space in the room and creates an exhibit with the artifacts brought to class. All use markers, colored paper, and other supplies to display and label their exhibits.

3. Students participate in a half-and-half gallery walk. Half of the students stay with their exhibits and explain them while the other half takes 10 minutes to visit the exhibits. Then the halves switch for another 10 minutes. This is followed by a final 10-minute period when the whole class visits the exhibits.

4. On multiple bulletin boards or wall spaces, label large pieces of butcher paper "Our Heritage" to serve as graffiti boards. Encourage students to jot down discoveries and connections they make as they visit each of the museum exhibits.

5. During a sustained silent reading period invite students to read the books and other print materials that were brought in. They can add additional new discoveries to the "Our Heritage" graffiti boards.

6. After a whole-class conversation about new discoveries and insights made at the exhibits and at the "Our Heritage" graffiti boards, assign a five-minute quickwrite response to the statement, "We have now indeed become a world community of immigrants" (or a more appropriate statement depending on the content of your class discussion).

7. As a follow-up to the five-minute freewrite, lead a whole-class discussion. You might also point out what students see or fail to see as the implications of this statement for how we as individuals and a nation might more productively position ourselves in the world. For example, because of a large immigrant population from the same country at your school, students may not be aware of immigrant contributions to our nation from other groups.

8. As an extension, the inquiry can move in historical directions by creating a timeline where students map out world events that triggered immigration and compare the motivations of current immigrants with those of early immigrants.

Learning Center Extension: *Picture Book Study on Immigration*

The museum experience is a good place to launch a picture-book study on immigration in which your class explores the difficulties, hardships, and hopes of immigrants, as well as how our ethnic, cultural, and family differences have contributed to the strength of our society.

Materials for Learning Center Extension

- At least 10 picture books about immigration; there is a wonderful range of children's books that focus on immigration (see sidebar)
- Table 10.21.1, Learning Center Directions
- "Literature Response Cube" handout (Table 10.21.2)
- Chart paper with the word "Questions" at the top

Books About Immigration

Angel Child, Dragon Child
(Surat, 1989)
Coming to America:
A Muslim Family's Story
(Wolf, 2003)
My Diary from Here
to There/Mi Diario
De Aquí Hasta Allá
(Pérez, 2002)
Amelia's Road
(Altman, 1993)
Molly's Pilgrim
(Cohen, 1983)
Going Home
(Bunting, 1996)
Happy Birthday, Mr. Kang
(Roth, 2001)
Tomás and the Library Lady
(Mora, 1997)
América Is Her Name
(Rodríguez, 1997)
El Chino
(Say, 1990)

Picture-Book Study on Immigration

1. With a partner, read at least two picture books at this center.

2. Individually, fill out a "Literature Response Cube" for each book.

3. Discuss your response sheets with your partner.

4. Write the questions from your response sheets on the "Questions" poster at this center.

5. You and your partner decide on one question from the "Questions" poster to answer. It can be one you wrote or a question written by someone else in the class.

6. Collect as much information as you can to answer your question. You might interview family or community members, go to the library, read more books, or use the Internet.

7. As a team, plan and present your research findings at class meeting time.

8. **Reflection**: What are your current understandings of immigration issues in the United States and around the world?

Literature Response Cube

Immigration	
Book Title:	
What did you learn from this book?	What surprised you?
What connections, if any, can you make between the story and people you know?	What questions do you have about immigration?

Taking Action

There are many ways your students may want to take action following this invitation. One is to have students collect news articles on current immigration controversies in this country; Google News is a great resource. Students can debate different sides of the controversies, take a stand on the issue (different students may take different stands), and decide on action they would like to pursue.

References

Ababa, A. (2003, June 24). *Ethiopia wary of GM seeds.* BBC News UK Edition. Available from http://news.bbc.co.uk/1/hi/business/3016390.stm

Aid agency warns on North Korea (2003, July 18). BBC News UK Edition. Available from http://news.bbc.co.uk/1/hi/world/asia-pacific/3077501.stm

Anderson, G. L., & Irvine, P. (1993). Informing critical literacy with ethnography. In C. Lankshear & P. L. McLaren (Eds.), *Critical literacy: Politics, praxis, and the postmodern* (pp. 81–104). Albany: State University of New York Press.

Anderson, H. (2004, July 24). *Sudan's cruel and slow starvation.* BBC News. Available from http://news.bbc.co.uk/go/pr/fr//1/hi/programmes/from_our_own_correspondent/3922461.stm

Anderson, R. C., & Pearson, P. D. (1984). A schema-theoretic view of basic processes in reading comprehension. In P. D. Pearson (Ed.), *Handbook of reading research* (pp. 255–291). White Plains, NY: Longman.

Anyon, J. (1997). *Ghetto schooling: A political economy of urban educational reform.* New York: Teachers College Press.

Babbs, F. (1998). *Go to your studio and make stuff: The Fred Babb poster book.* New York: Workman Publishing.

Bakhtin, M. (1983). *The dialogic imagination: Four essays.* Austin: University of Texas Press.

Baratz, J., & Shuy, R. (1969). *Teaching black children to read.* Washington, DC: Center for Applied Linguistics.

Barnes, D. (1975). *From communication to curriculum.* New York: Penguin.

Bearak, B. (2003, July 13). Why famine persists, *New York Times Magazine,* 32–37, 5, 60–61.

Bigelow, B. (2006). Hunger on trial: An activity on the Irish Potato Famine and its meaning for today. *Rethinking School, 20,* 44–46. Also available at http://www.rethinkingschools.org/.

Birchak, B., Connor, C., Crawford, K., Kahn, L., Kaser, S., Turner, S., et al. (1998). *Teacher study groups: Building community through dialogue and reflection.* Urbana, IL: National Council of Teachers of English.

Bleich, D. (1979). *Subjective criticism*. Baltimore, MD: John Hopkins Press.

Bleich, D. (1993). *Double perspective: Language, literacy, and social relations*. Urbana, IL: National Council of Teachers of English.

Bloome, D., & Green, J. (1984). Directions in the sociolinguistic study of reading. In P. D. Pearson (Ed.), *Handbook of reading research* (pp. 395–452). White Plains, NY: Longman.

Booth, W. (1988). The company we keep: An ethics of fiction. Berkley: California University Press.

Bomer, K. (2005). Missing the children: When politics and programs impede our teaching. *Language Arts, 82*(3), 168–176.

Bomer, R., & Bomer, K. (2001). *For a better world: Reading and writing for social action*. Portsmouth, NH: Heinemann.

Boozer, M. E., Maras, L. B., & Brummett, B. (1999). Exchanging ideas and changing positions: The importance of conversation to holistic, critical endeavors. In C. Edelsky (Ed.), *Making justice our project: Teachers working toward critical whole-language practice* (pp. 55–76). Urbana, IL: National Council of Teachers of English.

Borko, H. (2004). Professional development and teacher learning: Mapping the terrain. *Educational Researcher, 3*(8), 3–15.

Bourdieu, P. (1986). The forms of capital. In J. G. Richardson (Ed.), *Handbook of theory and research for the sociology of education* (pp. 241–258). New York: Greenwood Press.

Bowser, B. A. (2003, October 29). *Ethiopia*. NewsHour with Jim Lehrer. Available from http://www.pbs.org/newshour/bb/africa/july-dec03/ethiopia_10-29.html

Bread for the World. (2006). *Hunger facts: International*. Retrieved September 18, 2006, from http://www.bread.org/learn/hunger-basics/hunger-facts-international.html

Britton, J., Burgess, T., Martin, N., McLeod, A., & Rosen, H. (1975). *The development of writing abilities*. London, England: Macmillan.

Brown, R. (1970). *Psycholinguistics*. New York: Macmillan.

Burke, C. L. (1969). *A psycholinguistic description of grammatical restructurings in the oral reading of a select group of middle school children*. Unpublished doctoral dissertation, Wayne State University.

Cazden, C. B. (1988). *Classroom discourse: The language of teaching and learning*. Portsmouth, NH: Heinemann.

Chomsky, C. (1972). Stages in language development and reading exposure. *Harvard Educational Review, 42*(1), 1–33.

Chomsky, N. (1965). *Aspects of the theory of syntax*. Cambridge, MA: MIT Press.

Christensen, L. (2000). *Reading, writing, and rising up: Teaching about social justice and the power of the written word*. Milwaukee, WI: Rethinking Schools.

Christensen, L. (2003, March). *Acting for justice*. Paper presented at the Critical Literacy in Action Workshop, Bloomington, IN.

Clay, M. (1993). Reading recovery: A guidebook for teachers in training. Portsmouth, NH: Heinemann.

Clyde, J. A. (2003). Stepping inside the story world: The subtext strategy—A tool for connecting and comprehending. *The Reading Teacher, 57*(1), 150–160.

Codell, E. R. (2001). *Educating Esmé: Diary of a teacher's first year*. Chapel Hill, NC: Algonquin Books.

Coles, G. (2003). *Reading the naked truth: Literacy, legislation, and lies*. Portmouth, NH: Heinemann.

Comber, B. (2001). Negotiating critical literacies. *School Talk, 6*(3), 1–3.

Combs, A. (1971, April). *Perceiving, behaving, becoming: Lessons learned*. Presentation given at the annual meeting of the American Educational Research Association, Chicago, IL.

Creps, M. (2006, February 20). Clothing is a message in gold for 4 IU grads. *Herald-Times*, p. 5.

Crisis in Sudan (2004, August 4). News Hour with Jim Lehrer. Available from http://www.pbs.org/newshour/bb/africa/july-dec04/sudan_8-4.html

Damico, J., Campano, G., & Harste, J. (2005). What *Voices in the Park* do we hear and what *Voices in the Park* do we not hear? A critical look at multiple perspectives books. *Talking Points, 16*(2), 30–33.

Davis, B. (2003). *Frogs and snails and feminist tales: Preschool children and gender*. Cresshill, NJ: Hampton Press.

Delgado, R., & Stefancic, J. (2001). *Critical race theory: An introduction*. New York: New York University Press.

Denny, D. (2006, October 25). Banquet an exercise in real-world inequalities. *Herald-Times*, p. A3.

Denny, Dan (2005, July 22). *Cupboard bare at food pantries: Demand increasing as donations dwindle. Herald-Times*. Retrieved July 22, 2005, from http://www.hoosiertimes.com.

Dewey, J. (1916). *Democracy and education*. New York: Macmillan.

Dewey, J. (1933). *How we think*. Lexington, MA: Heath.

Dodds, T. (2004, November 24). Players' Union Blames Refs, Security in Appeal. *Indianapolis Star*. Retrieved 10/18/05 from http://www.indystar.com/articles/4/197070-9444-179.html

Douglas, W. O. (1951). *United States Supreme Court: Adler v. Board of Education*. Washington, DC: Government Printing Office.

Eco, U. (1970). *The role of the reader*. Bloomington: Indiana University Press.

Edelsky, C. (Ed.) (1999). *Making justice our project: Teachers working toward critical whole language practice*. Urbana, IL: National Council of Teachers of English.

Edwards, A. D., & Westgate, D. P. G. (1987). Investigating classroom talk: An international perspective. Padstow, Great Britain: Routledge Falmer.

Evans, J. (2004). Beanie Babies: An opportunity to promote literacy development or a money-spinner for the business tycoons? In J. Evans (Ed.), *Literacy moves on: Using popular culture, new technologies and critical literacy in the classroom* (pp. 97–114). London, England: David Fulton Publishers.

Fairclough, N. (1989). *Language and power.* London: Longman.

Fairclough, N. (1995). *Critical discourse analysis: The critical study of language.* London, England: Longman.

Farrell, L. (1998, July). *Reconstructing Sally: Narratives and counter narratives around work, education and workplace restructure.* Paper presented at the Meeting of the Australian Association for Research in Education, Adelaide.

Finn, P. J. (1999). *Literacy with an attitude: Educating working-class children in their own self-interest.* Albany: State University of New York Press.

Freedom Writers & Gruwell, E. (1999). The freedom writers diary: How a teacher and 150 teens used writing to change themselves and the world around them. New York: Main Street Books.

Freire, P. (1970). *Pedagogy of the oppressed.* New York: Herder & Herder.

Freire, P. (1985). *The politics of education.* South Hadley, MA: Bergin & Garvey.

Freire, P. (1998). *Pedagogy of freedom: Ethics, democracy, and civic courage.* Lanham, MD: Rowman & Littlefield.

Freire, P., & Faundez, A. (1989). Learning to question. In A. M. A. Freire & D. Macedo, (Eds.). *The Paulo Freire reader.* New York: Continuum.

Freisinger, R. (1982). Cross-disciplinary writing programs: Beginnings. In T. Fulwiler & A. Young (Eds.), *Language connections: Writing and reading across the curriculum* (pp. 3–13). Urbana, IL: National Council of Teachers of English.

Fries, C. (1963). *Linguistics and reading.* New York: Holt.

Fry, J. (2005, February). *Making our teaching critical.* Presentation made at the annual Conference on Children's Literature, American University, Washington, DC.

Garan, E. (2004). *In defense of our children: When politics, profit and education collide.* Portsmouth, NH: Heinemann.

Gee, J. P. (1996). *Social linguistics and literacy: Ideology in discourse* (2d ed.). New York: Taylor & Francis.

Gee, J. P. (1999). *An introduction to discourse analysis: Theory and method.* London, England: Routledge.

Giroux, H. (1991). Modernism, postmodernism, and feminism: Rethinking the boundaries of educational discourse. In H. Giroux, (Ed.). *Postmodernism, feminism, and cultural politics* (pp.1–59). Albany: State University of New York Press.

Giroux, H. (1993). Literacy and the politics of difference. In C. Lankshear & P. L. McLaren (Eds.), *Critical literacy, politics, praxis, and the postmodern* (pp. 367–378). Albany: State University of New York Press.

Giroux, H. A. (1994). *Disturbing pleasures: Learning popular culture.* London, England: Routledge.

Gioux, H. A. (2001). *The mouse that roared: Disney and the end of innocence.* Lanham, MD: Rowman & Littlefield.

Giroux, H., & Giroux, S. (2004). *Take back higher education: Race, youth, and the crisis of democracy in the post-civil rights era.* New York: Macmillan.

Goodman, K. S. (1965). A linguistic study of cues and miscues in reading. *Elementary English, 42*(8), 639–643.

Goodman, K. S. (1967). Reading: A psycholinguistic guessing game. *Journal of the Reading Specialist, 4*(1), 126–135.

Goodman, K. S., Shannon, P., Goodman, Y., & Rapoport, R. (2004). *Saving our schools: The case for public education.* Brandon, OR: Robert D. Reed Publishers.

Goodman, Y. (1978). Kidwatching: An alternative to testing. *Journal of National Elementary School Principals, 57*(4), 22–27.

Hade, D., & Edmondson, J. (2003). Children's book publishing in neoliberal times. *Language Arts, 81*(2), 135–143.

Halliday, M. A. K. (1973). *Exploration in the functions of language.* London, England: Edward Arnold.

Halliday, M. A. K. (1975). *Learning to mean: Explorations in the development of language.* London, England: Edward Arnold.

Halliday, M. A. K. (1982). Three aspects of children's language development: Learning language, learning through language, and learning about language (pp. 7–19). In Y. Goodman, M. Haussler, & D. Strickland (Eds.), *Oral and written language development research: Impact on the schools.* Urbana, IL: National Council of Teachers of English.

Halliday, M. A. K. (1985). *An introduction to functional grammar.* London, England: Edward Arnold.

Harste J. C., Breau, A., Leland, C., Lewison, M., Ociepka, A., & Vasquez, V. (2000). Supporting critical conversations in classrooms. In K. M. Pierce (Ed.), *Adventuring with books* (12th ed.) (pp. 506–554). Urbana, IL: National Council of Teachers of English.

Harste, J., & Burke, C. (1977). A new hypothesis for reading teacher education research: Both the teaching and learning of reading is theoretically based. In P. David Pearson (Ed.), *26th Yearbook of the National Reading Conference* (pp. 127–143). Minneapolis, MN: Mason.

Harste, J. C., Leland, C., Schmidt, K., Vasquez, V., & Ociepka, A. (2004). Practice makes practice: Or does it? *Reading On-Line, 4*(1), 1–70.

AU: URL deleted because it was not an exact link to the article. If a URL is added please provide the exact URL and also a retrieval date. Thanks.

Harste, J. C., Short, K. G., & Burke, C. L. (1988). *Creating class-rooms for authors: The reading–writing connection.* Portsmouth, NH: Heinemann.

Harste, J. C., Woodward, V. A., & Burke, C. L. (1984). *Language stories and literacy lessons.* Portsmouth, NH: Heinemann.

Heath, S. B. (1983). *Ways with words.* New York: Cambridge University Press.

Heffernan, L. (2003). Morning meeting: Contradictions and possibilities. *School Talk, 8*(3), 4.

Heffernan, L. (2004). *Critical literacy and writer's workshop: Bringing purpose and passion to student writing.* Newark, DE: International Reading Association.

Heffernan, L., & Lewison, M. (2003). Social narrative writing: (Re)constructing kid culture in the writer's workshop. *Language Arts, 80*(6), 435–443.

Heffernan, L., & Lewison, M. (2005). What's lunch got to do with it? Critical literacy and the discourse of the lunchroom. *Language Arts, 83*(1), 107–117.

Hertzberg, M. (2003, June). Engaging critical reader response to literature through process drama. *Reading Online, 6*(10). Retrieved March 6, 2007, from http://www.readingonline.org/international/hertzberg/

Hinchey, P. H. (1998). *Finding Freedom in the Classroom, a Practical Introduction to Critical Theory.* New York: Peter Lang.

hooks, b. (1994). *Learning to transgress: Education as the practice of freedom.* New York: Routledge.

Horsch, P., Chen, J., & Nelson, D. (1999). Rules and rituals: Tools for creating a respectful, caring learning community. *Phi Delta Kappan, 3*(1), 223–227.

Huck, C. (1966). *Good books for all children.* Columbus, OH: Ohio State University Press.

Iser, W. (1980). *The act of reading: A theory of aesthetic response.* Baltimore, MD: John Hopkins Press.

Janks, H. (1999). *Critical and position.* Johannesberg, South Africa: Hodder & Sloughton.

Janks, H. (2000). Domination, access, diversity, and design: A synthesis for critical literacy education. *Educational Review, 52*(1), 15–30.

Janks, H. (2002, November). *Critical literacy: Deconstruction and reconstruction.* Paper presented at the National Council of Teachers of English Annual Conference, Atlanta, GA.

Johnston, P. H. (2004). *Choice words.* Portland, ME: Stenhouse.

Joseph, P. B., & Efron, S. (2005). Seven worlds of moral education. *Phi Delta Kappan, 86*(7), 525–533.

Kamler, B. (1999). This lovely doll who's come to school: Morning meeting talk as gendered language practice. In B. Kamler (Ed.), *Constructing gender and difference: Critical research perspectives on early childhood* (pp. 191–213). Cresskill, NJ: Hampton Press.

Kamler, B. (2001). *Relocating the personal: A critical writing pedagogy.* Albany: State University Press of New York.

Kauffman, N. (2006, September 23). MCCSC schools look at bullying. *Herald-Times,* p. 5.

Keller, D. (2006). Hidden curriculum in school signage: A semiotic analysis. *International Journal of Applied Semiotics, 5*(2), 12–24.

Ketner, K. L. (1976). Identity and existence in the study of human traditions. *Folklore, 87*(2), 192–200.

Kintsch, W. (1974). *The representation of meaning in memory.* Hillsdale, NJ: Erlbaum.

Kirby, A. (2003, December 11). West "risks new Ethiopia famine." BBC News. Available from http://news.bbc.co.uk/go/pr/fr/-/1/hi/sci/tech/3308231.stm

Kirby, A. (2004, March 3). Ethiopians "rely on food imports." BBC News UK Edition. Available from http://news.bbc.co.uk/1/hi/sci/tech/3525571.stm

Kohn, A. (2004). Challenging students—and how to have more of them. *Phi Delta Kappan, 86*(3), 184–194.

Kress, G. (2003). *Literacy in the new media age.* London, England: Routledge.

Kress, G., & van Leeuwen, T. (1998). *Reading images: The grammar of visual design.* London, England: Routledge.

Labov, W. (1972). *Language of the inner city.* Philadelphia: University of Pennsylvania Press.

Ladson-Billings, G. (2002). I ain't writin' nuttin': Permissions to fail and demands to succeed in urban classrooms. In L. Delpit & J. K. Dowdy (Eds.), *The skin that we speak: Thoughts on language and culture in the classroom.* New York: New Press.

Ladson-Billings, G. (2004). Landing on the wrong note: The price we paid for brown. *Educational Researcher, 33*(7), 3–13.

Lakoff, G. (2004). *Don't think of an elephant: Know your values and frame the debate.* White River Junction, VT: Chelsea Green.

Lankshear, C. (1997). Language and the new capitalism. *International Journal of Inclusive Education, 1*(4), 309–321.

Lankshear, C., & Knobel, M. (2006). *New literacies* (2d ed.). Oxford, England: Open University Press.

Lankshear, C., & McLaren, P. L. (1993). Preface. In C. Lankshear & P. L. McLaren (Eds.), *Critical literacy, politics, praxis, and the postmodern* (pp. xii–xx). Albany: State University of New York Press.

Larson, C., & Ovando, C. (2001). *The color of bureaucracy.* Belmont, CA: Wadsworth/Thomson Learning.

Leland, C., & Harste, J. (2000). Critical literacy: Enlarging the space of the possible. *Primary Voices, 9*(1), 3–7.

Leland, C., Harste, J., Berghoff, B., Bomer, R., Flint, A., & Lewison, M. (2002). Critical literacy. In J. Kristo and A. McClure (Eds.), *Adventuring with books* (13th ed.) (pp. 465–487). Urbana, IL: National Council of Teachers of English.

Leland, C., Harste, J., & Huber, K. (2005). Out of the box: Critical literacy in a first-grade classroom. *Language Arts, 82*(4), 257–268.

Lensmire, T. (2000). *Powerful Writing, Responsible Teaching.* New York: Teachers College Press.

Lester, N. B. & Mayher, J. S. (1987). Critical professional inquiry. *English Education, 19*(4), 198–210.

Lester, N. B. & Onore, N. B. (1986). From teacher-teacher to teacher-learner: making the grade. *Language Arts, 63*(7), 698–704.

Leu, D. J., Kinzer, C. K., Coiro, J. L., & Cammack, D. W. (2005). Toward a theory of new literacies emerging from the Internet and other information and communication technologies. In R. B. Ruddell & N. J. Unrau (Eds.), Theoretical models and processes of reading (5th ed.) (pp. 1570–1613). Newark, DE: International Reading Association.

Lewison, M. (1995). Taking the lead from teachers: Seeking a new model of staff development. In J. Lemlech (Ed.), *Teachers and principals at work: Becoming a professional leader* (pp. 76–113). New York: Scholastic.

Lewison, M., Flint, A .S., & Van Sluys, K. (2002). Taking on critical literacy: The journey of newcomers and novices. *Language Arts, 79*(5), 382–392.

Lewison, M., & Holliday, S. (1999). Investigating a school-university partnership through the lenses of relationship, self-determination, reciprocal influence, and expanding power. In D. Byrd and D. J. McIntyre (Eds.), *Research on professional development schools: Teacher education yearbook VII* (pp. 79–96). Thousand Oaks, CA: Corwin Press, Inc.

Lewison, M., Leland, C., Flint, A. S., & Möller, K. (2002). Dangerous discourses: Using controversial books to support engagement, diversity, and democracy. *New Advocate, 15*(3), 215–226.

Lewison, M., Leland, C., & Harste, J. (2000). Not in my classroom! The case for using multi-view social issues books with children. *Australian Journal of Language and Literacy, 23*(1), 8–20.

Loewen, J. (1995). *Lies my teacher told me: Everything your American history textbook got wrong.* New York: Touchstone.

Loewen, J. W. (1999). *Lies across America.* New York: Touchstone.

Loyn, D. (2002, February 15). *Life hanging by a thread.* BBC News South Asia. Available from http://news.bbc.co.uk/1/hi/world/south_asia/ 1822916.stm

Luke, A. (1998). Getting over method: Literacy teaching as work in "new time." *Language Arts, 75*(1), 305–313.

Luke, A., & Freebody, P. (1997). Shaping the social practices of reading. In S. Muspratt, A. Luke, & P. Freebody (Eds.), *Constructing critical literacies* (pp. 185–223). Cresskill, NJ: Hampton Press.

Luke, A., & Watson, C. (1994). Teaching and assessing critical reading. In T. Husen & L. Postlewaite (Eds.), *International encyclopedia of Education* (2d ed.) (pp. 231–234). London, England: Pergamon Press.

MacGinitie, W. (1983). The power of uncertainty. *Journal of Reading, 5*(1), 677–679.

Marsh, J. (2000). Teletubby tales: Popular culture in the early years' language and literacy curriculum. *Contemporary Issues in Early Education, 1*(8), 119–133.

Marsh, J. (2005). Children of the digital age. In J. Marsh (Ed.), *Popular culture, new media and digital literacy in early childhood* (pp. 183–200). Padstow, Great Britain: Routledge Falmer.

Matson, R. J. (2006, May 3). Political cartoons. *St. Louis Post Dispatch.* Retrieved March 9, 2007, from http://www.cagle.com/teacher/2.asp

McIntosh, P. (1989). *White privilege: Unpacking the invisible knapsack.* Wellesley, MA: Wellesley College Center for Research on Women.

Merchant, G. (2005). Barbie meets Bob the Builder at the workstation: Learning to write on screen. In J. Marsh (Ed.), *Popular culture, new media and digital literacy in early childhood* (pp. 183–200). Padstow, Great Britain: Routledge Falmer.

Microsoft Corporation (1999). *Encarta® World English Dictionary.* London, England: Bloomsbury Publishing.

Moll, L. C., Amanti, C., Neff, D. & Gonzalez, N. (1992). Funds of knowledge for teaching: Using a qualitative approach to connect homes and classrooms. *Theory Into Practice, 31*(2), 132–141.

Moore, T. (2004, Summer). Beyond the bake sale: An elementary school club helps students explore the roots of hunger. *Rethinking Schools, 18,* Retrieved March 9, 2007, from http://www.rethinkingschools.org/archive/18_04/bake184.shtml

Muir, J. (2002, February 21). *Food reaches Afghanistan's desperate.* BBC News South Asia. Available from http://news.bbc.co.uk/1/hi/world/south_asia/ 1833696.stm

N. Korea crops hit by heavy rains (2004, August 2). BBC News UK Edition. Available from http://news.bbc.co.uk/1/hi/world/asia-pacific/3526816.stm

New London Group (2000). A pedagogy of multiliteracies: Designing social futures. In B. Cope & M. Kalantzis (Eds.), *Multiliteracies: Literacy learning in the design of social futures* (pp. 9–38). London, England: Routledge.

Nieto, S. (1999). *The light in their eyes: Creating multicultural learning communities.* New York: Teachers College Press.

Nieto, S. (2003). What keeps teachers going? *Educational Leadership*, 60(8), 14–18.

Noddings, N. (2004). War, critical thinking, and self-understanding. *Phi Delta Kappan, 85*(7), 489–495.

North Korea's empty shelves (2003, February 13). BBC News. Available from http://news.bbc.co.uk/1/hi/world/asia-pacific/2757047.stm

Pearce, R. (1999). Advertising: Critical analysis of images. In I. Parker & the Bolton Discourse Group (Eds.), *Critical textwork: An introduction to varieties of discourse and analysis* (pp.78–91). Buckingham, England: Open University Press.

Peirce, C. S. (1931–58). *Collected Writings* (C. Hartshorne, P. Weiss, & A. W. Burks, Eds., Vols. 1–8). Cambridge, MA: Harvard University Press.

Pennycook, A. (1999). Introduction: Critical approaches to TESOL. *TESOL Quarterly, 33*(8), 329–348.

Peterson, P. L., & Clark, C. M. (1978). Teacher's reports of their cognitive processes during teaching. *American Educational Research Journal, 15*(7), 555–565.

Peterson, R., & Eeds, M. (1999). *Grand conversations*. New York: Scholastic.

Poole-Kavana, H. (2006, Summer). 12 myths about hunger. *Institute for Food and Development Policy Backgrounder, 12*(2). Retrieved March 9, 2007, from http://www.foodfirst.org/12myths

Postman, N., & Weingartner, C. (1969). *Teaching as a subversive activity*. New York: Delta.

The Principals Vanish, Editorial, (2006, May 27). *New York Times*, p. 12.

Q&A: Sudan's Darfur conflict (2004, August 9). BBC News. Available from http://news.bbc.co.uk/go/pr/fr/-/1/hi/world/africa/3496731.stm

Robidoux, C. (2005, April 24). Kids at the mall, *New Hampshire Sunday News*, p. A22.

Rogers, R. (2001). Family literacy and the mediation of cultural models. In C. M. Fairbanks, J. Worthy, B. Maloch, J. V. Hoffman, & D. L. Schallert (Eds.), *50th Yearbook of the National Reading Conference* (pp. 96–114). Mahwah, NJ: Lawrence Erlbaum Associates.

Rosenberg, M. (2004, November 20). Malice at Palace. *Detroit Free Press*. Retrieved 10/15/05, from http://www.freep.com/sports/pistons/mrosey20e_20041120.htm

Rosenblatt, L. (1938). *Literature as exploration*. New York: Appleton-Century.

Rosenblatt, L. (1987). *The reader, the text, the poem*. Carbondale: Southern Illinois Press.

Rumelhart, D. (1980). Schemata: The building blocks of cognition. In R. J. Spiro, B. C. Bruce, & W. F. Brewer (Eds.), *Theoretical issues in reading comprehension* (pp. 33–58). Hillsdale, NJ: Erlbaum.

Sach, J. (2003). *The activist teaching profession*. Philadelphia: Open University Press.

Said, E. W. (2006). *On defiance and taking positions—Beyond the academy: A scholar's obligations* (Occasional Paper No. 31). New York: American Council of Learned Societies.

Schallert, D., & Tierney, R. J. (1982). *Learning from expository text: The interaction of text structure with reader characteristics* (NIE-6-79-0167). Washington, DC: National Institute of Education.

Schön, D. A. (1983). *The reflective practitioner: How professionals think in action*. New York: Basic Books.

Schön, D. A. (1987). *Educating the reflective practitioner*. San Francisco, CA: Jossey-Bass.

Shannon, P. (1995). *Text, lies, & videotape: Stories about life, literacy, & learning*. Portsmouth, NH: Heinemann.

Shor, I. (1987). Educating the educators: A Freirean approach to the crisis in teacher education. In I. Shor (Ed.), *Freire for the classroom, A sourcebook for liberatory teaching* (pp.7–32). Portsmouth, NH: Boynton/Cook.

Short, K. G., & Burke, C. L. (1989). New potentials for teacher education: teaching and learning as inquiry. *Elementary School Journal*, 90(1), 193–206.

Short, K., Harste, J., & Burke, C. (1996). *Creating classrooms for authors and inquirers* (2nd ed.). Portsmouth, NH, Heinemann.

Simpson, A., & Comber, B. (1995). Reading cereal boxes: Analyzing everyday texts. *Texts: The heart of the English curriculum* (Series 1). Adelaide, New South Wales: Department of Education and Children's Services.

Sims-Bishop. R. (1982). Dialect and reading: Toward redefining the issues. In J. Langer & M. T. Smith-Burke (Eds.), *Reader meets author/bridging the gap* (pp. 256–269). Newark, DE: International Reading Association.

Smith, F. (1971). *Understanding reading: A psycholinguistic analysis of reading and learning to read*. New York: Holt, Rinehart.

Smith, F. (1981). Demonstrations, engagement and sensitivity: the choice between people and programs. *Language Arts*, 58(2), 634–642.

Smith, F. (1982). *Understanding reading* (3d. ed.). New York: Holt, Rinehart, & Winston.

Smith, F. (1983). *Essays in literacy: Selected papers and some afterthoughts*. Portsmouth, NH: Heinemann.

Smith, P. (1996, May). *Improving literacy discussions*. Workshop conducted at the annual meeting of the International Reading Association, Anaheim, CA.

Smyth, J. (1989). Developing and sustaining critical reflection in teacher education. *Journal of Teacher Education*, 40(1), 2–9.

Sparks-Langer, G. M., & Colton, A. B. (1991). Synthesis of research on teachers; reflective thinking. *Educational Leadership*, 48(4), 37–44.

Stein, N., & Glenn, C. G. (1979). An analysis of story comprehension in elementary school children. In R. Freedle (Ed.), *New directions in discourse processing* (Vol. 2, pp. 53–120). Norwood, NJ: Ablex.

Strauss, S. L. (2004). *The linguistics, neurology, and politics of phonics: Silent "e" speaks out.* Mahwah, NJ: Erlbaum

Street, B. (1995). *Social literacies: Critical approaches to literacy, development, ethnography and education.* Boston, MA: Addison Wesley.

Suarez, R. (2001, March 29). *Afghanistan's agony.* NewsHour with Jim Lehrer. Available from http://www.pbs.org/newshour/bb/asia/jan-june01/afghanistan_3-29.html

Sumara, Dennis (1995, December). *Commonplace texts.* Presentation at the annual meeting of the National Reading Conference, San Antonio, TX.

Sumara, D. (2002). *Why reading literature in school still matters.* Mahwah, NJ: Lawrence Erlbaum Associates.

Sumara, D., & Davis, B. (1999). Interrupting heteronormativity: Toward a queer curriculum theory. *Curriculum Inquiry, 29*(2), 191–208.

The North Korean famine (1997, August 26). Online NewsHour Forum. Available from http://www.pbs.org/newshour/forum/august97/korea_8-26.html

Thomson, P. (2002). *Schooling the rustbelt kids: Making the difference in changing times.* Crows Nest, New South Wales: Allen & Unwin.

Tom, A. R. (1985). Inquiring into inquiry-oriented teacher education. *Journal of Teacher Education, 35*(2), 35–44.

Teaching Tolerance website (http://www.tolerance.org)

Tossing the teens out of the mall, into…what? [Letter to the Editor] (2005, April 26). *Union Leader*, p. A8.

Van Sluys, K. (2005). *What If and Why? Literacy invitations for multilingual classrooms.* Portsmouth, NH: Heinemann.

Vasquez, V. (2000). Our way: Using the everyday to create a critical literacy curriculum. *Primary Voices, 9*(3), 8–13.

Vasquez, Vivian (2006). *Negotiating critical literacy.* Mahwah, NJ: Erlbaum.

Wells, G. (1986). *The meaning makers: Children learning language and using language to learn.* Portsmouth, NH: Heinemann.

West, C. (1999). *The Cornel West reader.* New York: Basic Civitas Books.

Westheimer, J. & Kahne, J. (2004). What kind of citizen? The politics of educating for democracy. *American Educational Research Journal, 41*(5), 237–269.

White, B. (1994). *Mama makes up her mind: And other dangers of southern living.* New York: Vintage.

Wink, J. (2000). *Critical pedagogy: Notes from the real world.* White Plains, NY: Longman.

Zeichner, K. M. (1983). Alternative paradigms of teacher education. *Journal of Teacher Education, 34*(1), 3–9.

Zeichner, K. M., & Liston, D. P. (1987). Teaching student teachers to reflect. *Harvard Educational Review, 57*(1), 23–48.

References

An Annotated List of Picture Books, Chapter Books, Videos, Songs, and Websites*

Altman, Linda Jacobs (1991). *Amelia's road.* Illus. Enrique O. Sanchez. Lee & Low. Picture Book. Amelia and her family are constantly on the move from harvest to harvest. They live in labor camps for short periods of time, and then they are back on the road. Amelia fears that she will never have a place of her own. Eventually she finds a special spot.

Ancona, George (1997). *Mayeros: A Yucatec Maya family.* Lothrop, Lee & Shepard. Picture Book. That Ancona chose the title *Mayeros*—the name Yucatec Maya call themselves—sets the tone for his respectful and lively photodocumentary of the daily life of a Yucatec Maya family. We meet two young brothers, Armando and Gaspar, as well as their parents, sisters, grandparents, and extended family as they prepare and eat meals, build a ring for a bullfight, and dance to celebrate the feast of saints. Though there is room to ask questions about history and economic disparity, this is not primarily a story of poverty or oppression; rather, Ancona's lens portrays the life of the family as rich with tradition and resilient to change.

* Some of these materials have been edited and compiled here for your convenience from previous publications: *Adventuring with Books,* 12th ed., pp. 506–544 and 13th ed., pp. 465–487; *Talking Points,* 16(1), pp. 38–39, 16(2), pp. 30–32, 17(1), pp. 34–35, and 17(2), pp. 26–28. Reprinted with permission from the National Council of Teachers of English.

Ancona, George (2000). *Cuban kids.* Marshall Cavendish. Chapter/ Picture Book. This is a sympathetic look at the lives of Cuban children and presents an alternative to the typically negative image portrayed in the media. The book is a photo essay of snapshots from daily lives of children, with close-ups of a few. The photographs manage to make Cuba look both exotic and ordinary, so students will notice differences while still recognizing that Cuban kids go to school, have friends and families, and like to have fun.

Anzaldua, Gloria (1995). *Friends from the other side/Amgios del otro lado.* Illus. Consuelo Mendez. Children's Book Press. Picture Book. Prietita befriends Joaquin, a wetback and "illegal alien," new to the United States. What is powerful about this picture book is that it shows a human side to this national controversy.

Bartoletti, Susan (1999). *Kids on strike!* Houghton Mifflin. Chapter Book. Are children being exploited today in ways similar to the ways they were exploited during the Industrial Revolution in the United States? Bartoletti's historical account of children in the workforce is complemented by hundreds of authentic, gripping photographs of children at work on city streets, in coal mines, and in the garment industry. The images of the children and descriptions of their inhumane working conditions raise questions about human nature, progress, and American economic values.

Bennett, Cherie (2004). *A heart divided.* Delacorte. Chapter Book. After finding herself caught up in the tensions surrounding the flying of the Confederate flag at their school, Kate, a recent Yankee transplant, decides to write a play using the voices of the students she interviews as the text. One of the most powerful aspects of this book is Kate's play, which provides readers a demonstration of what they might do to address similar complex issues in their communities.

Birdseye, Debbie, & Birdseye, Tom (1997). *Under our skin: Kids talk about race.* Photographs by Robert Crum. Holiday House. Chapter/ Picture Book. Six 12- and 13-year-olds speak in their own words about their perceptions and experiences of race in America. They describe their own ethnic traditions, their experiences of racism and prejudice, and their ideas and hopes for race relations in America. This focus on kids' individual voices provides a great starting point for discussion of how students experience the impact of race and ethnicity in their own lives.

Birtha, Becky (2005). *Grandmama's pride.* Illus. Colin Bootman. Albert Whitman. Picture Book. It took a lot of "quiet dignity" for African Americans to face the indignities of the Jim Crow laws. In 1956, two young African American girls visit their grandmother and through her example come to understand how to maintain dignity and self-respect for themselves and their race despite deep and abiding social and racial segregation.

Booktrust (2006). *Education resources*. Illus. Anthony Browne. Available at http://www.booktrusted.co.uk/education,browne/browne.html. The Booktrust is an independent national charity in Great Britain that encourages people of all ages and cultures to discover and enjoy reading. This webpage gives all kinds of useful information about Anthony Browne—awards, a short biography, influences on Browne's illustrations, classroom links, and professional articles.

Breckler, Rosemary (1996). *Sweet dried apples: A Vietnamese wartime childhood*. Illus. Deborah Kogan Ray. Houghton Mifflin. Picture Book. This story is told from the point of view of a young Vietnamese girl whose life is changed by the encroaching war that surrounds her. What starts out as a distant threat gradually comes to encompass her family and her life. This book invites conversations about the different forms that social action can take and how this action affects people's lives.

Brown, Marcia (1971). *Cinderella*. Atheneum. Picture Book. In this version of the old French fairytale there is no mean stepmother, Cinderella's foot is anything by dainty (a triple EEE at least), and in the end she gives her stepsisters a home in her palace. Even if purists have trouble with the storyline, the illustrations are absolutely wonderful and tell a parallel story quite different from the one that is written.

Browne, Anthony (1986). *Piggybook*. Knopf. Picture Book. Mrs. Piggott gets no help around the house from her unappreciative husband and sons, so she leaves a note saying, "You are pigs," and disappears. Without Mom around to take care of them, the boys and their father gradually do turn into pigs; she finds them rooting around for scraps when she finally returns to check on them. After that, she stays—but everyone helps with the cooking and housework.

Browne, Anthony (1995). *Willy the wimp*. Walker. Picture Book. Willy is tired of being teased and sends away for a bodybuilding book. Charles Atlas he is not, but in the end he strikes up a companionship that lasts.

Browne, Anthony (1998). *Voices in the park*. DK Publishing. Picture Book. This book features four gorilla characters that dress and act like humans. The author used a different font for each character and structured the text so that each speaks from the first person in telling his or her version of what transpired in the park one day. This is a story about social class; it recounts the interactions of two families when they were in the park at the same time. One family consists of a bossy wealthy mother and her rather shy son. The other is a despondent out-of-work father and his outgoing young daughter. Readers are confronted with issues of prejudice and cultural stereotypes.

Classroom Resources

Browne, Anthony (2000). *Willy and Hugh.* Red Fox. Picture Book. Willy is being bullied. Hugh fears no one. Together they form the perfect team and in the process waylay their own fears.

Browne, Anthony (2001). *Through the magic mirror.* Walker. Picture Book. Toby is fed up with everything, but when he walks through the magic mirror, everything changes.

Browne, Anthony (2004). *Into the forest.* Candlewick. Picture Book. In this version of *Little Red Riding Hood* a young boy awakens to find his father missing. On his way to grandmother's house he encounters several characters from other fairy tales as well as finds a red coat, thus making his transition to *Little Red Riding Hood* complete. The story alludes to absentee fathers in its opening, but it ends happily.

Brumbeau, Jeff (2000). *The quilt maker's gift.* Illus. Gail de Marcken. Scholastic. Picture Book. A generous quilt maker "with magic in her fingers" sews the most beautiful quilts in the world and then gives them away to the poor and needy. A greedy king, "his storehouse stuffed with treasure," yearns for something that will make him happy. Although he is sure a quilt will do it, the quilt maker refuses, saying she will only make him a quilt if he gives everything away. Through helping others the king finds his own happiness.

Bunting, Eve (2001). *Gleam and glow.* Illus. Peter Sylvada. Harcourt. Picture Book. An 8-year-old boy named Victor narrates this story of wartime destruction and hope. Left at home with his mother and sister while his father fights in the Liberation Army, Victor becomes more and more frightened as he hears about burning villages from passing strangers who are trying to escape the violence. When his mother decides that they should leave as well, Victor releases two goldfish in the family's pond. After being reunited with his father at a refugee camp, Victor and his family finally return to find only the charred remains of what used to be their home. They feel more hopeful, however, after they find their pond filled with goldfish, a vivid contrast to the destruction all around them.

Bunting, Eve (1990). *How many days to America: A thanksgiving story.* Illus. Beth Peck. Clarion. Picture Book. After a hazardous adventure by sea, a Caribbean family arrives in the United States on Thanksgiving Day. This book is not only a great read at Thanksgiving but also is a wonderful addition to discussions on illegal aliens and what action we as a nation should or should not take.

Bunting, Eve (1991). *Fly away home.* Clarion. Picture Book. This story is narrated by a boy who lives with his father in an airport. He begins by saying that they do not have a home and "the airport is better than the streets." Readers learn that the main goal of living in an airport is not getting noticed. The boy and his father always have to be on the move to stay in crowded locations. Although they have made friends with other homeless families who are doing the same thing, there is a sense of hopelessness about their situation until the boy sees a trapped bird finally escape from the airport.

Bunting, Eve (1996). *Going home*. Illus. David Diaz. HarperCollins. Picture Book. When Carlos's mother says the family is going home to Mexico for Christmas, Carlos is not sure what to think. If Mexico is home, why did his parents ever leave? His father's answer is always the same: "We are here for the opportunities." This story raises crucial questions of economic disparity, the hard-working conditions of farm laborers in the United States, differences in language and culture that can exist within families, and the painful choices and sacrifices families living in poverty face.

Bunting, Eve (1998). *So far from the sea*. Illus. Chris K. Soentpiet. Clarion. Picture Book. In 1941, the Japanese bombed Pearl Harbor; two months later, President Franklin D. Roosevelt signed Executive Order 9066, decreeing that all people of Japanese ancestry living on the West Coast of the United States must be relocated to internment camps. Many of those interned were American citizens. Set in 1972, *So Far From the Sea* is a story of the Iwaskaki family and their visit to the internment camp in California where their father was held for three and a half years. The story raises important issues about the segregation of the Japanese during the war and offers a demonstration of how easily people can be "othered."

Bunting, Eve (1998). *Your move*. Illus. James Ransome. Harcourt Brace. Picture Book. As older brother, James has the responsibility of taking care of his little brother, Isaac, when his mother goes off to work. One evening James sneaks out to meet with a local gang called K-Bones. Bunting explores the reasons why James and even 6-year-old Isaac are attracted to the K-Bones. She also explores the challenges single mothers face, particularly in finding safe and affordable child care, and the way families and communities try to deal with violence.

Burnett, Karen Gedig (2000). *Simon's Hook: A story about teases and put-downs*. Illus. Laurie Barrows. GR Publishing. Picture Book. Simon is a boy who needs to learn how to deal with teasing and name calling. Fortunately, his grandmother helps him understand that he has choices and that how he responds will either encourage more teasing or make it no fun for the person teasing him. She uses a fishing metaphor to describe how Simon is "taking the hook" when he become upset or angry because someone called him a name. But if he walks away, makes a joke, or agrees with the name, then the person teasing will probably lose interest and stop. This is a story about patience, self-control, and, in the end, empowerment.

Classroom Resources

Coerr, Eleanor (1986). *Sadako and the thousand paper cranes*. Paintings by Ronald Himler. Yearling. Chapter/Picture Book. A Japanese legend holds that the making of a thousand paper cranes will prompt the gods to make a sick person well. This is a short book about a young Japanese girl who contracts radiation sickness 10 years after the bombing of Hiroshima in 1945 and the efforts to save her.

Cohen, Barbara (1983). *Molly's pilgrim*. Illus. Michael J. Deraney. Lothrop. Picture Book. Molly, an immigrant from Russia, is trying to fit in at her new school in America but is not succeeding. When her teachers ask students to make a pilgrim doll for their Thanksgiving table as homework, Molly worries that the doll her mother helps her make is not what the teacher wants. Despite her worries, the unusual doll helps Molly and her classmates understand that there are lots of different kinds of pilgrims.

Cofer, Judith Ortiz (2004), *Call me Maria*. Orchard. Chapter Book. As she struggles to lose her island accent, Maria does her best to find her place within the unfamiliar culture of a New York barrio. Using the multiple perspectives that genre offers—in this case poetry, journal entries, and prose—Maria, a recent immigrant from Puerto Rico, comes to grip with her parents' deteriorating marriage and the fact that she now has two homes and two identities.

Cole, Babette (1997). *Princess Smartypants*. Putnam. Picture Book. Princess Smartypants is not the typical princess. She is interested in nonprincess things and does not want to get married. By turning one of her suitors, Prince Swashbuckle, into a warty toad, she gains new friends, loses her "marriage appeal," and manages to live happily ever after.

Coleman, Evelyn (1996). *White socks only*. Illus. Tyrone Geter. Albert Whitman. Picture Book. This is a story of a young African American girl who decides to take a drink from a water fountain in segregated Mississippi. Thinking that she understands the "Whites Only" sign on the fountain, she sits down in the grass, takes off her patent leather shoes, and climbs up on the stool to take a drink with only her clean white socks on her feet. When some of the town's white residents attempt to chastise and humiliate the child, her fellow African Americans who witnessed the event decide to take action.

Coles, Robert (1995). *The story of Ruby Bridges*. Illus. George Ford. Scholastic. Picture Book. In 1960, a judge in New Orleans ordered the public schools in that city to stop the practice of racial segregation. He assigned 6-year-old Ruby Bridges to a formerly all white elementary school. As a result, Ruby found herself in the middle of a storm of anger and prejudice. Each day she displayed courage and dignity beyond her years as federal marshals escorted her to and from her first-grade classroom.

Cronin, Doreen (2000). *Click, clack, moo: Cows that type.* Illus. Betsy Lewin. Simon & Schuster. Picture Book. Farmer Brown has a problem. His cows have found an old typewriter in the barn and are using it to make demands. They want electric blankets to keep them warm at night and are willing to withhold their milk until they get them. What is worse, the chickens have joined the cows in their strike: No more milk! No more eggs! The ducks are the not-so-neutral party. They carry the cows' and chickens' message, which promises to turn over the typewriter in exchange for blankets. Once Farmer Brown capitulates, however, they have a few new demands of their own. The delightfully understated text and expressive illustrations add to the hilarity. This is a read-aloud must for teachers who wish to create space in their classroom for conversations about literacy and power with even the youngest of readers.

Crutcher, Chris (2004). *Ironman.* Harper. Chapter Book. Bo Brewster, a triathlete, needs anger-management classes after blowing up at one of his teachers. Told in the voices of the various characters that this event effects, Bo grows as an individual and in the process gains control of his emotions.

Cutler, Jane (1999). *The cello of Mr. O.* Illus. Greg Couch. Dutton. Picture Book. Set in an unnamed war-torn city, this is a story about courage from an unexpected source. Mr. O. is too old to be a soldier. He is one of the only men left in the city since all of the other men and older boys went off to fight. As the violence increases and the people become more frightened and dejected, Mr. O takes his cello into the town square and begins to play. His music serves to sooth the townspeople and to make their situation more bearable. When a bomb destroys Mr. O's cello, he returns the next day to play his harmonica.

Dahl, Roald (1982). *Revolting rhymes.* Illus. Quentin Blake. Puffin. Picture/ Chapter Book. This is a collection of Dahl poems that somewhat gruesomely reinterpret popular fairy tales, and it contains "Little Red Riding Hood and the Wolf"—a redo of the original story with a different kind of violence.

Dash, Joan (1996). *We shall not be moved: The women's factory strike of 1909.* Scholastic. Sophisticated Chapter Book. This historical account of the events leading up to a massive women's factory strike almost a century ago shows how taking social action and working together can help to improve conditions for those who lack power. This book is appropriate in an historical text set focusing on civil rights and suffrage issues as well as in one dealing with current and past labor practices.

De Brunhoff, Jean (1937). *The story of Babar.* Random. Picture Book. Babar, a little elephant, is the personification of a country bumpkin who comes of age during his visit to Paris. On his journey, Babar loses his mother to a hunter, gets a new wardrobe, becomes the hit of high society, marries his cousin, and is crowned King of the Elephants. The story is somewhat controversial because of its dark moments, and there have been many attempts to ban the book. However, seven decades after his birth, most of the word is still in love with this noble pachyderm.

Demarest, Chris (2005). *Alpha, bravo, charlie: The military alphabet.* McElderry. Picture Book. This book introduces young readers to the International Communications Alphabet used by the navy and armed forces to ensure accurate verbal communications. Each page is illustrated with a navy signal flag and some of the latest military weapons.

De Paola, Tomie (1979). *Oliver Button is a sissy.* Harcourt Brace. Picture Book. His classmates' taunts do not stop Oliver Button from doing what he likes best—dancing. He gains their respect when he performs his dance in a talent show and they realize that he has the courage to be himself in spite of their censure.

Edwards, Cory, Edwards, Tod, & Happily Ever After Agency (2005). *Hoodwinked!: The true story of Little Red Riding Hood.* Kanbar. This is the book version of the movie, *Hoodwinked* (Winestein Company, 2006).

Ellis, Deborah (2001). *Breadwinner.* Groundwood. Chapter Book. Since the Taliban took over Afghanistan, 11-year-old Parvana has rarely been outdoors—that is, until the Taliban hauls away her father and she has to disguise herself as a boy to become the family's breadwinner.

Ellis, Deborah (2002). *Parvana's journey.* Groundwood. Chapter Book. This sequel to *Breadwinner* follows 12-year-old Parvana, disguised as a boy, as she sets off from Kabul in search of her missing mother and siblings in Taliban-era Afghanistan. When war breaks out, Parvana and her collection of lost children join a long line of refugees, finally arriving at a camp where she finds some traces of her family.

Ellis, Deborah (2004). *Mud City.* Groundwood. Chapter Book. In this third book in the Breadwinner trilogy, Afghan orphan Shauzia ends up in a refugee camp in Pakistan. Mud city brings readers up to date in terms of Afghanistan history—including recent and continuing Taliban restrictions on women—and is meant to provide readers with a bird's eye view on the state of refugees in this part of the world.

Elya, Susan Middleton (2002). *Home at last.* Illus. Felipe Davalos. Lee & Low. Picture Book. The Patino family move to the United States, where everyone adjusts except Mama. When one of the twins gets ill, Mama finally decides to learn English. This is an important book in that it parallels the experiences of many immigrant children as they and their families both resist and try to adjust to a new culture.

English, Karen (1999). *Francie*. Farrar, Strauss & Giroux. Chapter Book. This story takes place during the Great Migration, and Francie's father has moved to Chicago for work. In his letters he promises to find a way to bring his family to join him. Francie begins tutoring an older boy as a way to earn money, but this boy becomes falsely accused of assaulting a white man. Through her feelings of compassion, Francie is drawn into a forcefully unjust system that surrounds both of them. In the details of relationships, we see the ways that unfairness and struggles for power are never simple, never just black or white, never just of an issue of male versus female.

Ernst, Lisa Campbell (1995). *Little Red Riding Hood: A newfangled prairie tale*. Simon & Schuster. Picture Book. Set on the Midwestern prairie, this is the traditional tale told with feisty heroines who, in the end, enlist the wolf in their entrepreneurial adventure and open a muffin bakery. Though disrupting some stereotypes about women, it perpetuates new stereotypes about farmers.

Fierstein, Harvey (2002). *The sissy duckling*. Illus. Henry Cole. Simon & Schuster. Picture Book. Elmer is not like the other male ducklings. While they boxed, Elmer baked. When they played football, Elmer built sand castles. Bullied by Drake and embarrassed in front of his father, Elmer runs away, only to witness his father being shot by hunters. Elmer tends him back to health and, come spring, wins the respect of the flock.

Fleischman, Paul (1997). *Seedfolks*. Illus. Judy Pedersen. HarperCollins. Chapter Book. This amazingly complex short novel is told from the perspectives of 13 different residents of an ethnically polarized inner-city neighborhood in Cleveland. Fleischman does a masterful job of intertwining the narratives and lives of each of the characters. Kim, a 9-year-old Vietnamese girl, plants dried lima beans in a trash-filled "vacant" lot in an attempt to spiritually connect with her father, a farmer who died soon after her birth. While Kim plants the seeds, she is watched by Ana, an elderly neighbor who lives across the street from the lot. Ana's suspicion of Kim hiding drugs leads to a series of human interactions that transform an ugly trash heap into a community garden, where people who had previously been distrustful of each other come together with a common purpose.

Fleischman, Paul (1998). *Whirligig*. Henry Holt. Chapter Book. The premise of this book is deceptively simple. The thoughtless act of an unhappy teenager has tragic results that set in motion a series of surprising events. As the story opens, the main character, Brent, is charged with the task of designing, constructing, and placing four memorial whirligigs at various locations throughout the United States. We then follow Brent's growth from a self-centered, care-less teenager to a thoughtful young man. Although Brent's story is engaging in its own right, Fleischman inserts four completely independent narratives with the only connection to Brent's story being the whirligigs. Each character in these four narratives has to rethink his or her own life as a result of his or her encounter with one of the whirligigs. Taken together the various layers in this novel provide the reader with an understanding of the impact one individual can have on others regardless of time or space.

Fletcher, Ralph (1998). *Flying solo*. Clarion Books. Chapter Book. Told from the perspective of different students in Mr. Fabiano's sixth-grade class, this is the story of what happens when a substitute teacher does not show up and the class decides they will run things by themselves for the day. The varying responses to the teacher on how the day went allows for great discussions on taking responsibility versus being irresponsible and on how school practices can both inhibit and empower kids.

Forrester, Sandra (1997). *My home is over Jordan*. Lodestar. Chapter Book. Life was not easy for newly freed slaves at the end of the civil war. Caught between the ruined economy and overt racism of the South, former slaves were often homeless and without means. Maddie Henry's family is better off than most since they have the money her Papa earned working as a soldier for the Union Army. This is a story about voice and how Maddie and other family members began to gain voices that refuse to be silenced.

Fox, Mem (1989). *Feathers and fools*. Illus. Nicholas Wilton. Harcourt Brace. Picture Book. This allegory tells the story of a group of swans and a group of peacocks that share a peaceful coexistence until they realize they are different. At that point they become suspicious of each other and "for safety's sake" begin collecting weapons to protect themselves. When a reed for nest making is mistaken for an arrow, an all-out war ensues, and both groups of birds are ultimately decimated. Fortunately, some eggs remain, and the new swan and peacock hatchlings notice their similarities instead of their differences.

Fox, Paula (1997). *Radiance descending*. DK Publishing. Chapter Book. This is a novel about an older brother, Paul, learning to accept a younger sibling, Jacob, who was born with Down's syndrome. At the start of the novel Paul would be quite happy if Jacob did not exist at all. Although there is no huge transformation, by the end of the novel Paul begins to see the world through less egotistical eyes. This book is an easy read that invites children to reflect on their own attitudes and behaviors toward others less fortunate than themselves.

Fradin, Dennis (2001). *My family shall be free! The life of Peter Still*. HarperCollins. Chapter Book. This book recounts the life of Peter Still and his family. Born into slavery, Peter and his brother, Levin, are separated from their mother and sister at the ages of 6 and 7. Deceived into believing that they are being taken to their mother—who has escaped to freedom with their sisters—the two boys are sold to a plantation owner 600 miles from their home. So begins the story of how Peter and Levin wait over half a century for their chance at freedom. The text provides useful information on the Underground Railroad and the work of abolitionists during the mid 1800s.

Fradin, Dennis, & Fradin, Judith (2001). *Ida B. Wells: Mother of the civil rights movement*. Clarion. Chapter Book. This book is a historical account of Ida's life as she crusaded against the unlawful treatment of African Americans in the early part of the 20th century. Through her writing and speaking, Ida championed voting rights for women, spoke out against lynching, and helped to establish the National Association for the Advancement of Colored People. She was outspoken in her beliefs, suggesting that those who did nothing to stop lynching and discriminatory practices were just as guilty as those who actually did them.

Frost, H. (2003). *Keesha's house*. New York: Farrar, Straus & Giroux. Chapter Book. Keesha and six other teenagers in trouble have found a safe place to live while they try to get their lives back on track. Through the use of traditional poetic forms, each of the teens tells his or her story. Readers hear from a pregnant girl, the confused father of the baby, an abused girl, a boy whose parents have disowned him because he is gay, a boy whose parents are in prison, a girl arrested for drunk driving, and a girl who is angry at her mother and stepfather.

Garden, Nancy (2000). *Holly's secret*. Farrar, Straus & Giroux. Chapter Book. Holly, who is 12 years old, has a secret: Her parents are gay. Rather than face a new round of painful jokes and secondhand gay bashing, she comes up with "The Plan," a new identity for herself. She uses the opportunity of a family move to change into Yvette, the epitome of sophistication, normalcy, and grown-up femininity. But keeping her two moms a secret is no easy task and maybe not such a great idea in the first place.

Garden, Nancy (2004). *Molly's family*. Illus. Sharon Wooding. Farrar, Straus & Giroux. Picture Book. Molly's picture of her family raises many questions when her kindergarten classmates notice that she drew two mothers and no father. Through talks with her two mothers and her teacher, she comes to understand that families can come in many different forms and that they do not all need to look the same.

Garland, Sherry (1977). *The lotus seed*. Ills. Tatsuro Kiuchi. Voyager. Picture Book. Being present when the last emperor of Vietnam abdicated the crown, the narrator of this story tells how his grandmother collected a lotus seed, brought it with her to the

United States, and lived long enough to see it bear fruit and seeds, which she then distributed to her grandchildren. This is a story of continuity and hope as cultures are crossed and cultural traditions maintained.

Giles, Gale (2002). *Shattering glass*. Roaring Brook. Young Adult. Rob Haynes, an out-of-state transfer student, has it all: good looks, unshakeable confidence, and a hold on everyone around him. To prove his power he talks his personal clique into taking on the seemingly impossible task of making Simon Glass, a textbook geek, into one of the most popular kids in the class. Unlike the others, Simon sees Rob's dark side and invites readers to ponder the problems in following a charismatic but amoral leader.

Glenn, Mel (2002). *Split image*. Harper. Young Adult. Laura Li is the dutiful Asian daughter in the daylight, but come midnight her reputation changes. Using multiracial and multiethnic voices of teachers and friends, Glenn poetically tells the story of what can happen when teenagers are denied the freedom to determine their own identity.

Grimes, Nikki (1999). *My man blue*. Illus. Jerome Lagarrigue. Dial. Picture Book. This is a beautifully illustrated book addressing the stereotypes that haunt African American males as they are often seen by visitors to the inner city. This is the story of a nurturing adult African American male, told in verse form from the perspective of an inner-city child.

Grimes, Nikki (2002). *Bronx masquerade*. Putnam. Chapter Book. "Open Mike Friday" is everyone's favorite period in Mr. Ward's English class. After Wesley writes a poem, 18 of his classmates clamor to use poetry to express frankly what is on their minds. The novel as a whole is a nice demonstration of the power of teaching as well as how teachers might use writing to inscribe the lives of the students they teach.

Grove, Vicki (1999). *The starplace*. Putnam. Chapter Book. Set in 1961 in Quiver, Oklahoma, where racial segregation has been an unquestioned way of life despite the 1954 *Brown v. Topeka* Supreme Court decision. Celeste is the first black student to enroll in Frannie's school, and the girls become friends. Without being heavy handed, the narrative exposes the attitudes of prejudice among the students, parents, and teachers at the school and recounts the story of the Ku Klux Klan's lynching of Celeste's grandfather.

Hansen, Joyce (1998). *Women of hope: African Americans who made a difference*. Scholastic. Chapter/Picture Book. Hansen's page-length, inspiring biographies depict the lives of 13 African American women, arranged chronologically. We meet celebrity authors Maya Angelou and Toni Morrison, as well as lesser-known women like Ida Wells-Barnet, a teacher and journalist at the turn of the century who exposed inequities in education for black students and the brutality of lynching in the South, and Dr. Mae C. Jemison, who was not only the first African American woman astronaut but also worked as a physician in West Africa. These artists, educators, health-care providers, and activists provide all of us with role models worthy of emulation

Haskins, James (1998). *Separate but not equal: The dream and the struggle*. Scholastic. Sophisticated Chapter Book. Perhaps no moment in time better dramatizes the institutional weight, violence, and injustice of segregated, inequitable education than when young Elizabeth Eckhart tried to pass through the line of armed National Guardsmen called out by Governor Orval Faubus to prevent black students from entering Central High in 1957. Haskins moves from this starting point to examine the history of black schooling in America, from violence against slaves who learned to read to the issues behind landmark legal decisions, most notably the stand for equality in education that the Warren Court took in 1954, with *Brown v. the Board of Education*.

Haskins, James, & Benson, Kathleen (2001). *Building a new land, African Americans in colonial America*. Illus. James Ransome. HarperCollins. Chapter Book. This book describes the brutality of slave life in colonial America. It presents many uncelebrated aspects of slavery including slave resistance, revolts, and rebellions and strengthens the argument that this country could not have been built without forced black labor.

Hautman, Pete, & Pritzker, Burton (2004). *Godless*. Simon & Schuster. Young Adult. Rather than follow in his father's footsteps, Jason Block decides to invent a new religion with a new god, the town's water tower. Finding converts is surprisingly easy as is the proliferation of new commandments and rituals. To create the mood, Hautman begins each chapter with a Bible-like verse written from the perspective of their new religion.

Heide, Florence, & Gilliland, Judith (1992). *Sami and the time of the troubles*. Clarion. Picture Book. "My name is Sami, and I live in the time of the troubles. It is a time of guns and bombs." These are the opening lines for a story about a 10-year-old boy who lives in a war-ravaged city where frequent bombings and gunfire make it unsafe for his family to leave the basement of his uncle's house. As Sami and his family pass the long hours by remembering better times, readers learn they used to enjoy picnics at the beach and that Sami's father owned peach orchards. We also learn that his father was killed in a bombing at the local market. There is some hope, however, as the story goes on because we read about a "good day" when the fighting stops temporarily and the family is able to leave the basement. Also, Sami's grandfather reminds him of a time in the past when hundreds of children marched in the streets to ask for peace, and this is what Sami is thinking about as the book ends.

Hesse, Karen (1998). *Just Juice*. Illus. Robert Andrew Parker. Scholastic. Chapter Book. This multi-layered story is told from the point of view of 9-year-old Juice Faulstich, a chronically truant child who is happier at home with her unsuccessful father and pregnant mother than at school, where she is constantly reminded of her inability to read. As the story unfolds, Juice comes to realize that her father is also a non-reader and that his lack of reading proficiency has brought the family to the brink of disaster in the form of eviction from their home. Juice begins to understand that although both she and her father are skilled in many ways, their acceptance by society and even by other family members is greatly affected by their status as illiterates. The book ends on a hopeful note as the family finds a way to avert the eviction and makes literacy a goal for all of them.

Hesse, Karen (2001). *Witness*. Hyperion. Chapter Book. In 1924, a small Vermont town finds itself under siege by the Ku Klux Klan. Told through the voices of the residents, this is the story of how a community comes to discover that they collectively must evict the Ku Klux Klan to once again feel safe. Part mystery, part social commentary, it explores race and identity from multiple viewpoints.

Hill, Kirkpatrick (2000). *The years of Miss Agnes*. McElderry. Chapter Book. An uplifting story of a dedicated teacher working in the outback of Alaska who builds curriculum from the cultural resources she finds in an Athabanian village in 1948.

Hirschi, Ron (1996). *People of Salmon and Cedar*. Illus. Deborah Cooper. Cobblehill. Chapter Book. Although this is a nonfiction text about the Native American tribes that populate the Northwest region of the United States, it is told like a story that invites the reader into these cultures to learn about their history and traditions. The text traces the history of the tribes of the Northwest, such as the Suquamish, S'Klallam, and Lummi, and realistically accounts their struggles since the Western culture invaded their land.

Hoffman, Mary (1991). *Amazing grace*. Illus. Caroline Binch. Dial. Picture Book. Grace uses her lively imagination to act out stories, assuming the roles of her favorite characters, so it is only natural that she would try out for the part of Peter Pan in the class play. Her classmates point out that she does not have a chance of getting the part because she is a girl and because she is black. But Grace is independent and persistent as well as imaginative. She believes in herself and gets others to believe in her as well.

Hoffman, Mary (1997). *An angel just like me*. Illus. Cornelius Van Wright & Ying-Hwa Hu. Dial . Picture Book. As Tyler's family prepares for Christmas, he discovers that the angel atop their tree has broken. Wondering why all the representations of angels he has seen are female, pale, and blond, Tyler sets out to find a black boy angel who looks more like him.

Holmes, Richard (2000). *Eyewitness: Battle*. DK Publishing. Picture/ Chapter Book. This is a nonfiction reference book that provides detailed illustrations of numerous combat weapons used in various wars throughout history. The book is problematic in the sense that although the message is that weapons are used for protection and therefore helpful to the people, these assumptions are left unquestioned.

Hurmence, Belinda (1997). *Slavery time: When I was chillun*. Putnam. Chapter Book. In these 12 stories selected from *Slave Narratives*, the 1930s Works Progress Administration interviewing project, we hear the voices and stories of African American men and women who lived under slavery. These are voices that have been largely erased or ignored by American history and culture. The stories range from nostalgic recollections of childhood games and plantation cuisine to painful memories of deprivation and abuse.

Isadora, Rachel (1984). *Max*. Aladdin. Picture Book. Max walks Lisa to ballet class each day. One day Lisa's ballet teacher invites Max, a crack baseball player, into the studio. While initially skeptical, Max finds out that ballet is a great way to warm up for hitting a home run.

Jackson, Ella (1994). *Cinder Edna*. Illus. Kevin O'Malley. Lothrop, Lee & Shepard. Picture Book. This updated version of the traditional Cinderella story adds an assertive and creative new neighbor, Cinder Edna, who decides that sitting in the cinders is "a silly way to spend time," so she keeps warm by mowing the lawn and cleaning parrot cages for the neighbors for $1.50 an hour. Whereas Cinderella approaches her problem of needing a dress for the ball by wishing for a fairy godmother who would change her rags into a beautiful gown, Cinder Edna uses her cage-cleaning money to put a dress on layaway. Whereas Cinderella rides to the ball in an elegant coach (also supplied by the fairy godmother), Cinder Edna takes the bus. The book ends with Cinderella marrying the handsome, but deadly dull, prince, and Cinder Edna marrying his goofy-looking, but definitely more fun, brother. Readers are invited to "guess who lived happily ever after." Readers are not invited to consider why this happy ending and so many others conclude with a heterosexual marriage, but the book provides an opportunity to ask this question.

Jiang, Ji-Li (1997). *The red scarf girl: A memoir of the cultural revolution.* HarperCollins. Chapter Book. "Chairman Mao, our beloved leader, smiled down at us from his place above the blackboard"—thus begins the true story of Jiang and her family from 1966 to 1969 during the cultural revolution in China. Mao commanded everyone to find and destroy the "four olds"—old ideas, old customs, old habits, and old culture. Because of her family's class status of being former landlords, Jiang and her family were publicly humiliated and threatened.

Jimenez, Francisco (1998). *The circuit: Stories from the life of a migrant child.* University of New Mexico Press. Chapter Book. Told from the point of view of the author as a young child, this book is a series of stories about what it means to be a child of a Mexican illegal immigrant without health insurance, job security, or even the right to an education. America is *La Frontera,* as are the strong familial bonds that maintain the family through all sorts of crises.

Johnson, Angela (2003). *The first part last.* Simon & Schuster. Young Adult. Using time and perception to give perspective, alternating chapters go back and forth between 16-year-old Bobbie's present-day attempts to cope with being a single teenage parent ("Now") and the story of how family and friends reacted to his girlfriend Nia's pregnancy ("Then").

Johnson, Donald B. (2000). *Henry hikes to Fitchburg.* Houghton Mifflin. Picture Book. This book is critical only to the extent that teachers take time to question with readers the underlying issues it raises: Why is our society always on the go, thinking faster is better? What social practices keep this lifestyle in place? Who benefits? What do we as a society lose? How could we, like Henry (a.k.a. Henry David Thoreau), make a difference? The story line is simple: Two friends agree to go to Fitchburg to see the country. They choose very different methods of travel based on their very different approaches to life.

Kaplan, William (1998). *One more border: The true story of one family's escape from war-torn Europe.* Illus. Stephen Taylor. Groundwood. Picture Book. In this historical nonfiction, Kaplan shares the story of his father's family as they escaped war-torn Europe during the late 1930s to avoid persecution for being Jewish. Through the story of the Kaplan family's escape, we learn about the oppression and marginalization of the Jews during the war. Inclusion of authentic artifacts such as photographs, maps, and the visa that allowed Bernard, Igor, and Nomi Kaplan to leave Europe provide a sense of realism.

Keith, Toby (2004). Courtesy of the red, white, & blue (The angry American). *Greatest hits 2*. Dreamworks Nashville. ASIN B00063F8CG. This song contains the lines, "My daddy served in the army/Where he lost his right eye/But he flew a flag out in our yard/Until the day that he died."

Koertge, Ron (2001). *The brimstone journals*. Candlewick. Chapter Book. Using the voices of the Branston High School class, poet Koertge portrays the anatomy of a would-be high school shooting through the voices of Boyd, an angry young man, and his classmates: the fat kid, the activist, the egghead, the jock, the anorexic, the rich boy, the stud, the dyke, and the list goes on. Topics addressed include racism, classism, homophobia, and an entire high school melting pot of "-isms."

Konigsburg, E. L. (2000). *Silent to the bone*. Atheneum. Chapter Book. This book invites readers into a mystery to uncover a secret kept by Branwell, a 13-year-old boy who has been accused by a nanny of dropping his baby sister and putting her into a coma. He is being detained at the Clarion County Juvenile Behavioral Center and has been silent since the accident. Branwell's father, Dr. Z, asks his son's friend Conner to see if he can get Branwell to talk about what happened that fateful afternoon. Through the visits at the detention center, Conner and Branwell discover that there are many ways to communicate without using speech. As clues are revealed, readers begin to see the many layers in the complex relationships among family members, friends, and peers.

Kyuchukov, Hristo, & Kyuchukov, Khristo (2004). *My name is Hussein*. Illus. Allan Eitzen. Boyds Mills. Picture Book. At end of this book, Hussein, about age 8, asks, "What would you call me?" This question is important since Hussein and his family were forced to take Christian names after their country, Bulgaria, was invaded, even though they were Muslins and their Muslin names had historical and familial significance. This is an important book in that readers get a sense of what life is like other parts of the world for children who live under repressive regimes.

Lawton, Clive (2004). *Hiroshima: The story of the first atom bomb*. Candlewick. Picture Book. This is a nonfiction account of Hiroshima before and after the bomb was dropped and recounts the history of the atomic bomb covering the Manhattan Project, Truman's decision to use the bomb, the Enola Gray mission, and the aftermath of the explosion.

Lears, Laurie (1998). *Ian's walk: A story about autism*. Illus. Karen Ritz. Albert Whitman. Picture Book. This book explores not only the range of emotions Julie feels as a sibling to an autistic child but also the ways Ian experiences and senses the world "differently." On the journey to the park, Ian wants to smell bricks, not flowers, and once there, he lies with his cheek on the concrete instead of feeding the ducks. After Ian becomes lost in the park, Julie tries hard to enter his world and figure out where Ian would go. In so doing, she finds not only her brother but also a way to connect with him and to share experiences together.

Lester, Julius (1998). *From slave ship to freedom road*. Illus. Rod Brown. Dial. Chapter/Picture Books. This disturbingly graphic picture book leads readers through the painful experience of slavery, beginning with the ocean passage and auction block and ending with freedom for those who were fortunate enough to be still alive when that happened. Haunting paintings by Brown anchor the story and serve as the main focus. Though the story recounts horrendous acts like throwing sick and dying slaves overboard during the long journey from Africa to the American colonies, it is usually the impenetrable strength and endurance of the Africans that stays with readers as the most memorable aspect of the book.

Lorbiecki, Marybeth (2006). *Jackie's bat*. Illus. Brian Pinkney. Simon & Schuster. Picture Book. Joey, the batboy, recounts Jackie Robinson's first season with the Brooklyn Dodgers. Torn between what he had been taught at home—"it ain't right, a white boy serving a black man"—and keeping his job, Joey grapples with his own prejudice, hostility from fans, and what it means to be a true sportsman.

Lorbiecki, Marybeth (1996). *Just one flick of a finger*. Illus. David Diaz. Dial Books. Sophisticated Picture Book. This is an urban tale of two boys trying to cope with the violence that handguns bring into their lives. The boys know well enough the dangers of handguns and can articulate the reasons to avoid using these weapons. Yet when one of the boys feels threatened by an older peer, he decides to ignore what good sense tells him and brings his father's gun to school. The use of street language and rhyme gives the story the feel of a rap song.

Lorbiecki, Marybeth (1998). *Sister Anne's hands*. Illus. K. Wendy Popp. Dial. Picture Book. Told in the style of a memoir from the 1960s, this book is the story of second-grader Anna Zabrocky, who is surprised to discover that her new teacher, Sister Anne, is African American. Since Sister Anne believes in active learning and the power of story, Anna is also surprised to discover how exciting school can be. Tension arises, however, when Sister Anne intercepts a paper airplane containing a racial slur. Skillful educator that she is, she uses this incident as an opportunity to teach her students about race, oppression, and social action. Hands become a metaphor for reaching across the racial divide.

Lowry, Lois (2000). *Gathering blue*. Houghton Mifflin. Chapter Book. Orphaned and physically flawed, Kira faces death in a futuristic society that shuns and discards the weak. When summoned to the Council of Guardians, Kira finds, much to her surprise, that the council has plans for her and her talent for weaving. While performing her new duties, Kira gathers "blue" (a metaphor for truth) and begins to question taken-for-granted notions of community, creativity, and values. Like Lowry's earlier book, *The Giver*, *Gathering Blue* is a provocative tale that inspires contemplation long after the last page is turned.

Martinez, Victor (1996). *Parrot in the oven: Mi vida.* HarperCollins. Chapter Book. In Mexico there is a saying about a parrot that complains how hot it is in the shade, while all along he is sitting in an oven. In this novel, the protagonist is known as Perico (*parrot* in Spanish), and the more we read, the more we come to appreciate the appropriateness of the book's title. Perico is growing up in an oven where his sister dates one of the roughest characters in the barrio, where gang membership is assumed, and where participation in what the gang does—even if it involves robbery—is considered common practice.

Maruki, Toshi (1980). *Hiroshima no pika* [The flash of Hiroshima]. Lothrop. Picture Book. This book follows a family in Hiroshima as they attempt to escape the devastation of the atomic bomb blast on August 6, 1945. The text and illustrations graphically describe the sudden change from peaceful life in the city to widespread chaos and destruction caused by the collapse of buildings and a huge fire that engulfs the area. Though the father of the family ultimately dies from radiation sickness, the girl and her mother survive and remember the event each year on its anniversary—with the wish that it never happens again. An "About This Book" section at the end describes how the author was inspired to write the story by meeting a survivor whom she later wrote about as the mother of the family.

Marx, Trish (2000). *One boy from Kosovo.* Photographs by Cindy Karp. HarperCollins. Chapter/Picture Book. Global conflicts involve each of us, whether our response is action or inaction. The story line focuses on Edi Fejzullahus, a 12-year-old Albanian, and his family as they are driven from their home in Kosovo by Serbian soldiers. An introductory chapter provides historical and political context not only for the conflict abroad but also for questioning our society's practices relative to the rest of the world. At issue are questions about the kind of people we wish to be, why we respond to some world crises and not others, what responsibilities we have to people in other nations, and how we might make a positive difference both locally and globally.

McCully, Emily (1996). *The ballot box battle.* Alfred Knopf. Picture Book. Set in the late 1800s, this story is a weaving of history and fiction that shares the parallel stories of two females and their attempts at challenging social norms and expectations. Cordelia is a young girl and neighbor to suffragist Elizabeth Cady Stanton. As the book unfolds, we learn of Cordelia's desire "to jump a four foot fence on horseback" and Elizabeth's story of going to the polls to attempt to vote and fight for women's suffrage.

McCully, Emily (1996). *The bobbin girl*. Dial Books. Picture Book. Rebecca Putney is a 10-year-old bobbin girl in 19th-century Lowell, Massachusetts, who works 13-hour days under unhealthy working conditions to help support her family. The story supports conversation about child labor, child abuse, and unfair labor practices. McCully's use of a dark palette sets the tone and captures the working conditions girls faced during this period in U.S. history.

McEwan, Ian (1987). *Rose Blanche*. Illus. Roberto Innocenti. Lectorium. Sophisticated Picture Book. A young German girl discovers a concentration camp in the woods outside her town. While she daily takes food and befriends several children, one day she discovers the camp abandoned and the people gone. This is an adult story cast in children's book form.

McGovern, Ann (1997). *The lady in the box*. Illus. Marni Backer. Turtle Books. Picture Book. Two children befriend a homeless woman who is trying to survive the winter living in a cardboard box next to a heat vent. Since they see her every day, they become concerned about her and begin to take food and warm clothes to her. When the lady is ordered to move away from the vent, they are horrified and tell their mother about the situation. Their mother takes action to get the lady back to the warm grate, and all three of them start to work as volunteers in a local soup kitchen.

McGuffee, Michael (1996). *The day the earth was silent*. Illus. Edward Sullivan. Inquiring Voices Press. Picture Book. The class makes a beautiful new flag, which they want to share with all the earth. The principal asks, "Why try?" But one child insists, "Why not try?" In this story, children keep asking their good questions, cooperating, and insisting on a unity among all people until the whole world is awed and healed by their vision. But this is not simply a story of visionary optimism; it is also about the importance of persistence and cherishing small yet significant moments of change. Sullivan's illustrations radiate the bright energy of kids engaged in creative expression and social action.

Mellencamp, John (2003). To Washington. *Trouble no more*. Sony. ASIN B0000940U1. This song contains the lines, "So a new man is in the White House/With a familiar name/Said he had some fresh ideas/But it's worse now since he came."

Meltzer, Milton (2001). *There comes a time: The struggle for civil rights*. Random House. Chapter Book. Meltzer traces the roots of racism back to slavery, describes the brutality of the segregated South in the first half of the 1900s, and chronicles the sit-ins, freedom rides, and other key events in the civil rights movement of the 1950s and 1960s. Children played an important role in this history, and Meltzer features them in the stories and black-and-white pictures.

Miller, William (1998). *The bus ride*. Illus. John Ward. Lee & Low. Picture Book. Based on the Montgomery bus boycott and framed through the experience of Rosa Parks, this book can be used as a vehicle through which conversations about how systems of meaning that "other" certain groups of people are maintained and opens up space to talk about the role the media can play in raising consciousness or maintaining inequities.

Mitchell, Margaree King (1997). *Granddaddy's gift*. Illus. Larry Johnson. BridgeWater. Picture Book. On her 18th birthday, Little Joe is able to register to vote simply by filling out a voter registration card. She does this while remembering her granddaddy's gift—his example of standing up for things he believed in and being proud, even when he was afraid. This book celebrates the gift given to us by preceding generations who made a difference in the struggle for human dignity and civil rights for all.

Mora, Pat (1997). *Tomás and the library lady*. Illus. Raul Colón. Knopf. Picture Book. Based on the life of Tomás Rivera, a migrant farm worker who became a national education leader and University of California chancellor, this story shows how literacy and access to good books can work together to given voice to people who historically have been marginalized. This book would be a good addition to a text set dealing with inequities and harsh working conditions in the workplace.

Mochizuki, Ken (1997). *Passage to freedom: The Sugihara story*. Illus. Dom Lee. Lee & Low. Sophisticated Picture Book. In July 1940, young Hiroki Sugihara, son of the Japanese consul to Lithuania, saw hundreds of Jewish refugees from Poland gathered at the gate of his family's house. These people wanted the consul to give them travel visas so that they could escape from imminent persecution. After Consul Sugihara was denied permission to give out visas to the refugees, for the next month he handwrote thousands of visas. This book raises important topics such as human rights; the relationships between compassion, courage, and sacrifice; nonviolent resistance; and the power of the pen as an instrument of social justice.

Morrison, Toni, & Morrison, Slade (1999). *The big box*. Illus. Giselle Potter. Hyperion. Picture Book. This seemingly humorous book has a haunting message about children who do not fit accepted definitions of what it means to be normal. In poetic form, the authors tell the stories of Patty, Mickey, and Liza Sue, who live in a big brown box with doors that open "only one way." Because of their behavior, the adults who are responsible for these children have concluded that they just cannot handle their freedom and must be locked away. Although they are provided with lots of toys and fun items like beanbag chairs and bubble gum, the children are portrayed as prisoners who have been separated from their families and peers. The story is reminiscent of children who are pulled out of their regular education classes and segregated in special education classes because they do not meet the standard definition of what children at any specific age should be able to do.

Munch, Robert (1983). *The paper bag princess*. Illus. Michael Martchenko. Annick. Picture Book. Just when she is about to marry Prince Ronald, a dragon smashes the feisty Princess Elizabeth's castle and everything she owns. Elizabeth sets out to find Robert in her disheveled state—slaying even the dragon—and comes to discover she is better off alone than trying to live happily ever after with the likes of Prince Robert.

Myers, Christopher (2000). *Wings*. Scholastic. Picture Book. Ikarus Johnson is a new kid in the neighborhood who is very different from everyone else: He has wings and flies. This Icarus-inspired character is relentlessly taunted and laughed at by other kids and ordered out of school by his teacher. The narrator, an extremely quiet girl who is also an outsider, feels a connection to Ikarus but remains silent for most of the book. After a policeman orders Ikarus off of the top of a building, the girl wonders, "Could the policeman put him in jail for flying, for being too different?" This realization brings her to action, and she invites conversations about difference and diversity.

Myers, Walter Dean (1999). *Monster*. Amistad. Sophisticated Chapter Book. *Monster* is what the prosecutor calls 16-year-old Steve Harmon for his role in the fatal shooting of a convenience store owner. Written as a screenplay that moves between Steve's journal entries and transcripts of his trial, the reader becomes both juror and witness.

Myers, Walter Dean (2002). *Patrol: An American solider in Vietnam*. Illus. Ann Grifalconi. HarperCollins. Picture Book. This tells the human story of war from the perspective of a young recruit who was supposed to shoot an equally young enemy but could not. The tale is a nice, down-to-earth counternarrative to use in a text set on war.

Newman, Leslea (2000). *Heather has two mommies*. Illus. Diana Souza. Scholastic. Picture Book. Preschooler Heather hears other children talking about their daddies and wonders if everyone has a daddy except her. Luckily, she is in the care of a smart teacher who asks the children in the play group to draw pictures of their families. When they look at them, they see that the family configurations are all different—and all are accepted as normal.

Nunez, Sandra, & Marx, Trish (1997). *And justice for all: The legal rights of young people*. Millbrook. Sophisticated Chapter Book. Nunez and Marx provide a valuable presentation of the legal rights of minors in the United States today. Each chapter focuses on a different issue, from children's rights to safety and protection to first amendment protections for minors to child labor laws.

Nye, Naomi Shihab (1997). *Sitti's secrets*. Illus. Nancy Carpenter. Aladdin. Picture Book. Mona, a U.S. citizen, travels to a Palestinian village in the West Bank to visit her grandmother where, to communicate, they have to develop their own language, full of hums and claps and aahhs. When Mona gets home she writes the president assuring him that if he would meet Sitti he would like her. Both she and Sitti vote for peace.

Paladino, Catherine (1999). *One good apple: Growing our food for the sake of the earth*. Houghton Mifflin. Picture Book. The saying goes, "What we don't know won't hurt us," but this book points out how important it might be to know more about the foods we purchase and eat. The story explains how the pesticides and fertilizers used to grow perfect fruits and vegetables are toxic to our bodies and the balance of nature. The author's cogent, urgent case for healthier agricultural practices raises many questions. Do the economic motivations of commercial farming justify the use of toxins? What are the alternatives? Whose needs are being met and whose are not? What can we do as consumers? Who is working on these issues? What other action is needed?

Parker, David (1998). *Stolen dreams: Portraits of working children*. Lerner. Chapter/Picture Book. It is impossible to read this book on the exploitation of children throughout the world and not feel the need to act on their behalf. Although the subject matter is difficult to read about, it is important to be aware of the injustices of child exploitation and labor. The final pages of the book are devoted to poignant letters and genuine questions from children speaking out eloquently against the exploitation of their peers. Throughout the book, stunning and disturbing black-and-white photographs of exploited children reveal their suffering and despair.

Perez, Amada Irma (2002). *My diary from here to there/Mi diario de aquí, hasta allá*. Illus. Maya Christina Gonzalez. Children's Book Press. Picture Book. Although everyone in her family seem excited about their move from Juarez, Mexico, to Los Angeles, California, Perez uses her personal journal to voice her reservations. The story is told in both Spanish and English.

Pinkney, Andrea Davis (2000). *Let it shine: Stories of Black women freedom fighters*. Illus. Stephen Alcorn. Gulliver. Chapter Book. Pinkney takes readers on a civil rights journey from the 18th century to the present with her compelling stories of Black women who fought for freedom and social justice. The stories in this book are about familiar "sheroes" like Sojourner Truth, Harriet Tubman, and Rosa Parks, as well as lesser-known black women like Biddy Mason, Ida Wells-Barnett, and Dorothy Irene Height. The stories are brief but powerful, highlighting the women's struggles against sexism, racism, and oppression. The book offers insight into the principled choices these women made when they were faced with challenges and compromising situations.

Randle, Kristen D. (2003). *Slumming.* Harper. Young Adult. Seniors Nikki, Sam, and Alicia have a "great idea" that each should choose a person "who is obviously untapped" and "by slumming" try to release that individual's potential. What they learn is that imposing one's ideals and values on others without a complete understanding of their situation is a life lesson worthy of serious reflection.

Rapp, Adam (1997). *The buffalo tree.* Front Street. Chapter Book. Told from the perspective of Sura, a juvenile who is doing six months in the Hartford Juvenile Home for "clipping" hood ornaments, this is a haunting tale of how the residents of the detention center—juveniles and adults alike—seem to be doing all that they can to make their collective experience there "a living hell." This book invites conversations about young people who most adults see as "anchorless" and their institutionalization as an answer to this problem.

Ringgold, Faith (1999). *If a bus could talk, the story of Rosa Parks.* Simon & Schuster. Picture Book. From the moment when Marcie, a young African American girl, steps onto the strange, driverless bus, readers learn about the events in the life of Rosa Parks told from the voices of famous passengers—all of whom participated in the Montgomery Bus Boycott. Although criticized for its condensed form, there is a remarkable amount of information about Parks presented in this picture book format. She is portrayed as a courageous political activist, and readers discover much about her life before and after the boycott. This book can open up conversations about the civil rights movement, segregation, and political activism.

Rockwell, Anne (2000). *Only passing through: The story of Sojourner Truth.* Illus. Gregory Christie. Dragonfly Books. Picture Book. This disturbingly graphic picture book begins with an auctioneer poking a stick at a young slave girl named Isabella. Her owner has died, and she is to be sold with the rest of his property. After enduring a series of owners, Isabella runs away and seeks the help of people who are known for their belief that slavery is immoral. These people purchase Isabella from her angry master and then promptly set her free. When Isabella learns that her son has been illegally sold in New York to a plantation owner in Alabama, she achieves what many consider to be an impossible task. She finds a lawyer to help her sue the man and have her son returned to New York, where slavery has been abolished. Later in life, she has a dream that directs her to become a sojourner who travels the country and serves as a voice for all the slaves still in bondage.

Rodriguez, Luis (1996). *America is her name*. Illus. Carlos Vasquez. Curbstone. Picture Book. In school, 9-year-old America Soliz passes some teachers in the hallway and hears her teacher, Miss Gable, whisper, "She's an illegal." How can a girl called America not belong in America? Miss Gable finds America's Spanish-speaking class "difficult," but when Mr. Aponte, a Puerto Rican poet, comes to visit, America rises to recite Spanish poetry, and the whole class listens and applauds. Encouraged, America begins to write poetry.

Roth, Susan (2001). *Happy birthday Mr. Kang*. National Geographic Society. Picture Book. Mr. Kang, a Chinese American, carries on the tradition of owning a caged hua mei bird. Every Sunday he and a group of his countrymen meet with their birds at the Sara Delano Roosevelt Park in New York City. Sam, his grandson, does not think that caged birds belong in America, the land of the free. Mr. Kang thinks about what Sam has said and, much to the surprise and horror of his fellow Chinese Americans, frees his hua mei bird. The book raises several critical issues: Who is an American? Who gets to decide? What social practices make immigrants feel that they must act like the dominant culture in order to be seen as American?

Rylant, Cynthia (1985). *Every living thing*. Illus. S. D. Schindler. Aladdin. Chapter Book. Rylant tells 12 short stories about people whose lives have been significantly altered because of their contact with animals. Though on the surface this text does not seem very critical, at a deep structure level it questions many of the social practices common in our society as we interact with others.

Sam the Sham & the Pharaohs. (1966). *Lil' Red Riding Hood*. Lyrics available at: http://top-lyrics.elizov.com/lyrics/Sam+The+Sham+& +The+Pharaohs.html.

Say, Allen (1990). *El Chino*. Houghton Mifflin. Picture Book. Billy Wong, the son of Chinese immigrants, buys into the American dream that you can be whatever you want to be if you work hard enough. Unable to play basketball because he is too short, Billy finally finds his sport in the bull rings of Spain. He is not accepted because of his ethnicity but eventually figures out that embracing rather than hiding his identity is the key to success.

Say, Allen (1993). *Grandfather's journey*. Houghton Mifflin. Picture Book. Done so as to recall a family photograph album, this story vacillates between Say's grandfather and his own life story. What is captured is the struggle that immigrants face as they leave one home country for another: "The funny thing is, the moment I am in one country, I am homesick for the other."

Sendak, Maurice (1963). *Where the wild things are*. HarperCollins. Picture Book. Having been sent to bed without his supper, Max, wearing a wolf suit uses his imagination to visit the wild things. When first published this book was banned because the monsters were thought to be too scary for young children. Since then the book has become known as a classic in children's literature, though some parental groups dislike the book because they think it encourages children to not honor their parents. Others dislike it because food is used as punishment.

Senisi, Ellen (1998). *Just kids: Visiting a class for children with special needs*. Dutton. Picture Book. Because she really does not know any special needs kids, Cindy makes a hurtful comment to a child in the special needs class. To help her better understand the special needs of some learners, Cindy is asked to join their class for a half hour each day over the course of two weeks. Through Cindy, the reader comes to know and appreciate the nine learners and their disabilities in this special needs classroom. It offers an entry point into discussions surrounding these sensitive issues.

Seurat, Marie (1990). *Angel child, dragon child*. Illus. Vo-Dinh Mai. Scholastic. Picture Book. Ut's American schoolmates call her "Pajamas" because her clothes do not match theirs, and they laugh at her accent when she tries to speak English. But she still tries to be the "angel child" her mother asked her to be when her family escaped from Vietnam. When Ut finally fights back, the principal assigns the boy who has been her chief tormentor to write her story as his punishment. When he discovers who Ut is and the problems she has faced, he helps organize a school fair to raise the money necessary to bring Ut's mother to the United States.

Seuss, Dr. (1984). *The butter battle book*. Random House. Picture Book. Engaged in a long-standing disagreement over whether bread should be eaten with the butter side up or down, the Yooks and Zooks erected a wall to make sure that each group remained on its own side. After border skirmishes that test the primitive weapons of each group, both sides get to work on bigger and better inventions to use against the other. As the weapons become more sophisticated and lethal, bands and pep squads are added to support the home teams and to get everyone involved. Finally, the Yooks announce that the "boys in the back room" have created a bomb that will annihilate the Zooks. But as the leader of the Yooks jumps to the top of the wall to drop the bomb on the Zooks, the leader of that side appears with an equally destructive bomb.

The story ends with the two staring at each other, and readers are left to wonder what will happen, providing an eerie reminder of the current world scene.

Shange, Ntozake (1997). *White wash*. Illus. Michael Sporn. Walker. Picture Book. Helene-Angel, an African American preschooler, walks home from school with her brother, who does not particularly enjoy the task of walking his little sister home. One day, a gang of White kids surrounds them, blackening Mauricio's eye and painting Helene-Angel's face white as they show her how to be a "true American" and "how to be white." Helene-Angel is, of course, traumatized; she hides in her room until her mother forces her to come out. As she emerges from the house, her classmates greet her and promise to stick together so that events like this will not happen again.

Shea, Pegi Deitz (2003). *The carpet boy's gift*. Illus. Leane Morin. Tilbury. Picture Book. This picture book tells the story of Nadeem, a young boy sold to a carpet maker so his family can live. He thinks his hard work is paying off the debt, but every time Nadeem gets close to working off his family's debt, his master penalizes him and the debt amount goes back up. In the course of the story, Nadeem meets Iqbal Masih, who opens Nadeem's eyes to new possibilities. There are great child labor resources at the end of the book.

Silverstein, Shel (1964). *The giving tree*. Harper & Row. Picture Book. This is the story of a tree that "loved a little boy." The tree was happy when the boy would eat her apples and swing from her branches. But as the boy grew older, he wanted money to buy things, so the tree told him to sell her apples. When he wanted to build a house, the tree offered up her branches. And when he wanted a boat, the trunk was ideal. The tree was happy to give right up until the end when there was little left of her except a stump for him (now an old man) to use as a chair. Though many readers find this a lovely tale, there are those who feel the book should have been titled "The Greedy Boy."

Sisulu, Elinor Batezat (1996). *The day Gogo went to vote*. Illus. Sharon Wilson. Little Brown. Picture Book. This story of the historic 1994 election in South Africa is told through the eyes of young Thembi, whose grandmother, Gogo, is determined to cast a ballot in the first election in which native people are allowed to vote. Even though she has not been out of the family's yard for years, the elderly Gogo makes the long journey to the balloting place, accompanied by her granddaughter and assisted by numerous community members. Thembi sees how much voting means to Gogo, the oldest voter in the township.

Skármeta, Antonio (2000). *The composition*. Illus. Alfonso Ruano. Groundwood. Picture Book. Pedro, a third grader, loves playing soccer with his friends. His parents listen to a "noisy" distant radio station every night to get news, which is annoying to Pedro. Although he has heard his parents talking about a dictatorship, the gravity of the situation he is living in does not touch Pedro until his friend Daniel's father is taken away by army troops. Soon after, a military captain comes to Pedro's classroom and has the students write on the topic, "What my family does at night." Even though the book deals with a very serious subject, Skármeta allows readers to experience tyranny from a child's perspective.

Smith, Frank Dabba (2000). *My secret camera: Life in the Lodz ghetto*. Photographs by Mendel Grossman. Gulliver. Picture Book. Grossman's life story is told in the afterword; the book consists of the photographs he secretly took showing life in the Lodz ghetto in Poland under Nazi rule. The book serves as a painful reminder of the results of hate, prejudice, and, to some extent, America's initial indifference and unwillingness to act.

Spinelli, Jerry (2003). *Milkweed*. Knopf. Chapter Book. By telling the story through the eyes and voice of Misha, a child who is struggling to understand the world during the time of the Holocaust, Spinelli invites readers to share Misha's innocence as they, too, discover the horrors of this period in history. *Milkweed* lays bare the worst in people as well as the best. Misha is both charming and resilient.

Spinelli, Jerry (1997). *Wringer*. HarperCollins. Chapter Book. If you grow up as a boy in society, you are expected to take, unflinchingly, "The Treatment" on your birthday, participate in hunting at a particular age, and be moderately ugly to girls even if they were, a year earlier, your best friends. While these behaviors might delight your peer group, amuse your father, puzzle your mother, annoy your female friends, and emotionally traumatize you, they are "what men do." Palmer LaRue is going to be 10 and is going through his own rite of passage in a town that annually holds a pigeon shoot. In this town it is the 10-year-olds who get to wring the necks of all the pigeons who are wounded but do not die outright. Boys may just be boys. This book invites explanation of the forces that operate in society to position boys in certain ways and not others.

Spinelli, Jerry (2000). *Stargirl*. Knopf. Chapter Book. "She was elusive. She was today. She was tomorrow. We did not know what to make of her. In our minds we tried to pin her to the corkboard like a butterfly, but the pin merely went through and away she flew" (back cover). Who is she? Stargirl. Or at least that is what she calls herself today. She is new to town and new to Mica High. She is as strange as her pet rat and as mysterious as her name. The students are fascinated, but even the ones who love her urge her to become the very thing that can destroy her: normal.

Springer, Jane (1997). *Listen to us: The world's working children*. Groundwood. Chapter Book. This book explores the difficult questions that surround child labor, including globalization, consumerism, and attitudes toward girls and women. Child activists and workers also speak for themselves in this volume, 10-year-old Nirmala, a Nepalese carpet weaver; 16-year-old Christine, a Canadian sex worker; and 18-year-old Naftal, kidnapped to be a soldier in the Mozambique National Resistance when he was 12 years old. This book leaves readers with critical questions about the economic and social systems that support the exploitation of children and what might be done to help them.

Stanley, Jerry (1997). *Digger: The tragic fate of the California Indians from the missions to the Gold Rush*. Crown Publishers. Chapter Book. Stanley has created a well-researched, highly readable portrait of the destruction of many of the Native American *tribelets* that inhabited what is now California at the time of the first Spanish, and then American, occupation. Sprinkled throughout the volume are maps, original photographs, drawings, and quotes from an interview with Ishi, a Yahi man believed to the last Californian Indian to live according to the customs of his people.

Steptoe, John (1997). *Creativity*. Illus. E. B. Lewis. Clarion Books. Picture Book. Charlie is surprised to learn that Hector, the new kid, is Puerto Rican. After all, both boys have the same brown skin and the same black hair, though Hector's is straight and Charlie's is curly. What separates them is their language. In exploring these issues, Charlie begins to see difference as "creative" rather than problematic. Although the book focuses on surface issues such as having the "right" shoes and t-shirt to fit into the group, bigger issues await discussion: how different languages can camouflage a common culture; how pop cultures are created to sell merchandise and define who is "in" and who is "out"; how language and issues of multiculturalism are related to power in our society.

Strasser, Tod (2002). *Give a boy a gun*. Simon Pulse. Young Adult. In an attempt to understand the psychology of a school shooting, Strasser has put together a narrative that consists of short, related statements from students, parents, school administrators, and even the shooters themselves. Running along the foot of many of the pages are media reports and statistics on gun usage in the United States and elsewhere. Issues addressed include gun control, bullying, and how social cliques within schools alienate students.

Tal, Eve (2005). *Double crossing*. Cinco Puntos. Chapter Book. Rich in historical detail—the separation from family, the ocean voyage, the inspection and arrival at Ellis Island—this book, on the surface, tells the story of Ukrainian Jews and their journey to America through the eyes of 12-year-old Raizel. The bigger story is one of assimilation and how, in this instance, an Orthodox Jew had to give up not only his religion but also his name.

Thomas, Rob (1997). *Slave day*. Simon & Schuster. Sophisticated Chapter Book (Sexual Content). This book explores how dominant systems of meaning position people and groups in certain ways. Through short, first-person narratives, the reader is able to follow the thoughts and actions of seven students and a teacher as they live through "Slave Day," an annual tradition at Robert E. Lee High School. Although the official purpose for the activity is to raise money for student activities, it is challenged by Keene, an African American student who sees it as racist and demeaning.

Tillage, Leon Walter (1997). *Leon's story*. Illus. Susan Roth. Farrar, Straus & Giroux. Chapter Book. Remembering his childhood as the son of a sharecropper in North Carolina, Tillage describes his personal experiences of segregation, racial violence, and the economic disenfranchisement of blacks in the South as he was growing up. This story is part of the American Heritage Oral History collection.

Tsuchiya, Yukio (1997). *Faithful elephants: A true story of animals, people, & war*. Illus. Ted Lewin. Houghton Mifflin. Picture Book. Narrated by the zookeeper, this is a perspective on war that is usually not seen or thought about. What happens to zoos in times of war? What if the animals should get out? One alternative the Japanese faced was to get rid of all the animals. Killing off two faithful elephants proved harder than one might think.

Twain, Mark (1948). *The adventures of Huckleberry Finn*. Grosset & Dunlap. Chapter Book. Because of its frequent use of the "N-word," this classic of American literature is often banned by school districts across the country. The narrative tells of Huck's travels and continual brushes with danger as he and a slave named Jim travel the Mississippi River. Placed in historical context, many of the passages that some see as offensive can now be read as Twain's appeals for broader racial understanding.

Trueman, Terry (2001). *Stuck in neutral*. Harper Collins. Chapter Book. Shawn is a 14-year-old with cerebral palsy. Since he cannot communicate, he has been diagnosed as profoundly developmentally disabled. His age-mates make fun of him, and his family members either resent what he has done to the family or feel sorry for him. The book leaves both adults and children feeling rather stunned. One cannot help but believe that everyone who experiences this book will interact with handicapped people differently and change the language they used in the past to "other" them. Several critical issues are raised, including, "What is normal? Who gets to decide?"

Van Camp, Richard (1998). *What's the most beautiful thing you know about horses?* Illus. George Littlechild. Children's Book Press. Picture Book. The author decides to ask his friends and family a question, "What's the most beautiful thing you know about horses?" The perspectives offered to Van Camp in response to his question sets up the possibility for a number of conversations to take place regarding stereotypes, ethnic differences, biracial issues, language and power, animal rights, and cultural perspectives.

Walter, Virginia (1998). *Making up megaboy.* Graphics Katrina Roeckelein. DK Ink. Sophisticated Chapter/Picture Book. In this remarkable book, Walter weaves together popular culture, ethnic tensions, youth violence, and strained interpersonal relationships into an extremely disturbing, realistic, and well-crafted tale. On his 13th birthday, Robbie Jones walks into Mr. Koh's convenience store, pulls out his father's gun, then shoots and kills the elderly Korean proprietor. The story is presented from the voices of community members as they try to figure out why this horrible killing happened. We hear his disbelieving mother, a glib TV news reporter; Robbie's disapproving father, a Vietnam veteran; the local barber; his classmates; the girl he had a crush on; Robbie's teacher; his best friend; a correctional officer; and many more. This book reads like a TV drama, and because of the disturbing content and treatment, it is probably best used as a read-aloud followed by a class discussion.

Whitman, Walt, & Long, Loren (2004). *When I heard the learn'd astronomer.* Simon & Schuster. Picture Book. Long uses Whitman's poem to illustrate the difference between an adult and a child perspective on knowing. Several social issues are raised implicitly, including what it means to learn and whose knowledge counts.

Weinstein Company (2006). *Hoodwinked.* This movie is a cross between the traditional Little Red Riding Hood tale and a Humphrey Bogart film noir. The four main characters of the story—Red, the Wolf, Granny, and the Woodsman—are interrogated by the policy, each giving their own version of the story.

Wiesner, David (2001). *The three pigs.* Clarion. Picture Book. In this delightful postmodern version of the Three Little Pigs, the story starts out traditionally with the wolf coming upon a house of straw and huffing and puffing and blowing the house down. The story takes an unexpected twist when the wolf also blows the first pig right off the page. Thus begins a refreshing tale of deconstruction, reconstruction, and liberation. When all three pigs get outside of the story, leaving the wolf trapped inside, they start a grand escapade by flying off on a paper airplane made from one of the folded pages of their story. On their adventure, they encounter other book characters, eventually bringing back a dragon they rescued along the way. This story is a great demonstration of how things do not have to be the way they have always been.

Wild, Margaret (2006). *Fox*. Illus. Ron Brooks. Kane/Miller. Picture Book. This is a story about Dog and Magpie. Magpie has been wounded, and Dog decides to nurse her back to health. Just as their friendship develops, along comes Fox, whom Magpie does not trust but over time is persuaded to simulate flying by riding on Fox's back. Fox takes Magpie far out in the desert and abandons her, telling the bird that now she too will know what loneliness really feels like. Despite this act of cruelty, the book ends hopefully as Magpie begins hopping back home.

Wiles, Deborah (2001). *Freedom summer*. Illus. Jerome Lagarrigue. Atheneum. Picture Book. This is the heartfelt story of two young boys who discover that even though the Civil Rights Act was passed, attitudes and beliefs do not change overnight. Readers are taken back to the summer of 1964 when, for the first time, the town swimming pool and other public places are open to all, regardless of skin color. As friends Joe and John Henry race to be the first ones to swim in water "so clear, you can jump to the bottom and open your eyes and still see," they are confronted head on with the power of discrimination. Rather than integrate, the town elders decided to have the swimming pool filled in with tar.

Willhoite, Michael (1990). *Daddy's roommate*. Alyson Wonderland. Picture Book. The story is told from the perspective of a boy whose parents recently divorced. Readers, even those who are skeptical of gay relationships, soon learn that the boy's father now lives with Frank, another male. It turns out that Frank is a lot like Daddy, and the boy ends up happy to have Frank join in the many activities he does with his father.

Wilson, Nancy Hope (1997). *Old people, frogs, and Albert*. Illus. Marcy D. Ramsey. Farrar, Straus & Giroux. Chapter Book. Albert is a fourth grader with more than just a reading problem—he is also very uncomfortable about walking by Pine Manor, a nursing home he passes on his way to and from school each day. The people who sit on the porch and call out to him are not only old and wrinkled but also are not in the best of health. When Mr. Spear, his reading tutor and friend, has a stroke and ends up at Pine Manor it is almost too much for Albert to bear. But when he surprises himself by reading a whole book without help and without focusing on the terrifying fact that he is reading, Albert gets the courage to overcome his fear and to share his success with the residents of Pine Manor.

Winslow, Vicki (1997). *Follow the leader.* Delacorte. Chapter Book. Set in 1971 in North Carolina, this is the story of a family that is trying to make a difference. Mrs. Adams remembers segregation laws from her childhood and now votes only for "people who want to make things better for everybody." Mr. Adams hires subcontractors according to their bids and not who they are and refuses to join a segregated country club, even though it would help him with business contacts and though he sees it as "the most beautiful golf course this side of Myrtle Beach." Both Mr. and Mrs. Adams support desegregation of the local schools, even though this means that their daughter, Amanda, will be bused out of their neighborhood to a downtown school. Resistant at first, Amanda eventually comes to appreciate the teachers and students in her new school and realizes that the friend she missed so much at first was not the kind of friend she wanted to keep. *Follow the leader* invites conversations about racist attitudes that continue to lurk at or just below the surface in contemporary life.

Wittlinger, Ellen (2000). *Gracie's girl.* Simon & Schuster. Chapter Book. As Bess Cunningham starts her middle school experience, her main concerns are to become popular in school and to get more attention from her busy parents. Although she initially complains about her mother's commitment to a community soup kitchen, she becomes more involved after meeting and befriending Gracie, a homeless elderly woman. She finds a vacant building for Gracie to sleep in at night and enlists the help of her brother and friends in bringing her food. Instead of spending her time thinking of ways to be cool, Bess becomes more concerned with providing food and shelter for Gracie and others like her. Although the story does not have a happy ending, it provides lots of opportunities for starting new conversations about how homeless people are positioned in society and what it means to take social action.

Wittlinger, Ellen (2000). *What's in a name.* Simon & Schuster. Chapter Book. "It's not just a name—it's an identity!" is more the rallying cry of a group of wealthy citizens determined to change the name of the town of Scrub Harbor to the posh-sounding Folly Bay. Through the backdrop of town politics, the various community members who author chapters struggle to understand their identities and how those identities change as a function of changing the name of the town. The jock, the exchange student, the working-class kid, the immigrant, the brain—each are confronted with the realization of how much of "who they are" is constructed by others. This novel offers critical insights into how personal identity directly intersects larger social issues of class, language, sexual orientation, and race.

Wolf, Bernard (2003). *Coming to America: A Muslim family's story.* Lee & Low. Picture Book. Wolf portrays the Mahmoud family as individuals rather than as stereotypical representations. Differences in religion do not equate with differences in fundamental human values. Readers are likely to walk away thinking of the Mahmouds as neighbors rather than as strangers or terrorists.

Wolff, Virginia (1998). *Bat 6.* Scholastic. Chapter Book. Just after WWII, everyone in the Oregon towns of Barlow and Bear Creek is gearing up for the yearly "Bat 6," the annual softball game between sixth-grade girls from each town. Both teams have great new players: Shazam, whose father was killed at Pearl Harbor and who has just come to live with her grandmother; and Aki, a Japanese American girl who has just returned home with her family after years in an internment camp. From the perspectives of 21 different characters, we hear first of the excitement and preparation leading up to the game and then how the game is cut short after a terrible incident of racial violence: Shazam knocks Aki in the head forcefully and intentionally, causing serious injury. What follows is the town's struggle to make sense of what happened that day—a search that brings many to question their acceptance of the war's racism and violence and their own complicity and silence.

Woods, Brenda (2004). *Emako blue.* Putnam. Young Adult. When Emako's brother is released from prison, Emako becomes the victim of a drive-by shooting. Told in the stark, contemporary voices of Emako's friends, this is this story of youth caught up in a world of violence despite their talents and plans to make something of themselves.

Woodson, Jacqueline (1995). *From the notebooks of Melanin Sun.* Scholastic. Chapter Book. Melanin Sun is an African American adolescent who is struggling with his own coming-of-age issues when his mother introduces him to her White lesbian lover and asks him to welcome her into their family. He has to deal not only with his own homophobic and racist feelings but also with the taunts and jeers of his friends.

Woodson, Jacqueline (2001). *The other side.* Illus. Earl B. Lewis. Putnam. Picture Book. This gentle story of friendship in the midst of racial tension is told from the perspective of an African American child. When a White family moves in next door, her mother warns her to stay away from them: "She said it wasn't safe." These words stop White readers in their track and challenge them to consider how they might be part of the problem in race relations. Readers are left with the hope that children might ultimately be able to point the way for their parents to achieving a more caring and safe world.

Woodson, Jacqueline (2004). *Behind you.* Putnam. Chapter Book. Despite the fact that Jeremiah is dead—killed by New York City police bullets at age 15—he looks over friends left behind, including his White girlfriend, Ellie, and his divorced parents as they struggle with racism, love, death, and grief. In some ways this novel is a little too realistic, having few answers and giving readers only glimmers of hope.

Wyeth, Sharon Dennis (1998). *Something beautiful.* Illus. C. Soentpiet. Doubleday. Picture Book. This book offers an opportunity to take a critical look at the places people inhabit as well as to initiate discussions around the multiple meanings of the word *beautiful.* The young girl in this book pursues a quest for beauty in her inner-city neighborhood. She initially is discouraged by the blighted areas around her, including the letters D-I-E on her own front door and the trash strewn around the yard. But she soon discovers that beauty can be found in a beautiful-tasting fish sandwich or in the beautiful sound of a baby's laugh or in simply the beauty inside each individual.

Yashima, Taro (1955). *Crow boy.* Viking. Picture Books. Chibi, a shy, small boy, is both belittled and ignored by his classmates until, in his last year of elementary school, a wise and sensitive teacher draws him out. His classmates come to realize how much he knows and how much they could have learned from him had they tried to befriend him earlier. Though this book is not unproblematic in that the children end up calling him *Crow Boy,* a name that still positions Chibi in particular ways, it does open up the possibility to talk about both the positive as well as negative effects of nicknames.

Index

C

Carpet Boy's Gift, The, 249, 250
Cello of Mr. O, The, 83
Center for Global Change, 109, 117
Center for Inquiry, 22, 87, 91
Certainty, action associated with, 35
Chart-a-Conversation, 209, 211
Child labor issues, 43, 50, 253
Children
    as consumers, 47
    displaced, 145
    working-class, self-interest of, 85
Children's literature, getting started with
        critical literacy using, 61–73, 153
    enactment of critical literacy, 68–69
    lingering questions, 69
    thought piece, 70–73
    vignette, 61–63
    what can be learned from experience,
        64–68
Cinder Edna, 81, 82
Cinderella, 249
Circuit: Stories from the Life of a Migrant Child,
    The, 27
Citizens, kinds of, 4
Civil War, 76
Classroom(s)
    assumptions about life in, 27
    community
        newcomers to, 25
        time for building, 1
    fear and, 73
    multilingual, 25
    performance differences of, 87
    racial diversity in, 62
    research, contradictions in, 2
Coexist clothing, 127
Collaboration
    learning and, 23
    power of, 65
Comfort zones, pushing out of, 116
Commonplace, disruption of, 7, 9, 14, 75–89,
    153
    critical literacy enactment, 85–86
    lingering questions, 86
    thought piece, 86–89
    vignette, 75–78
    what can be learned from museum
        experience, 78–85
Common text, definition of, 66
Community, poster demonstrating, 141
Competition, poster demonstrating, 140
Complex issues, simplistic responses to, 96
Complex systems, Hunger Project and, 121
Comprehension test, 255
Conscious engagement, 13
Consumer(s)
    children as, 47
    culture, impact of, 50

educators as, 45
    literacy, 52, 59
    teachers as, 45
Consumerism, 41, 159, 165–169
Controversial literature, 72
Conversation(s), 193–197
    big C, 47
    body image, 47
    intense, 67
    multiple perspectives of, 97
    significant, 193
    students talking about books, 65
    tension accompanying, 67
Cooperation, poster demonstrating, 141
Counternarrative(s)
    construction of, 84
    development of, 83
    war, 82
Crap detecting, 84
Critical inquiry, literacy as tool of, 133
Critical literacy(ies)
    curriculum, marginalized students and, 10
    description of, 3
    dimensions of
        considering multiple viewpoints, 14, 88
        disrupting the commonplace, 14, 88
        focusing on sociopolitical, 14, 88
        taking action to promote social justice,
          14, 88
    enactment of, 33, 51, 85, 100, 101, 122
    focus of, 3
    instructional model, 5, 6, 33, 50, 51, 147
    model of, context box of, 20
    movement between personal and social, 6,
        19
    roots of, 3
    use of language in, 49
Critical pedagogy, goal of, 4
Critical social practice, dimensions of, 7
Critical stance(s)
    adopting, 13
    alternate ways of being, 19
    being reflexive, 19
    consciously engaging, 19
    enactment of critical literacy, 33
    responsibility to inquire, 19
    risk taking and, 16
    use of tension as resource, 16
Critical thinking approaches, 3
Critique, language of, 8, 478
Cultural capital, 30
Cultural icons, 8
Cultural model, interrogation of, 43
Cultural texts, interrogation of, 46
Culture of origin, respect for, 149
Curricular structures, durability of, 9
Curriculum
    counternarratives in, 82
    critical language in, 80
    critical literacy, 10

Index

352
■

Index

Index

Index

Index